Information, Communication and Society

Information, Communication and Society

Bhaskar Mukherjee

Ess Ess Publications
New Delhi

Information, Communication and Society

ISBN: 978-81-7000-661-9

Rs.1150/-

First Published 2012

Published by:
Ess Ess Publications
4831/24, Ansari Road,
Darya Ganj,
New Delhi-110 002.
INDIA
Phones: 23260807, 41563444
Fax: 41563334
E-mail: info@essessreference.com
www.essessreference.com

Cover Design by *Patch Creative Unit*

Printed and bound in India at Salasar Imaging Systems.

Contents

Preface

Fritz Machlup and his colleague Stephen Kagan once pointed that "Information science, at present stage of its development, is a not fully integrated assemblage of systematic studies of the processes regarded as information, particularly of the system, operations and devices, technology, and organization by which men - which of course stands for men and women, transmit and receive, and therefore transfer, knowledge among one another. Truly, the field of Information Science has undergone many changes in the last few decades.

The goal of this book is to provide a conceptual background, and issues that constitute a new domain of information science in recent past. Each chapter in this book, as far as possible, follows *pedagogically,* where the theme moves from introduction towards critical discussion. Naturally, a course book of this nature cannot address all relevant issues related to information sciences, the aim of the book is to provide students with necessary course contents as provided in their syllabi. Due to that, each topic being an independent unit in itself also becomes a part of the larger whole. Various issues relating to information science, communication, information systems, information society, information profession, information industry, information protection, knowledge management etc. have been included. Ofcourse it is not only students who can benefit from a book like this but also teachers, researchers, experts and all those who find this area interesting.

As our world is becoming more interconnected and inter-dependable, information is becoming a vital and important aspect of life. The term "information" is used differently by individuals in different walks of life. Chapter 1 of this book maps the conceptual background of information science by defining fundamental concepts data, information and knowledge. Although, many scholars claim that data, information, and knowledge are part of a sequential order, the alternative views are also mentioned here as pointed in Delphi Study. In order to transmit information from one point to another, the foremost need is information has to be represented in some way, and conveyed through a channel of some kind. This chapter also discusses how information is represented through sign, symbol, and signals.

Nobel Prize receipient Joshua Lederberg once commented: 'Communication as the root of scientific progress'. Chapter 2 deals of information communication by elaborating various components of communication and media involved in communication process. In fact, communication process has two fold approach. Scientists from electronic engineering have taken communication through signal approach, whereas social science people took it as media approach. Considering the strong connection that library and information science has with social sciences, communication theories and models have been discussed in this chapter by social science approach by demonstrating how we have arrived at some of the models that are considered important today. The development of communication models, from the relatively simple, to those that are more complex, follows a more or less chronological sequence. So, I present the models ordered roughly by the time that they were developed, beginning with a discussion of the work of great philosopher Aristotle to Westley and MacLean's Conceptual Model. At the end of this chapter this book also discuss the concept of scholarly communication and the very famous concept of 'open access'.

Information science had its origins in a variety of reference disciplines with distinct theoretical research perspectives on the important issues to study and the methods to study them. The attachment of this science with so many scientific and social sciences discipline redefine its fundamental building blocks. A key to interpret information science is to find the meanings of information in information science, and those meanings are found in people, not in words. In chapter 3, due to that an attempt has been made to identify the concept 'information' in information science and then discusses information science from various information scientists view. The interdisciplinary nature of information science was proved in numerous studies, and interest in the field by professionals from various and related areas is undoubtedly on the rise. This chapter also includes the interdisciplinary relation of information sciences with few other disciplines.

Taking into account all of the behaviors of a system as a whole in the context of its environment is the systems perspective. While the concept of system itself is a more general notion that indicates separation of part of the universe from the rest, the idea of a systems perspective is to use a non-reductionist approach to the task of describing the properties of the system itself. Chapter 4 discusses information science in system perspective and explain various function oriented models like MIS (chapter 5) Expert System (chapter 6) and Decision Support system (chapter 7).

Post-industrial society is characterized by increasing demand of theoretical knowledge, the professionalization of everyone, and a economy which gives better value to services than goods itself. As a result, the concept of profession and professional knowledge becomes the central idea of post-industrial economy. The chapter 8 of this book has discusses the information profession, their duties, competencies and how the pervasive influence of digital computing is transforming the profession into a new direction. Some basic question: whether the traditional library will be transformed into a virtual entity with the majority of the information in electronic format? – has also discussed in this chapter.

Research methods have variously been classified as qualitative versus quantitative. Generally, the terms quantitative and qualitative have become associated with the positivist and humanistic approaches, while, in fact in many discipline, including information science, one can not restrict various method only by qualitative and quantitative. The next chapter provides a general framework regarding research methods that are useful in information science perspective and categorized research methods into three domains: Research Design methods, data collection methods and data analysis methods.

The importance of information in society is constantly on the rise, and many are involved in its various aspects, with a large number of studies, initiatives and businesses dedicated to information-related areas. The fact that information science has many competitors poses a certaindanger, numerous studies have sought to define the field and to examine links, relations and overlap between information science and other fields. The chapter 10 of this book synthesizes the essential facts and ideas regarding the information society and explains the role of ICTs in changing our society towards information society. This chapter also discusses the dimensions of the information society according to Daniel Bell and Yoneji Masuda.

A defining characteristic of an information society is an emerging or developing information industry. The next chapter discusses the characteristics of information industry and highlights information industry broadly into three categories: information creation industry, information delivery industry and information processing industry.

Information explosion, the technology revolution, and escalating library costs, have forced libraries and information centres to market their information products and services. This has emerged as an important area, especially as a means for improving user satisfaction and promoting the use of services by potential users. Due to that it is worthwhile to discuss the marketing concept in LIS domain. The chapter 12 considers the concept of marketing in the light of library and information services and mentions the why & how of marketing techniques in library and information centres. Here marketing difficulties to library and information services has also discussed

From the Internet to open acess, technologies are transforming our society and empowering us as speakers, citizens, creators, and consumers. At the same time, these modern technologies has changed the way we think, bringing many new challenges, including the amplification of the issues related to the rights and respect of information— intellectual property (IP) rights. On one extreme, a violation of intellectual property rights can lead to civil or criminal consequences. On another, as individuals and as a community, how we deal with intellectual property can inspire creativity and sharing, helping us all succeed. The recent strategies of open-source and "copyleft" licensing serve to encourage collaboration and innovation through the free sharing of information. The intension behind writing the chapter 13 - Protection of Information is to know the concepts like IPR, plagiarism, Digital rigts, fair use, creative common etc.

Since inception, libraries are actively involved in delivering stored resources to their clientless. However, after 1950s, the importance of managing and utilizing organizational knowledge started gaining popularity. In this knowledge-based economic system, the organizations are realizing the importance of their intellectual assets i.e., the knowledge possessed by the employees, their skills of the organization just like any other corporate resource and are now devising ways to harness this previously unforeseen power for organizational success. The final chapter, i.e. chapter 14, discusses various facets of knowledge management and its implication in libraries.

A famous write Wilson Mizner once quoted "To steal ideas from one person is plagiarism, to steal ideas from many is research." To write this document I have consulted number of sources. Consciously I have tried to mention all those in my references. However there might be some I forgot to mention, I apologise for not being able to mention them.

From the very first day of thinking to write such a book to its final stage, I received help, support and cooperation from many people, including my Moni, Baba, Maa, dada, Boudi, Wife, son and also from professional colleagues. I extend my thanks and sincere gratitude to all those who actively or passively supported me in writing this book.

Bhaskar Mukherjee

1
The Conceptual Background of Information

"Where is the Life we have lost in living? Where is the wisdom we have lost in knowledge? Where is the knowledge we have lost in information" — **T.S. Eliot**

Information is one of the most frequently used terms in our every day life. Since information is linked to data and knowledge, it is desirable to distinguish between these three terms. As, the formulation of systematic conceptions of data, information, and knowledge is crucial for the development of a systematic conception of Information Science, as well as for the construction of a systematic knowledge map of the field, this chapter maps the conceptual approaches for defining *data, information,* and *knowledge.* This might help the reader to a better understanding of the issues and the considerations involved in establishing the foundations of Information Science. We have sketch characteristics and attributes of information and attempt to understand how information is represent through signs, signals and symbols.

DATA - INFORMATION - KNOWLEDGE

The three concepts of data, information, and knowledge are very fundamental of information science. They are often regarded as the basic building blocks of the field. Due to that it is very crucial to understand these three concepts for the development of systematic conception of Information Science, as well as for the construction of a systematic knowledge map of the field. Following are some of the concepts revealed by Zins (2007) in his study based on opinion based-survey conducted among leading scholars in various major subfields and important aspects of the field. Many scholars claim that data, information, and knowledge are part of a sequential order, however, some scholars also identify their identity as unique. Lets take a look:

***Prof. Aldo de Albuquerque Barreto*, Brazilian Institute for Information in Science and Technology, Brazil**

Data is a symbol set that is quantified and/or qualified. **Information** is a set of significant sings that has the ability to create knowledge . . . The essence of the information phenomenon has been characterized as the occurrence of a communication process that takes place between the sender and the recipient of the message. Thus, the various concepts of information tend to concentrate on the origin and the end point of this communication process. **Knowledge** is information that has been appropriate by the user. When information is adequately assimilated, it produces knowledge, modifies the individual's mental store of information and benefits his development and that of the society in which he lives. Thus, as the mediating agent in the production of knowledge, the information, qualifies itself, in form and substance, as significant structures able to generate knowledge for the individual and his group."

Prof. Shifra Baruchson–Arbib, **Bar Ilan University, Ramat-Gan, Israel**

Data are sensory stimuli that we perceive through our senses. **Information** is data that has been processed into a form that is meaningful to the recipient (Davis & Olson, 1985). **Knowledge** is what has understood and evaluated by the knower."

Prof. Michael Buckland, **University of California, Berkeley, CA**

The word "data" is commonly used to refer to records or recordings encoded for use in computer, but is more widely used to refer to statistical observations and other recordings or collections of evidence. The word "information" is used to refer to a number of different phenomena. These phenomena have been classified into three groupings: (1) Anything perceived as potentially signifying something (e.g. printed books); (2) The process of informing; and (3) That which is learned from some evidence or communication. All three are valid uses (in English) of the term "information." I personally am most comfortable with no. 1, then with no. 3, but acknowledge that others have used and may use no 2. The word "knowledge" is best used to refer to what someone knows, which is, in effect, what they believe, including belief that some of the beliefs of others should not be believed. By extension the word "knowledge" is used more loosely for (1) what social groups know collectively; and (2) what is in principle knowable because it has been recorded somehow and could be recovered even though, at any given time, no individual knows (or remembers) it.

Dr. Quentin L. Burrell, **Isle of Man International Business School, Isle of Man**

Data are the basic individual items of numeric or other

information, garnered through observation; but in themselves, without context, they are devoid of information. **Information** is that which is conveyed, and possibly amenable to analysis and interpretation, through data and the context in which the data are assembled. **Knowledge** is the general understanding and awareness garnered from accumulated information, tempered by experience, enabling new contexts to be envisaged.

Burrell also explained **Data** are (or datum is) an abstraction. The concept of 'data' or 'datum' suggests that there is something there that is purely given and that can be known as such. The last one hundred years of (late) philosophic discussion and, of course, many hundred years before, have shown that there is nothing like 'the given' or 'naked facts' but that every (human) experience/knowledge is biased. This is the 'theory-laden' theorem that is shared today by such different philosophic schools as Popper's critical rationalism (and his followers and critics such as Kuhn or Feyerabend), analytic philosophy (Quine, for instance), hermeneutics (Gadamer), etc. Modern philosophy (Kant) is very acquainted with this question: experience ("Erfahrung") is a product of 'sensory data' within the framework of perception ("Anschauung") and the categories of reason ("Verstand") ("perception without concepts is blind, concepts without perception are void"). Pure sensory data are as unknowable as "things in themselves"." **Information** is a multi-layered concept with Latin roots ('informatio'_ to give a form) that go back to Greek ontology and epistemology (Plato's concept of 'idea' and Aristotle's concepts of 'morphe' but also to such concepts as 'typos' and 'prolepsis') (See Capurro, 1978; Capurro & Hjøerland, 2003). The use of this concept in information science is at the first sight highly controversial but it basically refers to the everyday meaning (since Modernity): "the act of communicating knowledge" (OED). I would suggest to use this definition as far as it points to the phenomenon of message that I consider the basic one in information science. **Knowledge** is 'no-thing' (contrary to "information-as-thing" as suggested by Michael Buckland, 1991a), i.e., it is the event of meaning selection of a (psychic/social) system from its 'world' on the basis of communication. The "act of communicating knowledge" (OED's definition of information) is then to be understood as the act of making a meaning offer (message) leading to understanding (and misunderstanding) on the basis of a selection of meaning (information). To know is then to understand on the basis of making a difference between 'message' (or meaning offer) and 'information' (or meaning selection). Human knowledge is, as Popper states, basically conjectural. Or, to put it in hermeneutic terms: understanding is always biased, i.e., based on (implicit) pre-understanding. In more classical terms we distinguish following Aristotle between 'empirical knowledge' (or 'know-how' 'empeiria') and explicit knowledge (or 'know-that', for instance, scientific knowledge or 'episteme').

Prof. Anthony Debons, **University of Pittsburgh, Pittsburgh, PA**

Data are symbols organized according to established algorithms. **Information** represents a state of awareness (consciousness) and the physical manifestations they form. Information, as a phenomena, represents both a process and a product; a cognitive/ affective state, and the physical counterpart (product of) the cognitive/affective state. The counterpart could range from a scratch of a surface, movement (placement)of a rock; a gesture(movement) speech(sound), written document, etc. (requirement). Information answers questions of what, where, when and who and permutations thereof. **Knowledge.** Knowledge represents a cognitive/affective state that finds definition in meaning and understanding. Knowledge is reflected in the questions of "how" and "why." Knowledge extends the organism state of awareness (consciousness/ information). Knowledge can be given physical representation (presence) in the material products (technology) thereof (books, film, speech, etc.).

Prof. Gordana Dodig-Crnkovic, **Mälardalen University, Västerås/Eskilstuna, Sweden**

Data-Information-Knowledge-Wisdom - According to Stonier (1993, 1997), data is a series of disconnected facts and observations. These may be converted to information by analyzing, cross-referring, selecting, sorting, summarizing, or in some way organizing the data. Patterns of information, in turn, can be worked up into a coherent body of knowledge. Knowledge consists of an organized body of information, such information patterns forming the basis of the kinds of insights and judgments which we call wisdom. The above conceptualization may be made concrete by a physical analogy (Stonier, 1993): consider spinning fleece into yarn, and then weaving yarn into cloth. The fleece can be considered analogous to data, the yarn to information and the cloth to knowledge. Cutting and sewing the cloth into a useful garment is analogous to creating insight and judgment (wisdom). This analogy emphasizes two important points: (1) going from fleece to garment involves, at each step, an input of work, and (2) at each step, this input of work leads to an increase in organization, thereby producing a hierarchy of organization."

Prof. Nicolae Dragulanescu, **Polytechnics University of Bucharest, Romania**

Data are a set of symbols representing a perception of raw facts (i.e., following Debons, Horne, & Cronenweth (1988), events from which inferences or conclusions can be drawn). **Information** is organized data (answering the following basic questions: What? Who? When? Where?).

Knowledge is understood information (answering following basic questions: why?, how?, for which purpose?)."

Prof. Raya Fidel, **University of Washington, Seattle, WA**

Data are a string of symbols. **Information** is data that is communicated, has meaning, has an effect, has a goal. **Knowledge** is a personal/cognitive framework that makes it possible for humans to use information.

Dr. H.M. Gladney, **HMG Consulting, McDonald, PA**

Data are representations of facts about the world. **Information** is data organized according to an ontology that defines the relationships between some set of topics. Information can be communicated. **Knowledge** is a set of conceptual structures held in human brains and only imperfectly represented by information that can be communicated. Knowledge cannot be communicated by speech or any form of writing, but can only be hinted at.

Dr. Donald Hawkins, **Information Today, Medford, NJ**

Data are facts and statistics that can be quantified, measured, counted, and stored. **Information** is data that has been categorized, counted, and thus given meaning, relevance, or purpose. **Knowledge** is information that has been given meaning and taken to a higher level. Knowledge emerges from analysis, reflection upon, and synthesis of information. It is used to make a difference in an enterprise, learn a lesson, or solve a problem.

Prof. Caroline Haythornthwaite, **University of Illinois at Urbana Champaign, Urbana, IL**

Datum is smallest collectable unit associated with a phenomenon. Normally, data occur in collections that are collected in order to monitor a process, assess a situation, and/or otherwise gain a referent on a phenomenon. This does not mean that data are always defined, collected or used appropriately for the question in hand, but that that is the intention when doing so. They are building blocks, even if the building is engineered incorrectly. **Information.** I would usually expect information to be an assessment or interpretation of data. Often information is not far removed from the 'smallest collectable unit' as I have defined "datum." But I expect it to be some abstraction from data.. Information does not inherently mean empirical or first hand analysis of data. It also does not guarantee correct interpretation of data although that is expected. **Knowledge** is more subject, and intangible compared to information or data. It is what an individual takes from information and data, and what they incorporate into their beliefs, values, procedures, actions, etc. It is heavily internally oriented, understood completely only to the person possessing it. Much work around knowledge implies how to get the knowledge "out of" one head and in to another. Such transfer entails encoding knowledge into transferable information and decoding again into knowledge. Knowledge and information are not the same, but they feed from and support each other. A message is the encoded information or codified/explicit knowledge that is disseminated to others. Very much a Shannon and Weaver transmission model, but I also consider that encoding and decoding have a heavy personal, contextual and historical influence.

Mr. Ken Herold, Hamilton College, Clinton, NY

Data are dynamic objects of cultural experience having the aspect of being meaning-neutral and a dual nature of description and instruction. **Information** is dynamic objects of cultural experience having the aspect of being belief-neutral and a dual nature of content and medium. **Knowledge** is dynamic objects of cultural experience having the aspect of being action-neutral and a dual nature of abstracting to and from the world.

Prof. William Hersh, **Oregon Health & Science University, Portland**

Data are the raw observations about the world collected by scientists and others, with a minimum of contextual interpretation. **Information** is the aggregation of data to make coherent observations about the world. **Knowledge** is the rules and organizing principles gleaned from data to aggregate it into information.

Prof. Michel J. Menou, **Knowledge and ICT management consultant, France**

Data are perceptible or perceived—if and when the signal can be interpreted by the 'user'—attributes of physical, biological, social or conceptual entities. **Information** is recorded and organized data that can be communicated (Porat & Rubin, 1977). However, it is advisable to distinguish between the various states or conditions of information (e.g. information-as an object (Buckland, 1991b), or semantic, syntactic and paradigmatic states (Menou, 1995). **Knowledge** is information that is understood, further to its utilization, stored, retrievable and reusable under appropriate circumstances or conditions.

Prof. Haidar Moukdad, **Dalhousie University, Halifax, Nova Scotia, Canada**

Data are sets of characters, symbols, numbers, and audio/visual bits that are represented and/or encountered in raw forms. Inherently, knowledge is needed to decipher data and turn them into information. **Information** is facts, figures, and other forms of meaningful representations that when encountered by or presented to a human being are used to enhance his/her understanding of a subject or related topics. *Knowledge* is a reservoir of information that is stored in the human mind. It essentially constitutes the information that can be "retrieved" from the human mind without the need to consult external information sources.

Prof. Charles Oppenheim, **Loughborough University, Leicestershire, UK**

Data are raw material of information, typically numeric. **Information** is data which is collected together with commentary, context and analysis so as to be meaningful to others. **Knowledge** is a combination of information and a person's experience, intuition and expertise.

Prof. Maria Pinto, **University of Granada, Spain**

Data are primitive symbolic entities, whose meaning depend on it integration within a context that allow their understanding by an interpreter. **Information** is the intentional composition of data by a sender with the goal of modifying the knowledge state of an interpreter or receiver. **Knowledge** is the intelligent information processing by the receiver and it consequent incorporation to the individual or social memory (Belkin & Robertson, 1976; Blair, 2002)

Prof. Paul Sturges, **Loughborough University, Leicestershire, UK**

Data are discrete items of information that I would call facts on some subject or other, not necessarily set within a fully worked out framework. **Information** is facts and ideas communicated (or made available for communication). **Knowledge** is the considered product of information. Selection as to what is valid and relevant is a necessary condition of the acquisition of knowledge.

Prof. Carol Tenopir, **University of Tennessee, Knoxville, TN**

Data are facts that are the result of observation or measurement. (Landry et al., 1970). **Information** is meaningful data. Or data arranged or interpreted in a way to provide meaning. **Knowledge** is internalized or understood information that can be used to make decisions.

Prof. Irene Wormell, **Swedish School of Library and Information Science in Boräs, Sweden**

Data are alphabetic or numeric signs, which without context do not have any meaning. **Information** is a set of symbols that represent knowledge. Information is what context creates/ gives to data. It is cognitive. Normally it is understood as a new and additional element in collecting data and information for planned action. **Knowledge** is enriched information by a person's or a system's own experience. It is cognitive based. Knowledge is not transferable, but through information we can communicate about it. (Note that the highest level of information processing is the generation of wisdom, where various kinds of knowledge are communicated and integrated behind an action.

Prof. Yishan Wu, **Institute of Scientific and Technical Information of China (ISTIC), Beijing, China**

Data are artifacts that reflect a phenomenon in natural or social world in the form of figures, facts, plots, etc. **Information** is anything communicated among living things. It is one of the three mainstays supporting the survival and evolution of life, along with energy and materials. **Knowledge** is a human construct, which categorize things, record significant events, and find causal relations among things and/or events, etc. in a systematic way.

DEFINING 'INFORMATION' THROUGH VARIOUS APPROACHES

Defining any term seeks to study the qualitative and quantitative behavior. It has been a contested project to define information among the savants. The term "information" is used differently by individuals in different disciplines, from people involved in less scholarly pursuits, to those working in information based professions, such as information management, as well as by specialists in the cognitive sciences. All definitions agree that information is something more than data and something less than knowledge.

The first definition in the *Random House College Dictionary* suggests for information, is "knowledge communicated or received concerning a particular fact or circumstance; news. In an approach similar to defining information as meaning, information is often understood in terms of knowledge that is transmitted to a sentient being. In this context, Peters defines information as " knowledge with the human body taken out of it" [Peters, 1988]. Dretske notes that "it is common among cognitive scientists to regard information as a creation of the mind, as something we conscious agents assign to, or impose on, otherwise meaningless events. Information, like beauty, is in the mind of the beholder" [Dretske, 1983]. Similarly, information may be understood as "that which occurs within the mind upon the absorption of a message" [Pratt, 1982]. In general, we may define Information as the characteristics of the output of a process, these being informative about the process and the input.

APPROACHES OF INFORMATION SCIENCE

Information has long been understood as a concept appropriate for discussion in the humanities and social sciences. For the library and information professionals no value is more fundamental than a commitment to provide the people with information. Any message received and understood by intended audience is information. Although it sounds simple, yet people have put forth multitudes of opinions depending on their nature of study and research on information. Due to that it would be disingenuous labor to present a singular vision on the topic. In lack of agreement of interpretations it would be fair to put forth some of the concepts explained by library and information science professional under various approaches. Broadly nine typologies of definition are available:

a. Communicatory or Semiotic approach

This approach attempts to depict the communicatory role of information from one point to another. How the transfer of information from the source to recipient affect the status of the recipient is explained through this approach. For example, Madden defines information as stimulus which expands or amends the world view of the informed. On the other hand, Bateson is of the opinion that information is a difference that makes a difference after understanding. Whitemore and Yovits argues that information is data of value to decision making.

b. Message Approach

Fritze Mackhlup considers information as flow of messages involving the act of being told. Similarly, Rowley surmises information as data that can be transmitted between individuals and each individual can use it accordingly. Bhattacharya opines that information is the message conveyed or intended to be conveyed by a systematized body of ideas, or its accepted or acceptable substitutes.

c. Meaning approach

According to Nauta information is the meaning that is common to all the different ways of expressing the meaning. Further, Losee argues that information is produced by all processes and it is the values in the characteristics of the process. He says "information is always informative about something, being a component of the output or result of the process. This aboutness or representation is the result of a processes or function producing the representation of the input which might be output of another function and represents its input and so forth". He cites an example of the process of baking of cake. Cake provides information about both the process and original ingredients. The choice of high quality ingredients will affect the outcome. Varying the process such as the amount of time in the oven also changes the final product.

d. Activity based approach

In this approach attempts have been undertaken to define, information as an event, which occurs at some unique point in time and space to some particular individual (Partt, 1977).

e. Propositional approach

This school of thought considers a piece of information to be claim of world or a proposition. Derr surmises that information is an abstract, meaningful representation of determinations which have been made of objects. Drestske opines that information is capable of yielding knowledge and since knowledge requires truth, information requires it also. Fox put forth that information is collective proposition claim of a set of statements in a given context, provided the agent is in a position to know.

f. Structural approach

Thompson argues that information is a product that results from applying the process of organization to the raw material of experience. According to him data to the scientist are like colors on the palette of the painter. It is by the artistry of his theories that we are informed. It is the organization that is the information. While Brookes (1980) has put forward a fundamental equation showing the relationship between information and knowledge. He argues that knowledge structure in the mind is changed in some way with the input of information. Mathematically it is represented as-

$$K[S] + \Delta I = K[S + \Delta S]$$

Where, K[S] = existing knowledge structure

$K[S + \Delta S]$ = modified information structure

ΔI = new information

ΔS = effect of modification to the existing knowledge

g. Social approach

Cornelius conceives that information should be seen as socially constructed within a set of practices. A practice is a coherent set of actions and beliefs which we conform to along with other people in our practice (profession or game) and it has its own internal logic and ethic. On the other hand, Gougen says an item of information is an interpretation of a configuration of signs for which members of some social groups are accountable.

h. Multityple information approach

According to Dervin information is external world (what information we seek), information is internal world (what information we already have). Information is the reconciliation between the two world.

Bates concludes that information is pattern of organization of matter and energy

i. Deconstructing approach

Lastly, Frohmann attempts to replace the centrality of information as the focus of information studies and science studies with the centrality of practices surrounding documents.

CHARACTERISTICS OF INFORMATION

Information is one of the basic elements in present day society. Knowing some of its characteristics will help us to identify our information need and evaluate what we are receiving. There are few characteristics which is essential for any information. They are:

Authoritativeness : Information can only be used if it generates from authoritative source that can be confirmed. In order to identify information from mis-information one should confirm the source or origin of information.

Accurateness : It is almost self-evident that information should be accurate, true and correct. It should be accurate enough for its intended purpose (or user), without being unnecessarily detailed. Inaccurate information cannot provide a valid representation of reality and can limit the effectiveness or worth of decisions based on it.

Frequency : This is a measure of how often information is updated since its origin. In present web era, it is very essential that every information available on a website should be updated at a regular interval to maintain its relevancy.

Comprehensiveness & Completeness : This defines the scope of information. How much information is available on a particular subject and whether it is complete on that field. It is very essential to provide intended users with all the information that is necessary to fulfill their information needs and requirements. Completeness also suggests that all necessary information is included in any report that the organisation produces. The assumption is that there would be no error or omission in the information.

Timeliness : Information in time make information in use, otherwise it become outdated.

Relevance : Information is useful only when it is relevant to the objective and the intended user. In other words write information to right user at right time. An analysis of the prime cost of a project should not include information on indirect costs, for example. It is important that any figures or reports should stick to the point and not provide more information than is necessary. Irrelevant information wastes time and can increase the cost of information production. Additionally, Information is relevant only if it is available for a requisite situation.

Cost-efficient : Valuable information should not cost more to produce than it is worth. This is the reason why information that is produced more regularly than required is less useful/ valuable than information that is produced to satisfy a specific need or requirement.

ATTRIBUTES OF INFORMATION

While investigating the validity of information as a resource, the natural approach would be to compare attributes of information with those of other resources, in order to find some commonality. Burk and Horton give nine basic similarities between information and other *traditional* resources to fit into a resource-management framework, namely:

- Information is acquired at a definite, measurable cost.
- Information has a definite value, which may be quantified and treated as an accountable asset.
- Information consumption can be quantified.
- Cost-accounting techniques can be applied to help control the costs of information.
- Information has a clear life cycle: definition of requirements, collection, transmission, processing, storage, dissemination, use, and disposal.
- Information may be processed and refined, so that raw materials (e.g., databases) are converted into finished products (e.g., published directories).
- Substitutes for any specific item or collection of information are available, and may be quantified as more expensive, or less expensive.
- Choices are available to management in making trade-offs between different grades, types and costs of information. (Burk & Horton 1988).

From these concept of Burk and Horton, information is seen as something tangible, physical and concrete. While from the viewpoints of information profession like Vickers (1985), White (1985), Cleveland (1985), Boulding (1968), Repo (1986), information is explained as intangible. There has yet not been any widely agreed definition or a sound theoretical base of information as intangible. However, it is described that information is an intangible product of human intellect which can neither be seen nor felt but can be only expressed. Eaton and Bawden combine the viewpoints of various authors to come to the following key distinctions:

Value of information : Unlike other tangible resources, information is not readily quantifiable - that is, it is impossible to predict the ultimate value of information to its users. Also, over time, there is no predictable change in the value of information.

Multiplicative quality of information : The results produced by the use of information differ greatly from those produced by the use of other resources - for instance, information is not lost when given to others, and does not decrease when 'consumed': sharing information will almost always cause it to increase - that is, information has a self-multiplicative quality.

Dynamics of information : Information cannot be regarded as a static resource to be accumulated and stored within the confines of a static system. It is a dynamic force for change to the system within which it operates. It adds value to an organisation through encouraging innovation and change without being tangible.

Life cycle of information : Information seems to have an unpredictable life cycle. Ideas come into, go out of, and finally come back into, fashion.

Individuality of information : Information comes in many different forms, and is expressed in many different ways. Information can take on any value in the context of an individual situation. This proves that, as a resource, information is different from most other resources. The very fact that information is characterised as a dynamic force, 'constantly altering and extending a store of knowledge' (Rogers 1992), corresponds with situations in development in which outside information is offered to focus groups to alter their understanding of certain practices, which in turn can help them solve problems (such as improving food security or standards of living). (Eaton and Bawden 1991: 162-163)

Apart from the attributes identified by Eaton and Bawden, the following, also containing elements of intangibility, may be added to the list:

Alleviation of uncertainty : According to Mark and Pierce (2001), Shannon , as long ago as 1948, defined information as the resolution of uncertainty. This is perhaps one of the intangible attributes best known among a variety of researchers.

Interdependency : Information almost always forms part of technology - it is the "soft" part (Röling 1990: 12). Without its information component, technology has little value as a resource for potential users who are not familiar with its workings or its background. With regard to developing rural communities, one should bear in mind that it is not necessarily new technology that brings about these achievements. All outside technology applied for the first time could be viewed as *new* to the user group or that particular situation, and could have similar effects.

Enhancement of economic growth : A frequent complaint is that information is often denied its role as a resource (Neelameghan 1980; Boon 1992). Yet, when looking at the effect of information in development situations, there seems to be an underlying awareness of its importance. Kaimowitz *et al.*, (1990: 238) refer to the impact of new technology (including information as the hidden component) in agriculture on the basis of such aspects as increased farm income, reduced risk, resource conservation, improved health, better (food) security, and overall economic growth.

Extension of the knowledge base : From a development point of view, there is more emphasis, first, on improving peoples' lives socially, and only secondly on economic improvement. In development, outside technology is often introduced with the help of education, training and visual demonstrations. Rogers (1992: 137) states that training helps people in rural communities to expand horizons, increase perceptions, enhance competencies, enlarge sense of perspective, and enhance self-esteem.

The above seem to emphasise the impact of the dynamic force of information, where the 'extension or altering of people's stores of knowledge' (Eaton & Bawden 1991) positively affected their social well-being. Thus, although information is an intangible entity, it has the ability to bring about change for the better; which is the ultimate goal of development.

Context dependency : The value of information as a resource in rural development depends largely on situation-specific issues: for example, one could argue that agriculture-related information is mostly technical in nature. However, people with little exposure to modern society have many related issues they need to know about. Ozowa (1995: 17), for example, identified certain types of basic information needed for the development of crop production by traditional farmers; *inter alia,* information about agricultural input (seeds, fertiliser, etc.), extension, technology (farming equipment, etc.), implementation techniques (ploughing, sowing, pest and weed control), soil, water and climatic conditions, conservation, credit, marketing and infrastructure.

Culture dependency : Another attribute of information that can influence its usefulness as a development resource is that it is culture dependent - involving conceptual and cognitive differentiation. Pickering (1996: 451) is of the opinion that because information is culture specific, it is incommunicable unless acculturated - that is, adapted for the cultural environment or the cultural mind-set of the recipient group. Here, Shields and Servaes (1989: 49) also point out that information is not totally value-free, but is socially conditioned and shaped by the social structures that apply it. This aspect has serious implications for developers' efforts to transfer information to the rural communities of developing countries.

Medium dependency : Information is not only culture dependent, but also medium dependent. Once information is concretised outside the human memory it should be packaged in some or other format (i.e., print, images, sound, electronic digits, etc..) to be communicated to someone else. Unless receivers know how to use that particular format, the information will remain inaccessible and rendered useless; for example, an electronic medium directed at users who are unfamiliar with such facilities can impede access to available information.

Thus, medium dependency of information can have serious implications for quite a number of rural people who are dependent on oral communication, owing to their oral tradition and the fact that many of them are not literate. This attribute could cause information to be a less useful resource when compared with other resources needed for development purposes.

Conversion dependency : It is a well-known fact that information is not used in the original form offered by its creator alone -.often, it needs to be adapted to suit a particular situation or specific circumstances. It can also happen that only a small chunk of the original information is used together with other chunks of information to form a new information package needed for a particular situation. In this way, more value can be added to the appropriateness of information. Particularly in a situation where outside information from the industrialised world is used to improve a practice in rural development, the information content needs to be adapted to bring it to the level of understanding of potential recipients.

Burt Nanun describe some peculiar properties of information. They are:

- Information is heterogenous in nature, the use of same information varies from person to person.
- It can not represent itself, rather it requires a context, structure, or model to interpret.
- The demand of any information is very associated with its supply, times etc.
- It severs as a vital element in any organization for its production, profit and prospect.
- It requires proper protection for conservation, storage.

TYPES OF INFORMATION

The intensive study and research on information in the last decades has started a new epoch seeking new awareness of information. People find it modish to deride earlier notions in light of novel ideas. As one senses a fatiguing fight of interpretations to define information, the fecund power of human brain has sprouted into various manifestations of information typologies.

On the basis of characteristics G. Bhattacharya has spotted two universally accepted varieties of information viz.

1. Discursive information; and
2. Non-discursive information

Discursive information is the message conveyed by a

systematized body of ideas or its accepted or acceptable substitutes, having one or many of the attributes like: ranging over a wide field; proceeding logically or coherently from topic to topic; proceeding from logical abstraction to logical interpretation relating to its treatment and/or expression. For example, the set of ideas conveyed by defining information science is discursive information.

Whereas, the organized bodies of idea taking the shape of statement that conveys information consisting of unit fact and does not show any attributes of discursive information are non-discursive information. For example, if one asks 'What is your age?' One can say 'I am 22 or 'twenty two. It consists of unit fact and does not show any attributes of discursive information. Henceforth it is non-discursive information. Non-discursive information is further divided into two groups:

(a) *Qualitative information* : Qualitative non-discursive information describes unit facts in relation to quality.

(b) *Quantitative information* : Quantitative non-discursive information describes unit facts in relation to quantity.

In another attempt, J.H. Shera in *Foundation of education for librarianship* has segregated information into six types:

1. Conceptual information : It refers to the formulation of mental conception of bare ideas and thoughts about any problem.

2. Empirical information : Information derived from or guided by experience or relating to experiment and observation rather than theory is said to be empirical information. They are verifiable by experience or experiment.

3. Procedural information : Information providing a well established method of acting or progressing in a course of action is known as procedural information.

4. Stimulatory information : These information are stimulated by existing theories.

5. Policy information : It provides a plan or definite course of action for the sake of expediency or facility to be pursued by an individual, government, party, business etc. It is an indispensable tool for decision making.

6. Directive information : It gives an authoritative instruction or direction for proper coordination work between team work or group activity.

On the basis of nature of production of information Moraine Valley Community College Library/Learning Resources Center have categorized information as:

1. Scholarly information : They report the advancements, new findings or ideas in a field in to quench the quest of information. They are available in books, articles in scholarly journals and websites.

2. Professional / Trade information : They inform, promote and usually strengthen the trade market or learned societies. They are available to the people in the form of trade magazines, journals and association websites.

3. Government information : They are an aid to inform the policies or programme of the government to the common people or the decision makers. They are commonly available as printed government publications or official government publications.

4. Information providing facts, definition or statistics: These information presents facts, definitions or statistics with little explanation or evaluation. They can be obtained from books and websites.

5. Information providing overviews : They provide overview or background on a subject. They can be found out from encyclopedias, dictionaries, other books and websites.

6. Information providing news or current events : They report daily events in a scheduled manner across the nation or worldwide. They are available as newspapers, newsmagazines, and news websites.

7. Information providing opinions : They contain the ideological thoughts put forth by anyone. It depends upon the reader to justify the credibility of the author and he may or may not follow him.

8. Uncredited information : They provide information on personal interests. No one is accountable of the thought content of the information. They are available in the form of personal websites and blogs.

On the basis of Shannon Weaver model of information transfer information can be further divided as:

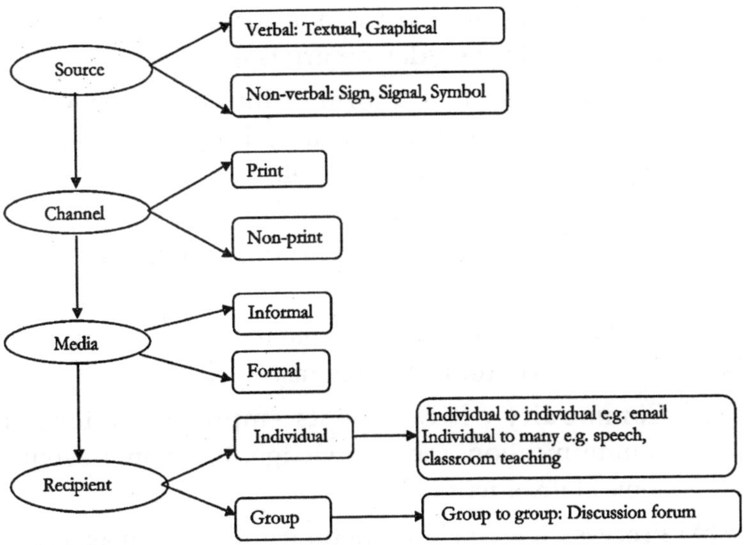

Kathy Tyner in his study pointed five types of information: facts, concepts, procedures, processes and principles. Fact is a bit of information that identifies an object, person, place or data. For example: 14.08.1947. If you recall the fact then you know that is the date when we got freedom. Whereas, concept is a group of items or ideas that share common features. For example: If you see cat and tiger you recall the concept that you have and distinguish between cat and tiger by their features. Procedure provides a series of steps to prepare or do something. For example, while preparing tea you recall the procedures and prepare tea. On the other hand, process describes how anything works or operates and principles are certain rules and well established guidelines that predict an outcome.

In a different look, Melvin J. Voigt has also put forth four categories of information. These are:

(a) **Current approach :** It is a type of information belonging to the time actually in progress or of the immediate present.

(b) **Everyday approach :** It is a form of information pertaining to everyday occurrence.

(c) **Catching up :** It is a form of information that one comprehends with the intellect. It has a tendency to grasp eagerly to update oneself.

(d) **Exhaustive approach :** It seeks to provide comprehensive or exhaustive information on a subject or a topic.

Lastly, Rathswol sates that the nature of information is taken in terms of four components:

(a) **Commodity :** It represents empirical content of communication and knowledge. E.g. Some events, some state of world.

(b) **Process :** It connotes structural and original aspect of communication and knowledge. Information as an process is represented as something. E.g. generic structure.

(c) **State of knowing :** Information as a state of knowing relates directly to the structural-functional aspects of human knowing activity. It is representative of the effect of information in terms of changes in a human knower.

(d) **Environment** : The concept of environment refers to man-machine, man-man system etc. command & control system within which certain data-information transformation occurs.

USAGES OF INFORMATION

The concept of information use is historically associated with the resource itself, rather than the information contained within. The emergence of self-serve searching and the web has changed the way we now view the object of use from those physical items to the information chunks. Taylor (1991, 230) proposed a taxonomy of eight classes of information uses, generated from the information need(s) perceived by users:

- **Enlightenment** : context information
- **Problem Understanding** : better comprehension of a specific problem
- **Instrumental** : what to do and how to do something
- **Factual** : precise data
- **Confirmational** : verify a piece of information
- **Projective** : future oriented
- **Motivational** : relates to personal involvement
- **Personal or Political** : relationships, statue, reputation, personal fulfillment.

These classes of information use were developed from expressions of perceived needs, rather than of observation, report or discussion of actual information use.

In examining the value of library and information services, Saracevic and Kantor (1997, 533-4) described a three-step model of information use, with the following components:

- **Acquisition** : getting information or objects potentially conveying information, as related to some intentions;

- **Cognition** : absorbing, understanding, integrating the information
- **Application** : use of this newly understood and cognitively processed information

This model clearly links the seeking and acquisition of information to its use; however, the discussion of use remains at a broad, conceptual level.

Choo (2002) views information use as "a dynamic, interactive social process of inquiry that may result in the making of meaning or the making of decisions." The very first type of information use involved with human understanding and integration with the user's knowledge base. This type of information use has no visible indicators except in the depth and breadth of one's personal knowledge base. The second form of information use concerns decision-making, this may be organizational decision-making or individual decision making. Interestingly, his approach is also at a conceptual high-level matching of potential uses with stages of the decision-making process: identification, development, and selection.

REPRESENTATION OF INFORMATION

In order to transmit information from one point to another, the foremost need is information has to be represented in some way, and conveyed through a channel of some kind. As Marshall McLuhan in his book *Gutenberg galaxy* pointed that only electric light is pure information. Every other medium has to have another medium inside it. Representation of information is the act or instance of portraying a mental imagery of some term, character or idea. Information is nebulous, unformed, unshaped and nondescript entity that is beyond mental conceptualization. In order to clasp the essence of information, it needs to be configured, ordered, and structured.

Kevin McGarry in his book: *The changing context of information: an introductory analysis* opines that information should have a discriminable attribute if it has to be perceived by the receiver which can distinguish it from the surrounding phenomena. McGarry has identified three classes of vehicles for information carriage. These are:

- Signs
- Signals
- Symbols

Sign

According to the Oxford Dictionary of Current English sign is an object, quality, or event whose presence or occurrence indicates the probable presence or occurrence of something else. For example *flowers are often given as a sign of affection,* thunder is a sign of storm. For medical practitioners sign is an indication of a disease detectable by a medical practitioner even if not apparent to the patient. A conventional sign signifies by agreement, as a full stop signifies the end of a sentence.

The concept sign also explain as a gesture or action used to convey information or instructions: *she gave him the thumbs-up sign.* Or a notice that is publicly displayed giving information or instructions in a written or symbolic form: *I didn't see the stop sign.* Evan an action or reaction that conveys something about someone's state or experiences: *she gave no sign of having seen him.* Sometimes, it is regarded as an indication or evidence of what is happening or going to happen. A sign, in common use, is an indication that a previously observed event is about to occur again . Thus the range of uses of signs are varied. They might include: the indication or mark of something, a display of a message (i.e. a notice), a signal to draw attention, evidence of an underlying cause (for instance, the symptoms of a disease are signs of the disease), a character for a mathematical operation, a body gesture, etc. Signs carry information content to be delivered to agents. However, it is also useful to understand that some signs are more easily used as referents than others. In the beginning of the 20th century, Charles Sanders Peirce defined a typology of signs:

- **Icons** are direct representations of objects. They are similar to the thing they represent. Examples are pictorial road signs, scale models, and of course the icons on your computer. A footprint on the sand is an icon of a foot.
- **Indices** are indirect representations of objects, but necessarily related. Smoke is an index of fire, the bell is an index of the tolling stroke, and a footprint is an index of a person.
- **Symbols** are arbitrary representations of objects, which require exclusively a social convention to be understood. A road sign with a red circle and a white background denotes something which is illegal because we have agreed on its arbitrary meaning. To emphasize the conventional aspect of the semantics of symbols, consider the example of variations in road signs: in the US yellow diamond signs denote cautionary warnings, whereas in Europe a red triangle over a white background is used for the same purpose. We can see that convention establishes a code, agreed by a group of agents, for understanding (decoding) the information contained in symbols. For instance, smoke is an index of fire, but if we agree on an appropriate code (e.g. Morse code) we can use smoke signals to communicate symbolically.

McGarry mentioned that sign is a physical evidence of the thing or event it represents. However, it is also used to indicate that someone or something is not present where they should be or are expected to be. For example, smoke is a sign of fire but one can't be sure whether the smoke is due to fire or burning of charcoal or something else. One can't be sure till he does not conform it personally.

The distinctive feature of signs in that they denote something, regardless of whether that something exists or does not exist, is concrete or abstract, possible or impossible, a thing or an event, a substance or a determination, an individual or a collective. Analysis even of one single sign leads to a multiplicity of signs and their denoted items. For this reason we may say that the sign contains a reference to both the denote items considered per se, in isolation and the contents or situation in which the denoted item appears.

Characteristics of signs

1. Signs are used to represent information beyond any cultural limitation.
2. Signs are always contextual.
3. Signs are a tool to start the preliminary phase of investigations.
4. Signs can be misleading, hence needs to be confirmed.
5. Signs are uncertain in nature.

Signals

The word *signal* comes from the Latin word *signum,* meaning "sign," and from the Late Latin word *signalis,* meaning "of a sign." A *signal* is an event, message, activity, or, generally, any means of communication that encodes or transmits a message or some information between at least two parties, the sender and the receiver of the message. *The policeman raised his hand as a signal to stop.* It also server as an indication of a state of affairs: *the markets are waiting for a clear signal about the direction of policy.* It can be an event or statement that provides the impulse or occasion for something specified to happen: *the player's announcement that he is retiring is the **signal for** scores of journalists to gather at his* *last match or* an apparatus on a railroad, typically a colored light or a semaphore, giving indications to train engineers of whether or not the line is clear.

Anything that serves to indicate, warn, direct or command that can be through light or a gesture or an act is signal like a traffic signal, a signal to sit. They are an act or event that causes some action. Signal is an impulse response to a stimulus whose variations represent information.

According to Kevin McGarry signal is a form of sign with an emphasis on the need for some form of action to follow and requiring some form of response from the receiver.

Characteristics of signals

1. Signal display two noteworthy characteristics: *multiplex* as well as *transflective*.
2. Signals are dynamic in nature. They change with time.
3. Signals are purely contextual.
4. The semantics of signal varies from person to person.
5. Signals are always responsive.
6. Signals relates to a particular society, and its ideas, customs and art.
7. Signals are transmittable.

Symbols

The English word *symbol* derives etymologically from the Greek *súmbolon*, meaning "tally," "contract," or "ticket," which referred originally to a token that was broken in two so that each half could be used to confirm the identity of the other. The word stems from the Greek roots *syn* - ("together") and *ballein* ("to throw"), and thus has the approximate connotation of "to throw together." Symbols are especially useful in *showing* what one cannot *say* ; that is, they express ineffable concepts, abstract ideas, and particularly complex emotional significations that are difficult or impossible to fully articulate. Data is represented by symbols. Symbols convey meaning only when understood. The symbol itself is not the information, but merely a representation of it. Symbol meaning is one of convention. Symbols may convey one meaning to you and me, another meaning to others, and no meaning at all to those that do not know their significance.

At its most basic level, a symbol is anything that represents another thing by virtue of customary association due to a conceptual connection or perceived resemblance. Because virtually anything can serve as a symbol and because a symbol conveys information only insofar as it has meaning to a specific community, the connection between a symbol and its referent is not intrinsic to the symbol itself but rather is a function of agreed upon use, custom, or convention. It is in this sense that language is symbolic. The word *water* designates the liquid object only insofar as members of the English speech community agree that it does. The liquid has no inherent property that compels us to call it by that name. It could just as well be designated by other sounds, for instance *jal* in Bengali, or pani in Hindi.

Symbols are figure or character or mark or a combination of letters that suggests something else to the unconscious mind. Culture is based on symbols. Flags, traffic lights, diplomas, and mathematical notation are all, in their various ways, symbols. It is the primary way by which humans create meaning, classify knowledge, express emotion, and regulate society. The ineluctably human ability to generate and interpret symbols is, for example, what allows us to differentiate winks from blinks (Sapir 1932, p. 493). Because symbolism is fundamental to human thought and interaction, it is of concern to the social and cognitive sciences, particularly anthropology and linguistics, though it is also studied by psychology, philosophy, and sociology, and to a lesser extent political science and even economics.

The meaning of political and religious symbols, often charged with emotion, are likewise dependent on cultural contexts, even when the same or similar signs are employed across cultures. The *swastika* has come to be taboo in much of Europe and the United States due to its historic association with Nazi Germany and contemporary white supremacists, but elsewhere, as in the cases of Hinduism, Buddhism, and Native American religions, it remains a sacred symbol with positive connotations. In religions of Indic origin it is a symbol of auspiciousness, as reflected by its original Sanskrit name *svasti,* meaning luck, well-being, and fortune; in Hindu traditions it is a solar symbol, and in Buddhist regions it adorns the entrance to some temples. The swastika design is also seen in Native American traditions. In short, symbols are without specific meanings aside from the connotations assigned to them.

Characteristics of symbols

1. Symbols are the property of a group, not the exclusive property of an individual.
2. Symbols are static in nature and to some extent are contextual.
3. Symbols are independent of situation. They serve as stores of meaning within a culture.
4. It also serves as unifying forces within and across social and cultural groups.
5. Symbols are highly customizable and reusable.
6. Symbols are used to promote logo or symbol to influence consumers.

Signal, Sign, and Symbol

Semiotics, epistemology, logic, and philosophy of language are concerned about the nature of signs, what they are and how they signify. The nature of signs and symbols and significations, their definition, elements, and types, is mainly established by Aristotle, Augustine, and Aquinas. Various traditions define signs as a class beside symbols or even as a class of symbols. Occasionally, sign is also opposed to the index. According to Sebeock (1976), however, when a sign token mechanically or conventionally triggers some reaction on the part of a receiver, it is said to function as a signal. On the other hard, a sign without either similarity or contiguity, but with a conventional link between its signifier and its denotata, and with an international class for its designatum, is called a symbol.

A *signal* generally expresses a relationship between signifier and signified that is dynamic or causal. Animals as well as humans make use of signals, and in both cases the signifiers trigger or incite certain actions—as, for instance, when a male bird arouses the female by signaling with a mating call or car brake lights signal motorists behind to stop. A *sign* tends to have a singular meaning, in that signifier and signified are closely connected and typically come from the same context, and the signification itself is mostly *metonymic* —that is, a part or attribute stands for the whole. When, for example, a hunter sees a hoofprint of the deer he is pursuing, the hoofprint is a sign of his quarry. In military, technical, and commercial fields signs are often employed as codes, such as Morse code or the North American Industrial Classification System used to designate business type. When signs are used as codes it is because the relation between signifier and signified is conventional rather than intrinsic and because the signification is precise.

Symbols expand the notions of signs and signals. Symbols are characterized by rich meanings that are multiple, fluid, diverse, layered, complex, and frequently predicated on metaphorical associations that assert an analogy between things from different contexts that normally may not be connected. Given that the referents of symbols tend to be general, abstract, and ambiguous, their personally or socially constructed significations may not be apparent except to those who make them. The simple difference from sign to symbol is that a sign gives you some kind of direction, whereas a symbol is a representation of something else.

Whether a signifier is a symbol, signal, or sign is determined not by the object itself but rather by how it is used. In fact, the same signifier can function as all three depending on the situation; for example, the color red functions as a signal in stoplights, as a sign of blood in a painting of the crucified Christ, and as a symbol in a national flag. Moreover, the meanings of symbols, insofar as they are conventional, are context-dependent and variable, both across and within cultures. In ancient Rome red was associated with the god of war, Mars, whereas in China red is an auspicious color associated with luck, money, success, happiness, and traditional wedding attire. In the United States, a red rose is a statement of love, but being "in the red" means one has suffered economic losses, and "seeing red" means one is angry.

CONCLUSION

From "soft" sciences such as sociology right across to "hard" sciences such as physics, information has become a central concern. This chapter discusses the conceptual approaches data, information, and knowledge. In this chapter we have proceed from general by giving an overview of the concept information science the by specific application, i.e., how information represents through sign, signals symbols etc. We have also detailed the attributes, types, & use of information. This might help the reader to a better understanding of the issues and the considerations involved in establishing the foundations of Information Science.

The second half of the 20th Century shows a growing interest on the objective meaning that was already part of the classic pre-modern tradition and which is interpreted now within the framework of empirical science and information technology. Based on the opinion about the distinction between the date, information, and knowledge, data is always specified in a conceptual context. Information is the one which expresses data in a structured format. In fact, information is data in context, or to say: contextualized data. It provides an understanding of data (provides insight about statements of observation). Knowledge, on the other hand, is internalized or understood information that can be used to make decisions. Knowledge isn't contextualized information, and it is certainly distinct from information. Information has so many attributes and can be represent through various vehicles like sign, symbols, languages etc.

REFERENCES

Bates, Marcia J. (2006). *Fundamental Forms of Information, Journal of the American Society for Information Science and Technology,* 57(8), 1033-1045

Bateson,Gregory (1972). Steps to an ecology of mind Ballantine Books:New York.

Belkin, N.J., & Robertson, S.E. (1976). Information science and the phenomenon of information. *Journal of the American Society for Information Science,* 27, 197–204.

Bhattacharya, G. (1978). Information Sciences : a unified view through a system approach. Twenty-Fourty All India Library Conference held at Bangalore, Indian Library Association, Delhi

Blair, D.C. (2002). Knowledge management: Hype, hope or help? *Journal of the American Society for Information Science and Technology,* 53(12), 1019–1028.

Boon, J.A. (1992). Information and development: some reasons for failure. *Information Society,* **8**(3), 227-241.

Boulding, K. (1968). Knowledge as a commodity. In *Beyond economics: essays on society, religion and ethics.* Ann Abor, Michigan: University of Michigan Press.

Brookes,B.C. (1980). The foundation of information science Journal of Information Science, 2(3-4),125-133

Buckland, M. (1991a). Information and information systems. New York: Praeger. Buckland,

Buckland, M. (1991b). Information as thing. *Journal of the American Society of Information Science*, 42(5), 351–360.

Burk, C.F. & Horton, F.W. (1988). *Infomap. A complete guide to discovering corporate information resources.* Englewood Cliffs, NJ: Prentice Hall.

Capurro, R. (1978). Information. Ein Beitrag zur etymologischen and ideengeschichtlichen Begründung des Informationsbegriffs [A contribution to the etymological and conceptual history of the concept of information].

Choo, Chun Wei. (2002). *Information Management for the Intelligent Organization: The Art of Scanning the Environment.* Medford, NJ: Information Today.

Cleveland, H. (1985). The twilight of hierarchy: speculations on the global information hierarchy. *Information and Referral,* 7(1),1-31.

Cornelius, Ian. (1996). Information and interpretation. In Peter Ingwersen & Niels Ole Pors (Eds.), *Information science: Integration in perspective* (pp. 11-21). From the Second International Conference on Conceptions of Library and Information Science (CoLIS2). Copenhagen: The Royal School of Librarianship.

Derr, Richard (1985). The concept of information in ordinary discourse Information process management, 21(6),489-499.

Dervin, Branda (1977). Useful theory of librarianship: communication not information, *Drexel Library Quarterly,* 13(3): 16-32.

Drestske, Fred (1981). Knowledge and the flow of information Cambridge: MIT Press.

Dretske, Fred I. (1983). Précis of 'Knowledge & the flow of information. *Behavioral and Brain Sciences,* 6:55-90.

Eaton, J.J. & Bawden, D. (1991). What kind of resource is information? *International Journal of Information Management,*

11(2), 156-165.

Fox, Christopher (1983). Information and misinformation: an investigation of the notions of information, misinformation, informing and misinforming. Greenwood Press. USA.

Frohmann, Bernd (2004). Deflating information: From Science Studies to Documentation, University of Toronto Press

Gougen, Joseph (1997). Towards a social ethical theory of information. Available at: http://cseweb.ucsd.edu/~goguen/projs/soc.html

Kaimowitz, D., Snyder, M. & Engel, P. (1990). A conceptual framework studying the links between agricultural research and technology transfer in developing countries. In D. Kaimowitz (Ed.), *Making the link: agricultural research and technology transfer in developing countries* , (pp. 227-269). Boulder, CO: Westview Press.

Kathy Tyner, M.S. Available at: (*http://www.etc.edu.cn/eet/eet/articles/Infotypes/start.htm*)

Landry, B.C., Mathis, B.A., Meara, N.M., Rush, J.E., & Young, C.E. (1970). Definition of some basic terms in computer and information science, *Journal of the American Society for Information Science*, 24(5), 328–342.

Losee, Robert (1997). A discipline independent definition of information science. *Journal of Information Science*,48(3), 254-269

Madden,A.D. (2004). A definition of information *Journal of Documentation*, 60(1),9-23

Mark, A. & Pierce, L. (2001). The social nature of information. *Library Trends* , **49**(3), 472-485.

Menou, M.J. (1995). The impact of information (Part 2): Concepts of information and its value. Information Processing and Management, 31(4), 479–490.

Moraine Valley Community College Library/Learning Resources Center. Available at: http://www.morainevalley.edu/library/handouts/types_of_information_0705.pdf)

München Saur Verlag.Capurro, R., & Hjørland, B. (2003). The concept of information. *Annual Review of Information Science and Technology*, 37(8), 343–411.

Nauta, Doedi (1972). The meaning of information. The Hague: Mounton:

Neelameghan, A. (1980). Information systems for national development - the social relevance of information systems. *International Forum on Information and Documentation*, **5**(4), 3-8.

Ozowa, V.N. (1995). The nature of agricultural information needs of small scale farmers in Africa: the Nigerian example. *Quarterly Bulletin of the International Association of Agricultural Information Specialists* , **50**(1), 15-20.

Peters, John Durham (1988). Information: Notes toward a critical history. *Journal of Communication Inquiry*, 12(2):9-23, Summer.

Pickering, W.R. (1996). Principia informatica: conversations with R.T. Bottle. *Journal of Information Science* , **22**(6), 447-456.

Porat, M.V., & Rubin, M. (1977). The information economy: Definition and measurement (OT Special publication, Vol. 1, pp. 77–120). Washington DC: Office of Telecommunications, U.S. Department of Commerce.

Pratt, Allan (1977). The information of the image: a model of the communication process, *Libri*,27(3),204-220

Pratt, Alan D. (1982). *The Information of the Image*. Ablex, Norwood, NJ

Repo, A.J. (1986). The dual approach of the value of information: an appraisal of use and exchange values. *Information Processing & Management*, **22**(5), 373-383.

Rogers, A. (1992). *Adults learning for development*. London: Cassell.

Sapir, Edward (1932). Symbolism. In *Encyclopedia of the Social Sciences*, ed. Edwin R. A. Seligman and Alvin Johnson, 14, 492–495. New York: Macmillan.

Saracevic, Tefko and Paul B. Kantor (1997). Studying the value of library and information services. Part I. Establishing a theoretical framework. *Journal of the American Society for Information Science* 48, 527-542.

Sebeock, Thomas A. (1976). History of structuralism. – the sign sets. MA: Newbury House.

Shera, Jesse. *The foundations of education for librarianship*. New York, Becker and Hayes 1972.

Shields, P. & Servaes, J. (1989). The impact of the transfer of information technology on development. *Information society*, 6(1), 47-57.

Stonier, T. (1993). The wealth of information. London: Thames/ Methuen.

Stonier, T. (1997). Information and meaning—An evolutionary perspective. Berlin: Springer.

Taylor, Robert S. (1991). Information use environments. In *Progress in Communication Science*, eds. Brenda Dervin and Melvin J. Voigt. Norwood, NJ: Ablex: 271-254.

Thompson, Frederick (1968). The organization is information *American Documentation*.,19(3),305-308.

Vickers, P. (1985). Information management: selling a concept. In B. Cronin (Ed.). *Information management: from strategies to action*, London: Aslib.

White, P. (1985). Intelligence management. In B. Cronin (Ed.). *Information management: from strategies to action*, London: Aslib.

Zins, Chaim (2007). Conceptual approaches for defining data, information and knowledge. *Journal of the American Society for Information Science and Technology*, 55(4), 479-493.

2

Information Communication

"Think like a wise man but communicate in the language of the people"
-W.B. Yeats

The basic motto for generation of information is to communicate. In this chapter we will discuss the concept information communication and then identify what are the major components through which communication made. The evolution of different means has opened up a vast potential for communication. With a plethora of tools and methods to use, the communicator and the receptor too may find it difficult to receive right information at right time. There are so many barriers which hindered the communication process. A theory is some form of explanation of a class of observed phenomena. Karl Popper described theory as "the net which we throw out in order to catch the world—to rationalize, explain, and dominate it." Many who study communication adhere to an idea of communication theory that is akin to that found in other academic fields. In this chapter we also approaches communication theory from a media perspective, in an attempt to show theory development within a social context.

DEFINING COMMUNICATION

The word communication is derived from a latin root '*communicare* 'which means to share or to participate. Communication is the prime mover of information. Theodore Clevenger Jr. noted that "the continuing problem in defining communication for scholarly or scientific purposes stems from the fact that the verb 'to communicate' is well established in the common lexicon and therefore is not easily captured for scientific use. Indeed, it is one of the most overworked terms in the English language".

Since a long time, scholars have made many attempts to define *communication,* but establishing a single definition has proved impossible and may not be very fruitful. Due to that in this part we do not offer a single definition of communication, instead look at a range of theories that defines communication in a variety of ways. According to the Newman and Summer communication is used as an exchange of facts, ideas, opinions or emotions by two or more persons. However, Hoben defines that communication is the verbal interchange of thought or idea. He is not dealing with written and visual communication. We get a good definition about communication by Anderson who says, Communication is the process, by which we understand others and in turn endeavor to be understood by them. It is dynamic, constantly changing and shifting in response to the total situation.

Frank Dance took a major step toward clarifying the concept by outlining a number of elements used to distinguish communication. He found three points of "critical conceptual differentiation" that form the basic dimensions of communication. The first dimension is *level of observation,* or abstractness. Some definitions are broad and inclusive; others are restrictive. For example, the definition of communication as "the process that links discontinuous parts of the living world to one another" is general (Ruesch,

1957). On the other hand, communication as "a system (as of telephones or telegraphs) for communicating information and orders (as in a naval service)," is restrictive (Webster, 1986)

The second distinction is *intentionality.* Some definitions include only purposeful message limitation. The following is an example of a definition that includes intention: "Those situations in which a source transmits a message to a receiver with conscious intent to affect the latter's behaviors" (Miller, 1966). A definition that does not require intent follows: "It is a process that makes common to two or several what was the monopoly of one or some" (Cartier, 1959).

The third dimension used to distinguish among definitions of communication is normative *judgment.* Some definitions include a statement of success, effectiveness, or accuracy; other definitions do not contain such implicit judgments. The following definition, for example, presumes that communication is successful: "Communication is the verbal interchange of a thought or idea" (Hoben, 1954). The assumption in this definition is that a thought or idea is successfully exchanged. Another definition, on the other hand, does not judge whether the outcome is successful or not: "Communication is the transmission of information" (Berlson and Steiner, 1964). Here information is *transmitted,* but it is not necessarily *received* or understood.

The basic objective of any communication is to establish and disseminate the thought content. It facilitates the development of plans for the achievement of goals. In an organization like library, communication helps to manage and utilizes manpower and other resources in the most effective and efficient manner. It helps librarians to lead, direct and motivate employees to contribute right things.

COMMUNICATION TYPES

Communication can be of different types such as verbal communication, non verbal communication and written communication. In case of **verbal** communication, it is merely by using speech and language that the communication takes place. In case of **non-verbal** communication, there is no exchange of words, but it may be gestures or signs or facial expressions that are used for communication. In case of **written** communication, a letter is used to express oneself. This could again either be a hand written letter or a typed letter.

In a different look, communication can also be explained as one-way communication, two-way communication and transaction. **One-Way Communication** is focused on getting the message to the receiver. Self-action treats communication as a manipulation of others. It is very message centered. There is no way to know if the meaning is shared between the sender and the receiver. On the other hand, **Two-Way Communication** approach recognizes the role of the receiver as a communicator through feedback. It is message centered and is a very simplistic view of the communication process. Feedback allows senders to see if their message got across. **Transaction** approach focuses on meaning and sharing by accounting for all other factors in the communication process. It is concerned with the barriers that might affect the communication. Transaction is best described as effective communication. This is when the communication process is applied and carried out completely. The sender gives a message that is passed on to the receiver. In return, the receiver can give clear feedback that allows the sender to know whether or not the message was perceived as intended. If the message wasn't received as intended, then the sender will continue the communication process again in order to ensure effective communication.

According to Prasher there are six forms of communication:

a. One- way communication e.g. radio or television
b. Two-way communication e.g. text chatting
c. Non-verbal communication e.g. facial communication
d. Verbal communication. e.g. letter, reports
e. Informal communication
f. Formal communication
   f.1 Downward communication
   f.2 Upward communication
   f.3 Horizontal communication
   f.4 Diagonal communication

After understanding the concept 'communication', let's take a closer look at the elements in the communication process. By analyzing the parts of the process, we are better able to understand the whole.

PROCESS OF COMMUNICATION

Galvin and Wilkinson, discussed the communication process as a constant symbolic interaction of sharing, exchanging, and coordinating meanings. In general, communication is a continuous process by which we assign and convey meaning in an attempt to create shared understanding. The means of communication could be auditory such as speaking, singing and sometimes tone of voice and non-verbal or physical means such as writing, body language, touch and eye contact. The message must be conveyed through some medium to reach to the recipient. It is essential that this message must be understood by the recipient in same terms as intended by the sender. He must respond within a time frame. Thus, communication is a two way process and is incomplete without a feedback from the recipient to the sender on how well the message is understood by him. The main **components of communication process** are as follows:

1. Thought : First, information exists in the mind of the sender. This can be a concept, idea, information, or feelings.

2. Context : Communication is affected by the context in which it takes place. This context may be physical, social, chronological or cultural. Every communication proceeds with context. The sender chooses the message to communicate within a context.

3. Sender : Normally, communication is known as interpersonal, wherein the information or message is transferred from one person to the others. Transmitting person of the message is called the sender or transmitter. Sender may be an individual or a group or an organization. The views, background, approach, skills, competencies, and knowledge of the sender have a great impact on the message. The verbal and non verbal symbols chosen are essential in ascertaining interpretation of the message by the recipient in the same terms as intended by the sender.

4. Encoding : A sender makes use of symbols (words or graphic or visual aids) to convey the message and produce the required response. The process of converting information that has to be sent, into a format which the receiver can understand is known as encoding.

5. Message : Message is a key idea that the sender wants to communicate. It is a sign that elicits the response of recipient. Communication process begins with deciding about the message to be conveyed. It must be ensured that the main objective of the message is clear.

6. Media : Media is a means used to exchange / transmit the message. The sender must choose an appropriate medium for transmitting the message else the message might not be conveyed to the desired recipients. The choice of appropriate medium of communication is essential for making the message effective and correctly interpreted by the recipient. This choice of communication medium varies depending upon the features of communication. For instance - Written medium is chosen when a message has to be conveyed to a small group of people, while an oral medium is chosen when spontaneous feedback is required from the recipient as misunderstandings are cleared then and there.

7. Decoding : Information which is transferred to the receiver has to be interpreted. Interpretation is known as decoding.

8. Recipient : Recipient is a person for whom the message is intended / aimed / targeted. The degree to which the receipient understands the message is dependent upon various factors such as knowledge of recipient, their responsiveness to the message, and the reliance of encoder on decoder.

9. Feedback : Feedback is the main component of communication process as it permits the sender to analyze the efficacy of the message. It helps the sender in confirming the correct interpretation of message by the decoder. Feedback may be verbal (through words) or non-verbal (in form of smiles, sighs, etc.). It may take written form also in form of memos, reports, etc.

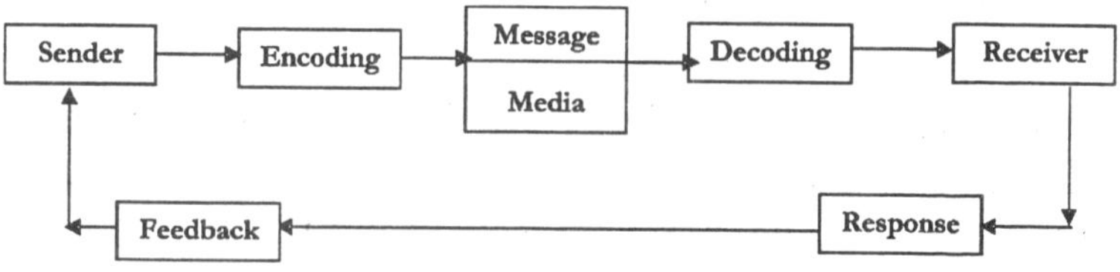

MEDIA OF INFORMATION COMMUNICATION

From the above diagram it is clear that message transmit through some media. In the next part we will discuss various media used in communication process. In communications, media (singular medium) are the storage and transmission channels or tools used to store and deliver information or data.

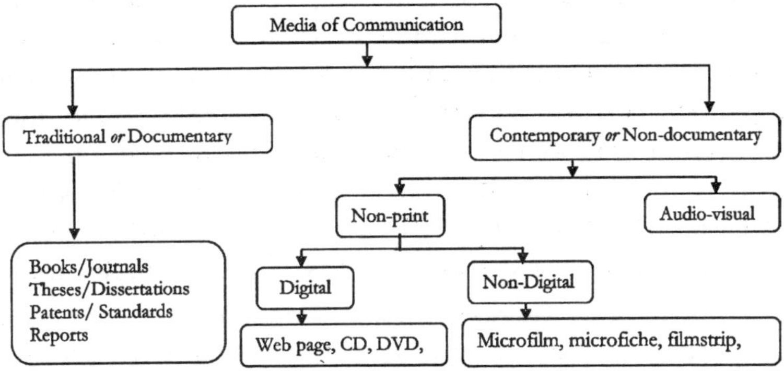

Parthasarthy has put forth two different means (he termed it as channel) of communication: Informal and formal. Communication, through formal and informal channels both is the lifeblood of any organization.

1. Informal channels : Informal channels are of stiffly conventional nature. They are not in accordance with any prescribed official manner. Some of common informal channels are:

a) Face-to-face discussion
b) Telephone
e) Internet
f) Voice messaging/ emailing/ instant messaging
g) Information intermediaries
h) Conference, meeting
i) Open forum

Traditionally, the main forms of informal communication in science, technology, medicine etc. have been through oral communication channels - personal contacts with colleagues and teachers - seminars, lectures, and discussions at conferences, fairs etc. These oral channels are often rapid and effective for conveying information. They allow a high degree of flexibility and are easy and pleasant to use. There is the possibility of a two-way communication between the producer and the receiver of the information. However, oral communication is seldom comprehensive; for example, it can be difficult to give detailed information about methods, constructions or results in a verbal presentation. Oral communication sometimes stimulates the hearer to look for some form of printed communication, but some information does not exist in a printed form, and can, therefore, only be reached by means of oral communication.

A widespread network of personal contacts is of great importance for gathering information. Research workers are particularly interested in obtaining the most recent information about developments within their own subject fields. Informal verbal communication is valued for the speed of information transfer. Established research workers gradually build up "the invisible college," an informal communication network.

2. Formal channels : A formal communication channel transmits information such as the goals, policies, and procedures of an organization. Messages in this type of communication channel follow a chain of command. These channels are in accordance with prescribed or customary forms. They ensure a formal authorization. Prasher (2003) has put forth various formal channels of communication, which include:

a) Authors

b) Libraries and information centres

c) Universities

d) Government

e) Professional societies

f) Research associations

g) Public or private research establishments
h) Learned societies and autonomous bodies
i) Industrial houses
j) Book trade
k) Manufacturers and traders brochure
l) Mass media- Pres, Radio, Television

Formal communication channels follow the organisational structure or hierarchy and flow in four directions: These four directions in which communication can travel are: downward; upward; lateral or horizontal; and diagonal. While in downward, communication involves communication from higher to lower levels so that leadership can communicate goals, strategies or role expectations. In upward, communication flows from lower levels to higher levels of the organisation, for example, when there is a need to communicate problems, results or suggestions. Horizontal communication occurs across the same level and involves for example, coordination of activities with peers (teams, committees), dissemination of useful information from one department to another (for example sales forecasts from the sales department to production, and problems such as a problem with product design from the production department to research and development). Horizontal communication facilitates the l inking of different areas of expertise and this may encourage innovation. The diagonal channels may potentially cause conflict as they involve communication between the lower level of one department to a higher level in another.

BARRIERS TO INFORMATION COMMUNICATION

Effective communication is achieved when the message sent is received by cent accuracy, which is a rare phenomenon. It is because of various hurdles or barriers in the communication process. The hindrances distort the messages and the communication becomes ineffective and incomplete. Some of the barriers are:

1. Physical barrier : Physical barriers are communication interferences that occur in the environment in which communication occurs. Some of the interferences are:

(a) *Noise* : Sudden distracting noise drowns the quality of voice message.

(b) *Physical distance* : When receiver is far away from the sender it is difficult to determine whether the receiver has received, understood, accepted and properly acted upon the message or not for an effective communication.

(c) *Information overload* : Unrestricted flow may result in overloading of information. For example people getting too many emails may tend to ignore mails that should be answered. People respond to information overload by simply escaping from the task of information communication.

2. Semantic barrier : Semantic is the science of meaning, words seldom mean the same thing to two persons. The sender and the receiver have to choose one meaning from among many. If both of them choose the same meaning the communication will be perfect. But people use either the same words in different ways or different words in the same way.

Hence, semantics may be a barrier to communication and it is not only the words but actions, implication and the entire situational contents that produce misunderstanding. Also, technical language may not be easily understood by the receiver which is also a barrier in communication process.

3. Organizational barrier :

(a) *Status differences* : Organizations often express hierarchical rank through a variety of symbols (titles, offices etc.). Such differences may distort communication. If the sender has a higher status than that of the receiver, then he has a tendency of not disclosing all the information to the receiver just to maintain his importance. On the other hand if the status of the sender is lower than that of the receiver he will have to transmit those information that can please the superior.

(b) *Organizational facilities* : An organization needs to hold meetings, suggestion boxes, and complaint boxes for effective communication to increase information potency.

(c) *Choice of channel* : Choice of channel is a prerequisite for an effective communication. For illiterate people using written communication is a failure. Similarly face to face communication as well as demonstrations is highly effective for sales person.

(d) *Organization policies* : Some organization don't share the information to all which affects the communication

4. Psychological or emotional barrier : The importance of communication depends on the mindset of both sides. Different persons can apprehend the message differently that adversely affects the free flow of communication. Some of the psychological barriers are:

(a) *Listening* : Many a times, people find are reluctant to accept the nascent information if it conflicts with their pre existing conception and perception. This rigid attitude of receiver is a barrier to information communication.

(b) *Psychological behavior* : When a receiver is emotionally disturbed or not in a state to receive information then he may fail to communicate effectively leading to communication gap.

(c) *Emotional behavior* : At times when the superior have

an attitude of losing their temper then subordinates may develop an attitude to keep themselves away of the communication cycle.

5. Personal barriers : These factors connote the personal issues between the sender and the receiver.

(a) *Trust* : If the source of information lacks a justifiable authority then information can lose its grounds on account of trust which is a big barrier.

(b) *Ability* : Many people generally tend to keep themselves away from communication process which prevents the free flow of messages making it a big barrier.

(c) *Attention* : Sometimes the receiver may not be interested in the message of the sender which obstructs the communication process.

6. Financial barriers : Sometimes people can't communicate their ideas and opinions in lack of necessary funds. Many international seminars or learned societies demand fund to present their papers or publish their writings thus blocking the healthy flow of communication process.

7. Technological barriers : Time and again, technological innovation has kicked loose plenty of options like SMS, MMS, email, voicemail etc which needs one to be acquainted with the technology. Failure of the knowhow of a technology is hurdle to efficient communication.

8. Communication barrier : Inadequate information can be misleading. Many a times out of confusion sender creates befuddle messages like "I will reach there at sharp 10:00 tomorrow" "I will have midday meal at your home" whose semantics is unclear. The receiver cannot figure out what sender means to say.

In nut shell, all barriers can be shows as :

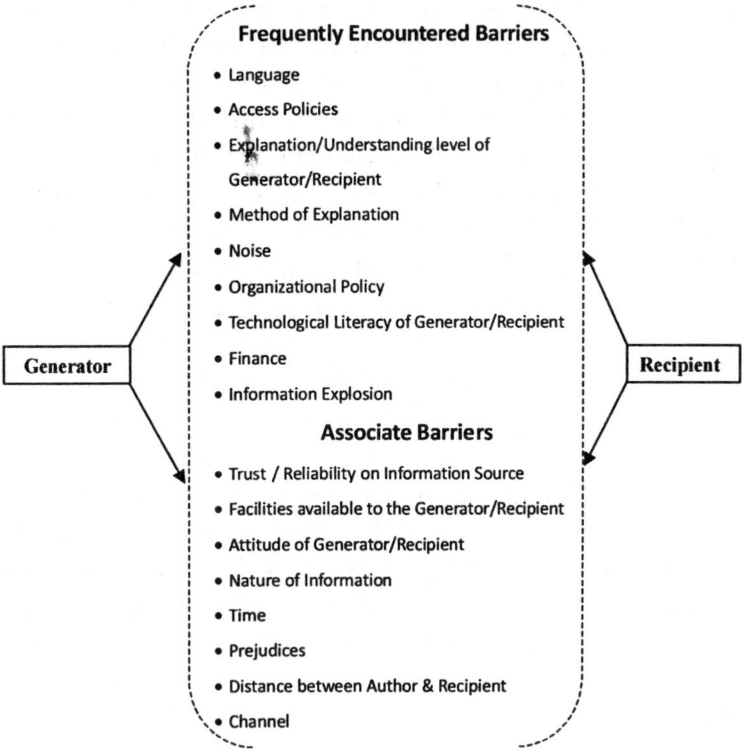

COMMUNICATION THEORIES & MODELS

There is a common consensus that there is no such thing as a successful body of communication theory, but that we have been relatively more successful in generating models of communication. Although we have Uncertainty Reduction theory (URT), Leon Festinger's Cognitive Dissonance theory (CDT) in the domain of interpersonal communication, these theories are linked to studies into language, social cognition, and social psychology. Due to that, in information communication context, in the preceding parts we will concentrate on communication models only.

According to Mortensen: "In the broadest sense, a model is a systematic representation of an object or event in idealized and abstract form. Models are somewhat arbitrary by their nature. Karl Deutsch in his seminal 1952 article "*On Communication Models in the Social Sciences*", describe model as "a structure of symbols and operating rules which is supposed to match a set of relevant points in an existing structure or process." In other words, it is a simplified representation or template of a process that can be used to help understand the nature of communication in a social setting. Such models are necessarily not one-to-one maps of the real world, but they are successful only insofar as they accurately represent the most important elements of the real world, and the dynamics of their relationship to one another.

Deutsch suggests that a model should provide four functions. It should organize a complex system (while being as general as possible), and should provide a heuristic function. He goes on to suggest models should be as original as possible, that they should not be obvious enough that they fail to shed light on the existing system. They should also provide some form of measurement of the system that will work analogously within the model and within the actual system being observed. There are two good reasons for having models. The first is that models guide research process and serves as a means for academic discussion. The second reason is that models serve as a blue print to implement a conceptual framework.

In communication study, models, allowing for the simplification of complex dynamics to help scholars and students better understand the components and processes that are involved. As with other models, communication models also provide important insights into the perspectives of the designers. Let's see some of communication model from very early to present.

A. Classical Communication Model

One of the first scholars to examine the communication

process in terms of its component parts was Aristotle (385-322 B. C. E.), who characterized communication (then called "rhetoric") in terms of an orator (i.e., a speaker) constructing an argument to be presented in a speech to an audience (i.e., listeners). He defined 'Rhetoric' as the faculty of observing in any given case the available means of persuasion. In his model, the ethos is the speaker and his or her character as revealed through the communication. The pathos is the audience and the emotions felt by them during the rhetoric. The logos is the actual words used by the speaker.His model has four elements: 'Invention', 'Arrangement', 'Style' and 'Delivery'. At invention stage, a speaker discovers rationale

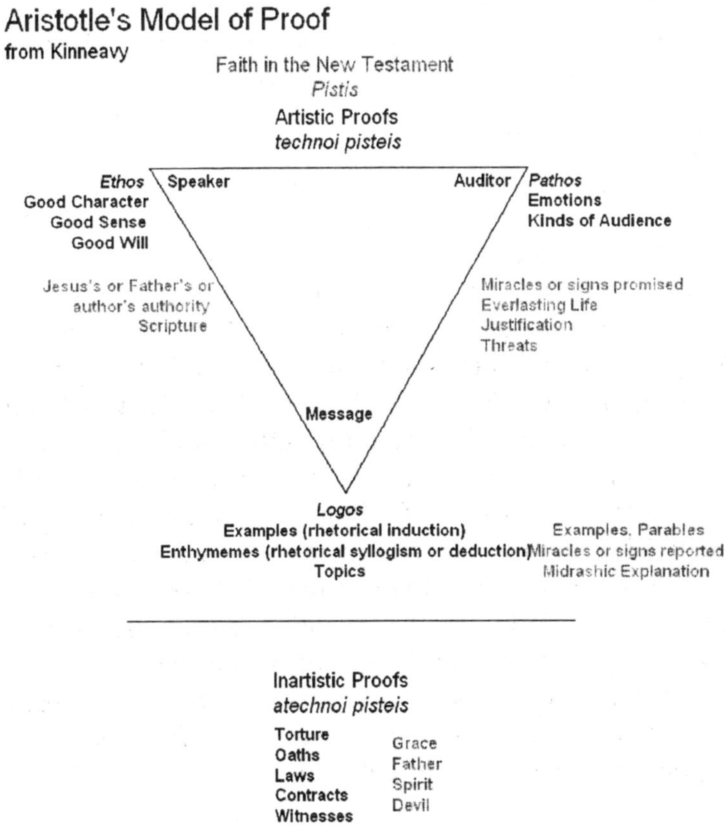

emotional and ethical proofs. At arrangement stage speaker arranges those proofs strategically and at style stage speaker clothes the ideas in clean and compelling words. At deliver stage speaker deliver the product appropriately. As need speaker also memorise the proofs.

Beginning with the formal study of communication by Aristotle and his contemporaries, communication came to be viewed as a process through which a speaker conveys messages to influence or persuade one or more receivers. However, the Aristotelian view of communication usefully highlighted the perspectives of communication thinkers until the midtwentieth century. In the late 1940s, and through the 1950s and 1960s, a number of new communication models were advanced. Many of the new models preserved the basic themes of the Aristotelian perspective.

B. Early Linear Models

A very well-known model of communication developed by Shannon and Weaver (1949), as the prototypical example of a transmissive model of communication: a model which reduces communication to a process of 'transmitting information'. Claude Shannon and Warren Weaver were not social scientists but engineers working for Bell Telephone Labs in the United States. Their goal was to ensure the maximum efficiency of telephone cables and radio waves and to formulate a theory to guide the efforts of engineers in finding the most efficient way of transmitting electrical signals from one location to another. Later Shannon introduced a mechanism in the receiver which corrected for differences between the transmitted and received signal; this monitoring or correcting mechanism was the forerunner of the now widely used concept of feedback (information which a communicator gains from others in response to his own verbal behavior).

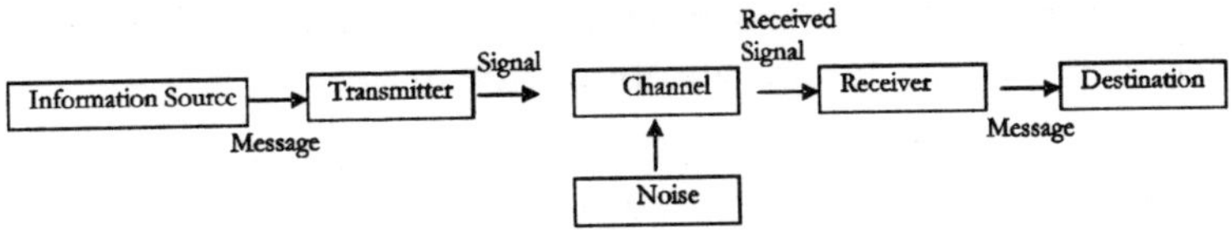

Shannon and Weaver 's original model consisted of five elements:

1. An *information source,* which produces a message.
2. A *transmitter,* which encodes the message into signals
3. A *channel,* to which signals are adapted for transmission
4. A *receiver,* which 'decodes' (reconstructs) the message from the signal.
5. A *destination,* where the message arrives.

A sixth element, *noise* is a dysfunctional factor: any interference with the message traveling along the channel (such as 'static' on the telephone or radio) which may lead to the signal received being different from that sent.

This model is the best-known example of the 'informational' approach to communication. Although no serious communication theorist would still accept it, it has been the most influential model of communication which has yet been developed, and it reflects a commonsense understanding of what communication is. In words of John Fiske's, Shannon and Weaver 's model is 'widely accepted as one of the main seeds out of which communication studies has grown' (Fiske 1982: 6). Shannon and Weaver's work proved valuable for communication engineers in dealing with such issues as the capacity of various communication channels in 'bits per second'. It contributed to computer science. It led to very useful work on redundancy in language. And in making 'information' 'measurable' it gave birth to the mathematical study of 'information theory'. Some commentators, however, claimed that Shannon and

Weaver's model has a much wider application to human communication than a purely technical one.

James Carey, however, critically commented that Shannon and Weaver's highly mechanistic model of communication can be seen as being based on a *transport* metaphor. He commented "within the broad scope of transport I tend to see the model primarily as employing a postal metaphor. It is as if communication consists of a sender sending a packet of information to a receiver, whereas I would insist that communication is about meaning rather than information. One appalling consequence of the postal metaphor for communication is the current reference to 'delivering the curriculum' in schools, as a consequence of which teachers are treated as postal workers. But the influence of the transmission model is widespread in our daily speech when we talk of 'conveying meaning', 'getting the idea across', 'transferring information', and so on. We have to be very alert indeed to avoid falling into the clutches of such transmissive metaphors".

With only slight changes in terminology of Shanon & Weaver model, a number of nonmathematical schemas have elaborated on the major theme. For example, Harold Lasswell (1948) conceived of analyzing the mass media in five stages: "Who?" "Says what?" "In which channel?" "To whom?" "With what effect?" Lasswell's model was closely allied to behaviouristic approaches. In apparent elaboration on Lasswell and/or Shannon and Weaver, George Gerbner (1956) extended the components to include the notions of perception, reactions to a situation, and message context.

2. *Schramm's Interactive Model, 1954*

Wilbur Schramm (1954) was another who altered the mathematical model of Shannon and Weaver. He conceived of decoding and encoding as activities maintained simultaneously by sender and receiver; he also made provisions for a two-way interchange of messages. Notice also the inclusion of an "interpreter" as an abstract representation of the problem of meaning.

Schramm's Model of Communication, 1954

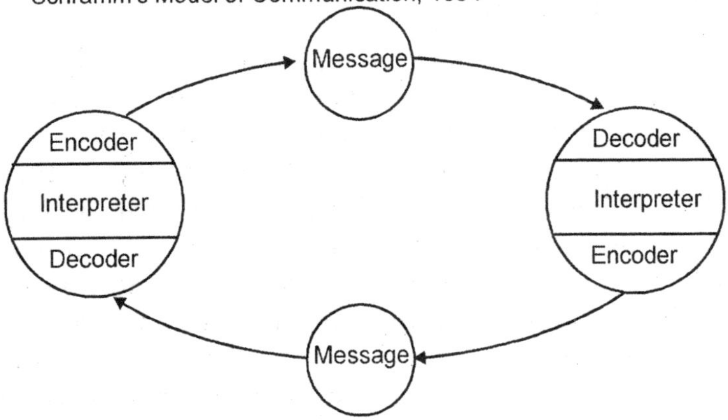

3. *Berlo's S-M-C-R, 1960*

This is an adaptation of the Shannon-Weaver model. In this model the idea of "source" was flexible enough to include oral, written, electronic, or any other kind of "symbolic" generator-of-messages. "Message" was made the central element, stressing the transmission of ideas. The model recognized that receivers were important to communication, for they were the targets. The notions of "encoding" and "decoding" emphasized the problems we all have (psycho-linguistically) in translating our own thoughts into words or other symbols and in deciphering the words or symbols of others into terms we ourselves can understand.

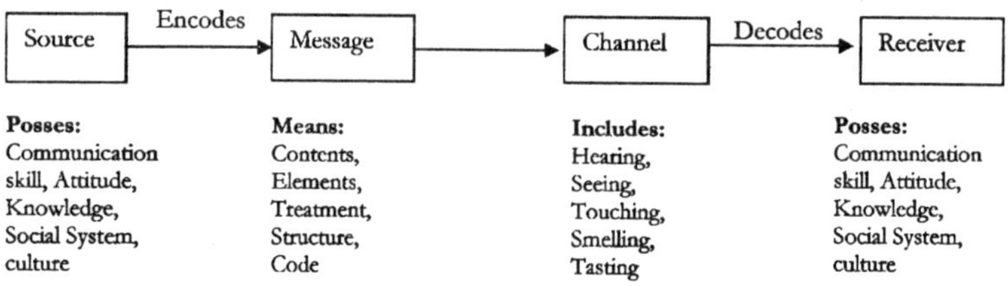

C. Contemporary Liner Models

1. Foulger Model, 2002

Some of the shortcoming as discussed earlier has overcome by the new model given by Foulger. model, which is focuses on the important role that intermediaries often play in the communication process. Many of these intermediaries have the ability to decide what messages others see, the context in which they are seen, and when they see them. They often have the ability, moreover, to change messages or to prevent them from reaching an audience (destination). In extreme variations we refer to such gatekeepers as censors. Under the more normal conditions of mass media, in which publications choose some content in preference to other potential content based on an editorial policy, we refer to them as editors (most mass media), moderators (Internet discussion groups), reviewers (peer-reviewed publications), or aggregators (clipping services), among other titles . Delivery workers (a postal delivery worker, for instance) also act as intermediaries, and have the ability to act as gatekeepers, but are generally restricted from doing so as a matter of ethics and/or law.

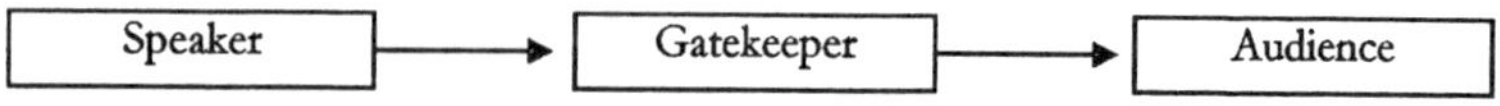

The gatekeeper model are also used in teaching organizational communication, where gatekeepers, in the form of bridges and liaisons, have some ability to shape the organization through their selective sharing of information.

These variations are generally more complex in depiction and often take the form of social network diagrams that depict the interaction relationships of dozens of people. They network diagrams often presume, or at least allow, bi-directional arrows such that they are more consistent with the notion that communication is most often bidirectional.

2. *An Interactive Model*

All these above liner models are well known as Intermediary Models of interpersonal communication. There are two variants too: the interactive model and the transactive model. The interactive model, a variant of which is shown below, elaborates Shannon's model with the cybernetic concept of feedback (Weiner, 1948, 1986), often without changing any other element of Shannon's model.

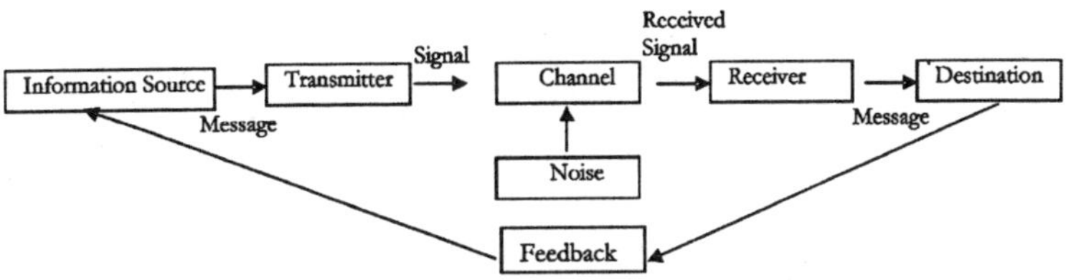

The key concept associated with this elaboration is that destinations provide feedback on the messages they receive such that the information sources can adapt their messages, in real time. The source of feedback is an information source. The consumer of feedback is a destination. Feedback is transmitted, received, and potentially disruptable via noise sources. None of this is visible in the typical depiction of the interactive model.

3. *Transactional Model*

The earliest model was a simple sender-channel-message-receiver model. Modifications added the concept of feedback, leading to a loop. The next development was that receivers normally selectively perceive, interpret and retail messages.

This Transactional model acknowledges neither creators nor consumers of messages, preferring to label the people associated with the model as communicators who both create and consume messages. The model presumes additional symmetries as well, with each participant creating messages that are received by the other communicator. This is, in many ways, an excellent model of the face-to-face interactive process which extends readily to any interactive medium that provides users with symmetrical interfaces for creation and consumption of messages, including notes, letters, C.B. Radio, electronic mail, and the radio.

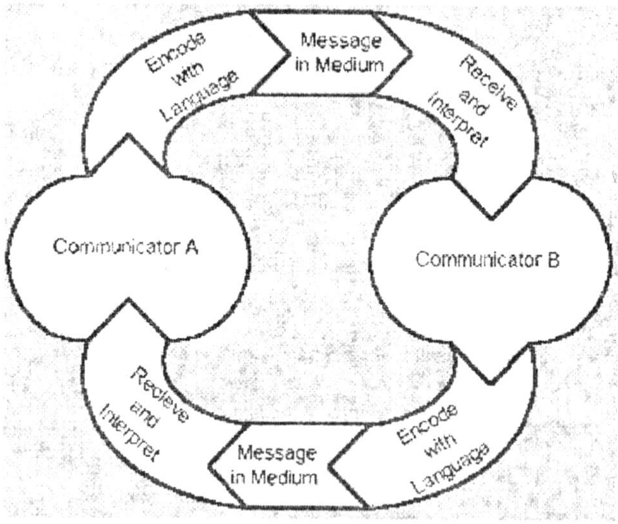

Source: Foulger, 2004, Model of Communication.

4. Ecological Model

The ecological model of communication, shown in below figure, given by Davis Foulger in 2004, attempts to provide a platform on which these issues can be explored. As explained by Foulger, this model asserts that communication occurs in the intersection of four fundamental constructs: communication between people (creators and consumers) is mediated by messages which are created using language within media; consumed from media and interpreted using language. In the ecological model , the "who" are the creators of messages, the "says what" are the messages, the "in which channel" is elaborated into languages (which are the content of channels) and media (which channels are a component of), the "to whom" are the consumers of messages, and the effects are found in various relationships between the primitives, including relationships, perspectives, attributions, interpretations, and the continuing evolution of languages and media.

A number of relationships are described in this model:

1. Messages are created and consumed using language
2. Language occurs within the context of media
3. Messages are constructed and consumed within the context of media
4. The roles of consumer and creator are reflexive. People become creators when they reply or supply feedback to other people. Creators become consumers when they make use of feedback to adapt their messages to message consumers. People learn how to create messages through the act of consuming other peoples messages.
5. The roles of consumer and creator are introspective. Creators of messages create messages within the context of their perspectives of and relationships with anticipated consumers of messages. Creators optimize their messages to their target audiences. Consumers of messages interpret those messages within the context of their perspectives of, and relationships with, creators of messages. Consumers make attributions of meaning based on their opinion of the message creator. People form these perspectives and relationships as a function of their communication.

6. The messages creators of messages construct are necessarily imperfect representations of the meaning they imagine. Messages are created within the expressive limitations of the medium selected and the meaning representation space provided by the language used. The message created is almost always a partial and imperfect representation of what the creator would like to say.

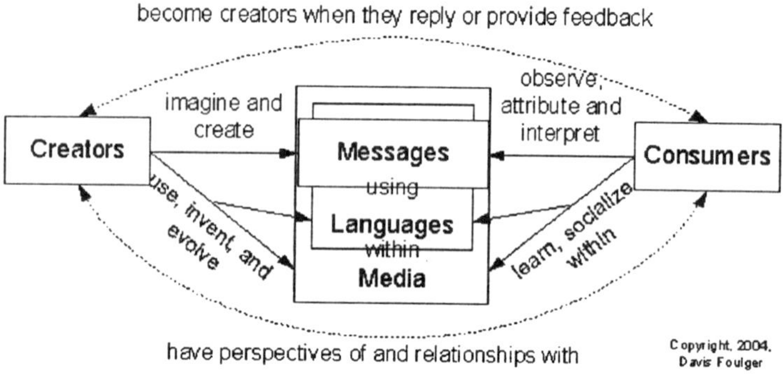

7. A consumers interpretation of a messages necessarily attributes meaning imperfectly. Consumers intepret messages within the limits of the languages used and the media those languages are used in. A consumers interpretation of a message may be very different than what the creator of a message imagined.
8. People learn language by through the experience of encountering language being used within media. The languages they learn will almost always be the languages when communicating with people who already know and use those languages. That communication always occurs within a medium that enables those languages.
9. People learn media by using media. The media they learn will necessarilly be the media used by the people they communicate with.

10. People invent and evolve languages. While some behavior expressions (a baby's cry) occur naturally and some aspects of language structure may mirror the ways in which the brain structures ideas, language does not occur naturally. People invent new language when there is no language that they can be socialized into. People evolve language when they need to communicate ideas that existing language is not sufficient to.
11. People invent and evolve media While some of the modalities and channels associated with communication are naturally occurring, the media we use to communicate are not.

D. Non-linear Models

1. Dance's Helical Spiral, 1967

Dance model depicts communication as a dynamic process. The helix represents the way communication evolves in an individual from his birth to the existing moment. According to Dance "at any and all times, the helix gives geometrical testimony to the concept that communication while moving forward is at the same moment coming back upon itself and being affected by its past behavior, for the coming curve of the helix is fundamentally affected by the curve from which it emerges. Yet, even though slowly, the helix can gradually free itself from its lower-level distortions. The communication process, like the helix, is constantly moving forward and yet is always to some degree dependent upon the past, which informs the present and the future. The helical communication model offers a flexible communication process". The helix implies that communication is continuous, unrepeatable, additive, and accumulative; that is, each phase of activity depends upon present forces at work as they are defined by all that has occurred before. All experience contributes to the shape of the unfolding moment; there is no break in the action, no fixed beginning, no pure redundancy, no closure. In short, the helix underscores the integrated aspects of all human communication as an evolving process that is always turned inward in ways that permit learning, growth, and discovery.

A Helical Model of Communication
from Dance, 1967

Source : http://www.shkaminiski.com/communication_models

2. *Westley and MacLean's Conceptual Model, 1957*

Westley and MacLean realized that communication does not begin when one person starts to talk, but rather when a person responds selectively to his immediate physical surroundings.

Each interactant responds to his sensory experience (*X1* . . .) by abstracting out certain objects of orientation (*X1*

... *3m)*. Some items are selected for further interpretation or coding (X′) and then are transmitted to another person, who may or may not be responding to the same objects of orientation (X,b),

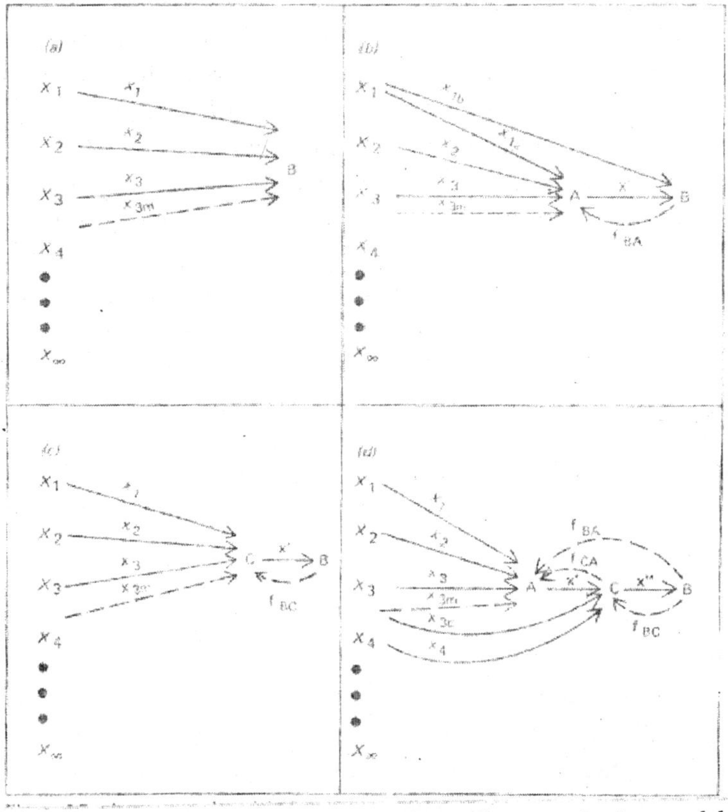

Source : http://www.shkaminiski.com/communication_models

The authors were keen to create a model which showed the complexities of mass communication - hence the emphasis on having to interpret a mass of Xs (events which are communicated in the media). It oversimplifies the relationships between participants by not showing power relations between participants. It makes the media process seem more integrated than it may actually be. It doesn't show the way different media may have different interests of the state (eg difference between a state broadcaster and private one)

SCHOLARLY COMMUNICATION

Nobel Prize recipient Joshua Lederberg made a speech in 1991 entitled "Communication as the Root of Scientific Progress" (Lederberg 1993). In this speech, he indicated the significance of scholarly literature, scholarly publishing, and scholarly communication for the progress of science. The new information resulting from modern scientific research led to the development of a "knowledge society." For a knowledge society, knowledge generated through research is a critical national resource. It is not enough to focus on the generation of knowledge. It is equally essential to spread and share it. The system of scholarly communication consists of the generation of knowledge and the means to share and communicate it. The concept of scholarly communication (SC) can be seen in ancient cultures such as the Greeks, although it was not known by that name and clear distinctions between formal and informal communication did not exist (Feather and Sturges 2003). In Western Europe, scholarly communication was primarily a product of universities and this is now established worldwide. The term "scholarly" is generally used in the academic domain, especially higher education, for activities that entail research or investigation. Scholarly communication is generally used to describe how research is communicated among peers and evaluated.

Definitions from the Literature

There is no single definition of the term "scholarly communication." It is sometimes narrowly defined to include only the peer-reviewed literature published upon completion of research (Rowlands, Nichols, and Huntington 2004) but a broader definition includes all communication among peers

(Harnad 1995). Borgman (2000) describes scholarly communication as "the study of how scholars in any field (e.g. physical, biological, social and behavioural sciences, humanities and technology) use and disseminate information through formal and informal channels. The study of scholarly communication includes the growth of scholarly information, the relationships among research areas and disciplines, the information needs and uses of individual user groups, and the relationships among formal and informal methods of communication." University College London (n.d.) states that, "scholarly communication is the method and route by which academic information is passed from author to reader, via various intermediaries such as libraries and publishers." Scholarly communication can be seen as a process in which research results are made available through publication and preservation. Computer mediated communication (CMC) has redefined scholarly communication. The CMC literature explores how computer networks are used to communicate, independent of print journals (Peek and Pomerantz 1998). Scholarly electronic communication includes the distribution of articles, research papers, and messages by electronic means as opposed to their distribution in print. Lyman and Chodorow (1998) assert that scholarly communication originated when information technology became more prominent in scholarly research. They observe that scholarly communication is a term "invented to frame both print publication and digital communication within a single functional schema." ACRL (2004) defines scholarly communication as "the system through which research and other scholarly writings are created, evaluated for quality, scholarly community, and preserved for future use. The system includes both formal means of communication, such as publication in peer-reviewed journals, and informal channels, such as electronic listservs"

Means of Scholarly Communication

Communication through informal means includes face-to-face discussion, exchange of personal communication, sharing views, opinions, etc. The term "invisible college" is sometimes used to describe this informal communication network (de Solla Price 1963). The channels established are fast and easy. New researchers may lack this informal network. Formal communication uses public and permanent vehicles such as books, journals and monographs. The advantages of formal channels are:

- information can be disseminated to a widely scattered group of readers;
- detailed information, such as descriptions of methods, tables, diagrams, results etc. can easily be given;
- printed documents contain information which can be critically examined and verified;
- the documents can easily be referred to as and when required; and
- published documents provide a means for establishing "priority" of academic work, and thereby
- contribute to establishing academic merit for the author(s).

Formal scholarly communication can research articles, letters, memos, conferences, technical reports, monographs, edited books, and so on. Scholarly electronic communication uses a number of genres. Kling and Callahan (2003) categorise them as:

- social and socio-technical research literature like journals, research monographs, specialized
- research conference;
- technological research literature which includes analytical examination of technological standards
- and design strategies;

- practitioner literature (professional writing) where primary audience includes publishers,

All these genres have well defined advantages and disadvantages. In scholarly communication process, however, the primary scholarly literature is composed of social and socio-technical research literature especially journals or its electronic counterpart e-journals. This type of literature is not only efficient in providing most up-to-date and advanced information but it also fulfills certification requirement rather well because it also provides reviewed output as print.

Scholarly Communication through Traditional Print Journals

The historical evidences reveal that some three hundred and forty years ago, there were only two scholarly journals in existence. They were *Journal des Scavans* edited by Denis de Sallo first published on Monday, January 5th, 1665 in Paris followed by *Philosophical Transactions of Royal Society* edited by Henry Oldenburg first published on 6th March 1665 in England (Fjallbrant, 1997). These journals of the learned societies contained not only original scientific material - papers read at the meetings of the society, but also reviews of scientific work in specific subject areas. Over the last two hundred years, the traditional print journals have proliferated, and these have overwhelmed university libraries. Major portion of library budgets has been allocated to journals as opposed to other materials, such as books. But there is a 'crisis' in this formal scholarly communication means. There are many reasons for the crisis including information overload, printing delay etc. However one of major crisis was economic crisis. McDonald once mentioned:

"Scholarship today has become victimized by a predatory commerce that is preying on its weakness. The knowledge chain in which libraries are the penultimate link is under particular pressure beyond the volume and complexity of communication. It is traumatically stressed by the aggressive efforts of those who would live off the avails of scholarship; those who I've referred to elsewhere as the `pimps and pushers of scholarly publishing.' In the past decade or more, commercial publishers have markedly increased their incursion into the scholarly publishing process. We are now faced with an unwelcome economic concentration focused particularly in the areas of science, technology and medicine. The noisy bleating and moaning of your librarians as they crumble under the weight of cost increases is merely symptomatic of these wolves at the door." (MacDonald, 1990).

It is widely documented that the traditional scholarly journal publication process was fraught with delays and inefficiency (Prosser, 2003). But some other studies examined the diverse cause of journal prices. Some said that commercial publishers have increased their market power and pushed up price (Hunter, 1998; Odlyzko, 1998), others said that the increase in number of new titles over time lowers the average circulation of journals and thereby raises fixed cost (first copy) as a proportion of the total cost (King & Tenopir, 2000). Whatsoever may be the cause, but frustrated with excessive delays between submitting a manuscript and its publication along with phenomenal increase of price in paper-based journal, the scholarly community was looking to electronic technologies as one possible solution (Diospatonyi, Horvai, & Braun, 2001). Some scientists argued that "electronic media are almost always better than paper" because of the following reasons: electronic publishing is dramatically less expensive than paper publishing; access to electronic publications is easier and wider; and electronic publishing can speed up scientific communication (Brent, 1995). New communication and dissemination methods and formats, that take advantage of the unique capabilities of the Web and challenge traditional methods of collecting, publishing, storing and preserving research have also been discussed by various scientists. For example, Kling & McKim (1997a) estimated the role of the Internet in reducing publication delays theoretically. In another study OECD estimated that there might be a decrease from 128-308 days (traditional mail), to 3 to 284 days, depending upon the kind of digital communication employed. Organisation for Economic Co-operation and Development (OECD) estimated that publication delays might be 104-284 days (with e-mail attachments), 100-280 days (publication via an electronic journal, with issue packaging), 54-84 days (pure electronic journal, with individual articles), 50-80 days (with an online preprint system, article sent at time of acceptance), or even 3 days (published, un-refereed, in an online repository, manuscript submitted to the repository and to a journal on the same day) (OECD, 1998).

Scholarly Communication through e-Journals

The term 'e-journal' can be defined as a publication, often scholarly, accessible in a computerized format and distributed electronically. This distribution can be both off-line (e.g. CD-ROMs) and On-line (e.g. Internet). The *Electronic Journals: A Selected Resource Guide* explicitly defines electronic journals as "... serial publications available in digital format. Some are distributed on CD-ROMs, some over the internet. Of the internet-available ones, some are delivered over the World Wide Web, some by e-mail. Some are ASCII texts, some are HTML WWW pages; some use proprietary formats such as Adobe's PDF (portable document format). Some have paper equivalents, some are purely electronic. Some are published in electronic form; some are digitally reformatted print journals. Some are free; some are available by subscription only. Some are peer-reviewed scholarly journals; many are not quality-controlled" (Harrassowitz, n.d.).

In scholarly communication system, the term "electronic journal" is often characterized in conflicting ways. Michael Strangelove in his writing used term e-serial (electronic serial) instead of e-journal. According to him e-serial attempts "to emulate the characteristics of their print counterparts through organization, periodicity and topical focus" (Strangelove, 1993). Like print, they also have "the intervention of editors, reviewers, and so forth". He categorised e-journals as a subset of e-serials, and described them as "not merely informational in design but . . . add to the corpus of a discipline through the organized dissemination of original research or knowledge" (Strangelove 1993). Others described an electronic journal simply as looking "like a paper journal, except for format" (Quinn 1994). Kling and Covi (1995) mentioned e-journal "as an edited package of articles that is distributed to most of its subscribers in electronic form". Harter and Kim (1996) argued "Articles from an e-journal may, and probably will, be printed for careful reading, and might be stored in libraries in a printed form, for archival purposes. However, e-journals are accessed primarily in electronic form". MIT Press's Janet Fisher (1996) commented that "in the period from 1993 to 1995, the number of e-journals has increased, but they are still almost entirely free and created almost entirely by dedicated groups of individuals without production subsidy from institutions or scholarly associations" referred primarily to journals or journal-like publications that were distributed in electronic form only, like *Bryn Mawr Classical Review*, *Postmodern Culture*, and *Psycholoquy*. Odlyzko (1995) proposed still a different view of electronic journals, as collections of unpackaged, but potentially refereed documents, available for download from a central server.

The development of World Wide Web was a boon to electronic journal project (basically before Web, electronic journals were ASCII text based) which is now reflected in terms of output and use of electronic publications. In one respect the speed of change today belies the fact that the development of early electronic journals (ASCII text based), from the viewpoint of some of the first experimenters, struggled to keep pace with technology (McKnight, 1993). Yet it was approximately 200 years after the invention of print that the first scientific journals appeared in 1665 (Fjallbrant, 1997); it is just 20 years since the feasibility of an electronic journal (ASCII text based) was discussed by Senders (1977). Many of e-journals publishers developed their Web sites during 1995 to 1997. They established their Web sites as media for product marketing to a wide range of scholars. Almost all publishers began to host their journals on the Web and wide range of e-journal in every discipline began to be available on Web.

The increasing quantity of e-journals publication has been reported in various studies. For example, Clement's study on October, 1994 was based on 25 peer-reviewed e-journals [Science, universal archive] whereas it was 39 [full-text] in December (Roes, 1994). In January, Hitchcock, Carr and Hall (1996) and in May, Harter and Kim (1996) found 77 [scholarly] and 115 [STM full text] such titles, respectively. This number reached up to 508 [STM] in December 1996 (Goldie, 1996 -cited by Hitchcock, Carr & Hall, 1996). In 1997, ARL's *Directory of Electronic Journals, Newsletters, and Academic Discussion Lists* (7th Edition) claimed 1,002 peer-reviewed e-journals (Mogge, 1997). Thomas Baker (1998) asserted that "this is all the more likely to happen because the advantages of electronic publication are not just economic, but scholarly".

The phenomenal increase in e-journals during last few years is evidenced in *Ulrich International Periodical Directory*. The 44th edition (2006) of *Ulrich International Periodical Directory* has listed 188,500 serials under 900 subject headings out of which 45,000 serials were available exclusively online or in addition to other media, 6700 serials were indicated as available on CD-ROM.

Varieties of Electronic/Online Journals

Looking back into the history, it can be said that there are two distinct eras of e-journals' development. They are ASCII text based pre-web era and graphics enabled post-web era. In the pre-web era, these ASCII text based e-journals appeared in four different forms. They were (a) Newsletters; (b) Un-refereed e-journals; (c) Refereed e-journals (eg. Mental Workload); and (d) Tailored and Structured 'Journals' (eg. *Legitech*) (Peek & Pomerantz, 1998).

With the arrival of Web, e-journal in all disciplines has proliferated, finding widespread, and enthusiastic acceptance by end user. Some electronic publications replicate existing print publications, others start only in electronic form. Kling and McKim (1997b) have distinguished at least four kinds of e-journals in the post-web era. They are:

a) Pure e-journals which are originally distributed only in digital form e.g. *Electronic Journal of Communication, Journal of Digital Information, Information Research.*

b) E-p journals which are primarily distributed electronically, but may have very limited distribution in paper form. e.g. *Journal of Artificial Intelligence Research, Electronic Transactions on Artificial Intelligence.*

c) P-e journals which are primarily distributed in paper form, but are also distributed electronically. E.g. *Nature, Science, Physical Review.*

d) P+e journals which are initiated with parallel paper and electronic editions that may be widely distributed. e.g. *Organic Letters.*

OPEN ACCESS (OA) PUBLISHING

The escalating cost of providing access to research materials, together with the license constraints placed on the use of digital contents by commercial publishers, are seriously eroding the ability of libraries to provide students and faculty with the resources. The Open Access (OA) movement has been an important catalyst for change in this regard, prodding publishers to re-examine their access policies and in some cases, to move towards news access models. According to Peter Suber, open-access literature is characterised by two essential properties. First, it is free of charge to everyone. Second, the copyright holder has consented in advance to unrestricted reading, downloading, copying, sharing, storing, printing, searching, linking, and crawling. The first property solves the pricing crisis. The second property solves the permission crisis (Suber, 2003). The open access movement seeks to change the traditional subscription based model of scholarly publishing to one where readers have unrestricted electronic access to the scholarly literature. This paradigm has been supported by a number of initiatives worldwide.

Definition of OA Publication

Open Access (OA) is not a simple concept; it has many different definitions and approaches, numerous supporters and abundant detractors. Wikipedia defines OA as "an ongoing publication practice which differs from the traditional methods of publishing papers, particularly in context of how the papers get submitted, reviewed, authenticated and finally published. The word 'open' here means a change in how publication is negotiated between author and publisher and 'access' has an inflex on how the audience can obtain the publication". Peter Suber (2004), on the other hand, provides a brief definition of open access as "digital, online, free of charge, and free of most copyright and licensing restrictions" whereas, Harnad (2005) advocates "immediate, permanent, free online access to the full text of all refereed research journal articles". But the detailed definition of OA is given by Budapest Open Access Initiative (BOAI) and Public Library of Science (PLoS).

BOAI and PLoS both define OA as: "the free availability of literature on the public Internet, permitting any users to read, download, copy, distribute, print, search, or link to the full texts of these articles, crawl them for indexing, pass them as data to software, or use them for any other lawful purpose without financial, legal, or technical barriers other than those inseparable from gaining access to the Internet itself" (Budapest Open Access Initiative, 2002 and Public Library of Science, 2005). PLoS offers unrestricted access to the scientific literature, while BOAI promotes open access to research articles in all disciplines. This definition of OA involves availability of scholarly literature free of cost. On the other hand, the Bethesda Statement on Open Access Publishing in April 2003 and Berlin Declaration on Open Access to Knowledge in the Sciences and Humanities, in the same year, discuss the process of open access in some different way. Both the statements include the definition of an open access publication as below:

- The author(s) and copyright holder(s) grant(s) to all users a free, irrevocable, worldwide, perpetual right of access to, and a license to copy, use, distribute, transmit and display the work publicly and to make and distribute derivative works, in any digital medium for any responsible purpose, subject to proper attribution of authorship, as well as the right to make small number of printed copies for their personal use.
- A complete version of the work and all supplemental materials, including a copy of the permission as stated above, in a suitable standard electronic format is deposited immediately upon initial publication in at least one online repository that is supported by an academic institution, scholarly society, government agency, or other well-established organization that seeks to enable open access, unrestricted distribution, interoperability, and long-term archiving (for the

biomedical sciences, PubMed Central is such a repository).

These definitions of open access differ only slightly and because they agree in the substance they are referred to collectively as the BBB statement (Suber, 2008).

A recent example of defining open access as principle is provided by Hall (2008): By open access, "I mean access that is digital, online, and free of charge to those able to connect to the Internet, without having to pay subscriptions either to publish or to [pay per] view, in its purest form, anyway".

Some Milestones Towards Open Access

The success story of open access was created with the establishment of some projects and initiatives worldwide. Many open access projects also involve collaborations by people around the world, both expected and unexpected. The first free scientific online archive http://www.arxiv.org was started in 1991, initially a preprint service for physicists, initiated by Paul Ginsparg. Self-archiving has become the norm in physics, with some sub-areas of physics, such as high-energy physics, having a 100% self-archiving rate. In 1997, The Association of Research Libraries developed the Scholarly Publishing and Academic Resources Coalition (SPARC), an alliance of academic and research libraries and other organizations, to address the crisis of scholarly communication and to develop and promote alternatives, such as open access. Around the same time, Scientific Electronic Library Online or SciELO's comprehensive approach to publish full open access journals, involving a number of Latin American countries is another important milestone. During 1997, also Bioline International, a not-for-profit organization, decided to help publishers in developing countries. Bioline is a collaboration of people in the UK, Canada, and Brazil; the Bioline International Software is used around the world. The U.S. National Library of Medicine made MEDLINE freely available in the same year. In 2001, 30,000 scholars around the world signed "An Open Letter to Scientific Publishers" calling for "the establishment of an online public library that would provide the full contents of the published record of research and scholarly discourse in medicine and the life sciences in a freely accessible, fully searchable, interlinked form" (Ramachandran, 2004). This led to the establishment of the Public Library of Science (PLoS), an advocacy organization. PLoS decided to become an open access publisher aiming to compete at the high quality end of the scientific spectrum with commercial publishers and other open access journals, which were beginning to flourish. The Budapest Open Access Initiative arose from a small but lively meeting convened in Budapest by the Open Society Institute (OSI) on December 1-2, 2001. The purpose of the meeting was to accelerate progress in an international effort to make research articles in all academic fields freely available on the internet. The initiative has been signed by the Budapest participants and a growing number of individuals and organizations from around the world who represent researchers, universities, laboratories, libraries, foundations, journals, publishers, learned societies, and kindred open-access initiatives (Chan *et al.*, 2002). In 2003, the Berlin Declaration on Open Access to Knowledge in the Sciences and Humanities was drafted and the World Summit on the Information Society included open access in its Declaration of Principles and Plan of Action. During the same year IFLA declared the "world-wide network of library and information services which provides access to past, present and future scholarly literature and research documentation, ensures its preservation, assists users in discovery and use, and offers educational programs to enable users to develop lifelong literacies" (IFLA, 2004). In 2005, the world's two largest funding agencies of medical researchers, the United

States National Institute of Health and the United Kingdom's Wellcome Trust, adopted policies to provide open access to the results of successful grantees. They decided to place articles in a central medicine-specific repository, either the U.S. PubMed Central or a UK central repository. Now, The U.S. National Institute of Health policy requests that researchers should place a copy of their article in PubMedCentral for secure archiving as well as Open Access, within 12 months of publication. The United Kingdom government's Science and Technology Committee in their report, entitled *Scientific Publications: Free for All?*, recommended that the results of all research funded by the United Kingdom government should be made freely accessible in a network of institutional repositories across the United Kingdom. While the United Kingdom government has rejected the mandated approach, the United Kingdom's Joint Information Systems Committee (JISC), is developing the institutional repository system, to be filled on a voluntary basis.

From the early 1990s, researchers have discussed the potential for open access (OA) publishing to revolutionize scholarly communication (e.g., Harnad, 1990; Harnad, 1991; Harter, 1996), and explored author role in OA (Harnad 1995), copyright issues in OA (Suber, 2003; Wellcome Trust, 2003), author experiences and opinions about publishing in open access journals and self-archiving (e.g., Swan & Brown, 2005).

Various scientists have discussed the publication amount in 'green' road and 'gold' road. For example, in 1999, Harnad estimated that out of total publication in the world 10% was in open access. Of these, one fourth or 2.5% appeared in gold publications while about three fourths or 7.5% appeared in green publications. He then suggested some measures to make all publication OA. He also explained how, with the support of universities (primarily through librarians and networks) and the use of interoperability standards (such as the Open Archives Initiative), scholars can 'self-archive' their work, and users could locate papers regardless of where they are stored. In contrast Jean-Claude Guedon (2004) argued against the efficacy of author self-archiving of peer-reviewed journal articles, the 'Green' road to OA, on the grounds:

(1) that far too few authors self-archive;

(2) that self-archiving can only generate incomplete and inconvenient access, and

(3) that maximizing access and impact is the wrong reason for seeking OA (and only favours elite authors).

He suggested that the right reason for seeking OA is to reform both the peer review system and the journal publishing system by creating new ways of 'creating value' and 'branding' whilst converting to OA ('Gold') publishing (in which the online version of all articles is free to all users). Harnad (2005) commented that "while either setting up an OA journal, or converting an established journal to an OA model, is extremely risky, depositing work in institutional repositories is virtually risk free", but Eysenbach (2006) in his paper showed the advantage of gold-OA over green-OA. Eysenbach compared citations to individual articles published between June 2004 and December 2004 in the same journal—namely, *Proceedings of the National Academy of Sciences* (PNAS).

The long term preservation in OA system may be threatened, some argued, as repositories themselves - either subject based or institutional - may not prove to be permanent. New technologies and new publishing models should not be at the expense of preserving the research record (Kling & McKim, 2000). They also estimated that many OA journals, which are established, do not survive more than a few years, and if repositories do not reach the critical mass, then there is the risk of "losing scientific reports that are published in what will soon become disestablished and little visited electronic islands" (Kling & McKim, 2000). Gustafsson (2002) calculated the number of titles of OA journals which have been alive between 1998 and 2002. For the situation in 1998, Gustafsson used the data provided by Wells (1999). Of 387 journals identified as active by Wells in 1998 only 193 or 50% were active in 2002. The result can be compared to a study by Crawford (2002), who found that out of 86 OA journals active in 1995, only 49 (57%) were active in early 2001.

Flavours of OA

The concept of OA has existed since the mid-1990s, with champions such as Stevan Harnad (1995) expressing his 'subversive proposal.' In a brief statement, Harnad claimed that authors of 'esoteric' articles, for which no payment is received, only want to publish their work and not sell them. He recommended a two step process to make access to such material 'open': first to place pre-prints, that is papers that have not yet been peer-reviewed or quality controlled, into globally accessible archives; then, once they have been peer-reviewed and made ready for publication, substitute this version into the archive. Alongside these archives, journals could still exist, but they would no longer be able to charge subscription fee, but would be forced to meet the costs before publication through 'authors' page charges, learned society dues, university publication budgets and/or governmental publication subsidies.' This original proposal sparked a heated debate, but the basic tenets of OA were set. Presently, OA advocates two types of strategies for promoting the free availability of scholarly literature: self-archiving and open access journals. These two strategies are also known as "Green" and "Gold" roads to OA, respectively. A green publisher (or journal) has given green light to its authors to self-archiving their papers (i.e make the research output open by depositing the full text on a toll free, publicly accessible Web site). Initially, self-archiving method created confusion among commercial publishers but the majority of publishers now do permit authors to post their articles online in form of preprint (the version originally submitted to the journal) or post-print (the final, peer-reviewed and accepted but not yet edited version) or final version as prepared for publication or even the final published version with all its formatting (typically in PDF format). The permitted posting may be either authors' personal Web sites, departmental or other institutional Web sites, or organized institutional repositories or subject based repositories. ArXiv, D-space, e-print, E-LIS are some of the examples of these repositories.

In gold road, OA publishers not only give the green light to both preprint and post-print self-archiving by the author, but the publishers themselves archive all their articles publicly on their Web sites. There are three shades of gold OA journals: (a) Delayed OA journals; (b) Partial OA journals and (c) purely OA journals. In Delayed OA, publishers make their previous issues freely available after a period varying from few months to more than a year. Most of the Learned societies follow this model of OA. The journals like *Libri, Information Technology and Libraries* are some of the examples of this category. Sometimes, a few publishers (e.g. Institute of Physics) make articles available free for a few months and then subject them to access control. Many commercial publishers routinely make particularly important or newsworthy articles freely available to attract more readers to their journals. These are known as Partial OA journals. The Florida Entomological Society in 1994 and Entomological Society of America in 1995 first developed the idea. Sometimes, some publishers adopt these models with their trial version. But the most popular model of OA is purely OA journal where each and every article of a whole journal is available free for all its issues. Journals like *Information Research, D-Lib Magazine* are under this category.

Who funds publication of scholarly materials with free and open access is a question most frequently asked of OA system. Numerous models have been proposed to address this issue. One of the most common business models is 'Author-Pay' model. In this new publishing model, instead of charging subscription fee from end user, OA journals either charge author(s) or their sponsoring bodies, universities, governments etc. for publication. There are two variants of author-pay OA business model. First the Public Library of Science (PLoS) is a low volume, high price publisher using the author-pay model that competes with top quality journals like *Nature, Science, Cell* etc. Second, BioMed Central is a high volume, low price publisher that, as ISI data show, competes with low impact journals. PLoS usually charges $1500 and in BMC journal's authors are charged fees ranging from $525 to $1500 depending upon the journal (Regazzi, 2004). But in purely open access journals' author does not pay any charges to the publisher and the article is permanently made available to the journal Web sites in its immediate issues. These journals get support either explicitly by grant funding or implicitly by subsidy from the institution which pays the staff and provides infrastructure. Many institutions now support this form of publishing because they realize that it is a solution to the problem of beating down the library budget and increasing the cost of commercially published e-journal. As per the statistics of 2004, less than 20% of journals listed by Directory of Open Access Journals (DOAJ) are author pay, 28% of journals listed in the DOAJ are free online versions of print subscription journals. Societies, government institutions or universities typically subsidize the remaining titles (Regazzi, 2004).

Besides the 'green' and 'gold' some other colour shades also have seen in OA publishing arena. For example, Association of College and Research Libraries (2004) categorizes OA e-journals in some different colour codes. They are:

1. Open Access Journals (OA Journals, color code: green) : These journals provide free access to all articles and utilize a form of licensing that puts minimal restrictions on the use of articles, such as the Creative Commons Attribution License. Examples: *Biomedical Digital Libraries, Information Research* etc.

2. Free Access Journals (FA Journals, color code: cyan): These journals provide free access to all articles and utilize a variety of copyright statements (e.g., the journal copyright statement may grant liberal educational copying provisions), but they do not use a Creative Commons Attribution License or similar license. Examples: *The Public-Access Computer Systems Review, D-Lib Magazine* etc.

3. Embargoed Access Journals (EA Journals, color code: yellow) : These journals provide free access to all articles after a specified embargo period and typically utilize conventional copyright statements. Examples: *Learned Publishing, Libri* etc.

4. Partial Access Journals (PA journals, color code: orange) : These journals provide free access to selected articles and typically utilize conventional copyright statements. Examples: *College & Research Libraries, Library Quarterly* etc.

John Willinsky in 2005 has identified ten types of open access. They are:

Types of open access	*Economic models*	*Journal or portal example*
Home page	University department maintains home pages for individual faculty members on which they place their papers and make them freely available.	http://www.econ.ucsb.edu/~tedb/

E-print archive	An institution or academic subject area underwrites the hosting and maintenance of repository software, enabling members to self-archive published and unpublished materials.	arXiv.org E-Print Archive
Author fee	Author fees support immediate and complete access to open access journals (or, in some cases, to the individual articles for which fees were paid), with institutional and national memberships available to cover author fees.	BioMed Central
Subsidized	Subsidy from scholarly society, institution and/or government/ foundation enables immediate and complete access to open access journal.	First Monday
Dual-mode	Subscriptions are collected for print edition and used to sustain both print edition and online open access edition.	Journal ofPost-graduateMedicine
Delayed	Subscription fees are collected for print edition and immediate access to online edition, with open access provided to content after a period of time (e.g., six to twelve months).	New England Journal ofMedicine
Partial Open	Access is provided to a small selection of articles in each issue—serving as a marketing tool—whereas access to the rest of the issue requires subscription.	Lancet
Per capita	Open access is offered to scholars and students in developing countries as a charitable contribution, with expense limited to registering institutions in an access management system.	HINARI

Indexing	Open access to bibliographic information and abstracts is provided as a government service or, for publishers, a marketing tool, often with links to pay per view for the full text of articles.	ScienceDirect
Cooperative	Member institutions (e.g., libraries, scholarly associations) contribute to support of open access journals and development of publishing resources.	German Academic Publishers

REFERENCES

Aristotle. (1954). *Rhetoric and Poetics*, tr. Robert W. Rhys. New York: Random House.

Association of College and Research Libraries (2004). Principles and strategies for the reform of scholarly communication. Available at: http://www.ala.org/ala/acrl/acrlpubs/whitepapers/principlesstrategies.htm

Baker, T. (1998). *TIAC white paper*. Available at: http://www.tiac.or.th/tiacweb/Baker/Section1_3.html.

Berelson, Bernard and Steiner, Gary (1964). *Human Behavior*. New York: Harcourt, Brace, & World, 254.

Borgman, C.L. (2000). Digital libraries and continuum of scholarly communication. *Journal of Documentation* 56(4), 412-430.

Budapest Open Access Initiative (2002). *Definition of open access*. Available at:: http://www.soros.org/openaccess/read.shtml

Carey, James (1989): *Communication as Culture*. New York: Routledge (Chapter 1, 'A Cultural Approach to Communication'). *New York: Routledge*

Chan, L., Cuplinskas, D., Eisen, M., Friend, F., Genova, Y., Guedon, J., *et al.* (2002). *Budapest open access initiative*. Available at: http://www.soros.org/openaccess/read.shtml

Schwartz, David G. Integrating knowledge transfer and communication-mediated communication: categorizing barriers and possible responses. Available at:: http://

www.palgravejournals.com/kmrp/journal/v5/n4/fig_tab/8500153f3.html)

Berlo, David K. (1960). *The Process of Communication.* New York: Holt, Rinehart, and Winston.

Diospatonyi, I., Horvai, G., & Braun, T. (2001). Publication speed in analytical chemistry journals. *Journal of Chemical Information and Computer Sciences,* 41(6), 1452-1456.

Cartier, F. A (1959). The President's Letter, *Journal of Communication* 9, 5.

Feather, J., & Sturges, P., (eds.) (2003). Scholarly communication. *International encyclopedia of information and library science* (2nd ed.) London: Routledge: 563-567.

Fisher, J. (1996). Traditional publishers and electronic journals. In R. Peek & G. Newby (Eds.), *Scholarly Publishing: The Electronic Frontier* (pp. 231-242). Cambridge, MA: MIT Press.

Fiske, John (1982): *Introduction to Communication Studies.* London: Routledge.

Fjallbrant, N. (1997). *Scholarly communication – historical development and new possibilities.* Available at: http://www.iatul.org/conference/proceedings/ vol07/papers/full/nfpaper.html

Foulger, D. (2002a). Roles in Media. Presented at National Communication Association Summer Conference, May, 2002. Available at: http://evolutonarymedia.com/papers/rolesInMedia.htm.

Foulger, D. (2004). An Ecological Model of the Communication Process. Available at: http://davis.foulger.info/ papers/ecologicalModelOfCommunication.htm

Dance, Frank E. X (1970). The 'Concept' of Communication, *Journal of Communication* 20, 201–10.

Miller, Gerald R. (1966). On Defining Communication: Another Stab, *Journal of Communication,* 16, 92.

Guedon, J-C. (2004). The "green" and the "gold" roads to open access: The case for mixing and matching. *Serials Review,* 30(4), 315-328.

Gustafsson, T. (2002). Open access: An empirical study of openly accessible journals on the Internet. Master's Thesis, Swedish

School of Economics and Business Administration, Helsinki, Finland.

Hall, G. (2008). Digitize this Book! The politics of new media or why we need open access now, University of Minnesota Press.

Harnad, S. (1990). Scholarly skywriting and the prepublication continuum of scientific inquiry. *Psychological Science,* 1, 342-343. Available at: http://www.cogsci.soton.ac.uk/~harnad/Papers/Harnad/harnad90.skywriting.html

Harnad, S. (1991). Post-Gutenberg galaxy: The fourth revolution in the means of production of knowledge. *Public Access Computer Systems Review,* 2(1), 39 - 53. Available at: http://www.cogsci.soton.ac.uk/~harnad/ Papers/Harnad/harnad91.postgutenberg .html.

Harnad, S. (1995). A subversive proposal. In A. Okerson & J. O'Donnell (Eds.), *Scholarly journals at the crossroads: A subversive proposal for electronic publishing*. Washington, DC: Association of Research Libraries. Available ar: http://www.arl.org/scomm/subversive/ toc.html

Harnad, S. (2005). Fast-forward on the green road to open access: The case against mixing up green and gold. *Ariadne,* 42. Available at: http://www.ariadne.ac.uk/issue42/harnad/

Harrassowitz (n.d.). *Electronic journals: A selected resources guide.* Available at: http://www.harrassowitz.de/ top_resources/ ejresguide/providers.html.

Harter, S.P. (1996). The impact of electronic journals on scholarly communication: A citation analysis. *Public Access Computer Systems Review,* 7(5), 5-34.

Harter, S.P., & Kim, H.J. (1996). *Electronic journals and scholarly communication: A citation and reference study*. Available at: http://php.indiana.edu/ ~harter/harter-asis96midyear.html.

Hitchcock, A., Carr, L., & Hall, W. (1996). *A survey of online STM journals 1990-95; a calm before the storm*. Available at: http://journals.ecs.sotom.ac .uk/survey/survey.html.

Hunter, K. (1998). Electronic journal publishing: Observation from inside. *D-Lib Magazine.* 4(July/August). Available at: http:/

/www.dlib.org/ dlib/july98/07hunter.html

International Federation of Library Associations and Institutions (2004). *IFLA statement on open access to scholarly literature and research documentation*. Available at: http://www.ifla.org/V/cdoc/open-access04.html

Hoben, John B. (1954). English Communication at Colgate Re-examined, *Journal of Communication* 4, 77.

Ruesch, Jürgen (1957). Technology and Social Communication, In *Communication Theory and Research,* ed. L. Thayer (Springfield, IL: Thomas, 462.

King, D.W., & Tenopir, C. (2000). *Scholarly journal and digital database pricing: Threats or opportunity*. Available at: http://www.si.umich.edu/PEAK-2000/king.pdf

Kling, R., & Callahan, E. (2003). Electronic journals, the Internet, and scholarly publishing. *Annual Review of Information Science and Technology,* 37, 127-177.

Kling, R., & Covi, L. (1995). Electronic journals and legitimate media in the system of scholarly communication. *The Information Society,* 11, 261-271. Available at: http://www.ics.uci.edu/~kling/klingej2.html

Kling, R., & McKim, G. (1997a). Speed of scientific communication and the pace of scientific innovation. (Working Paper No.WP-97-08). Indiana University, Bloomington, Center for Social Informatics.

Kling, R., & McKim, G. (1997b). *A typology for electronic-journals: Characterizing scholarly journals by their distribution forms*. Center for Social Informatics, SLIS Indiana University, Bloomington, Available at: Indiana University Web site: http://www.slis.indiana.edu/csi

Kling, R., & McKim, G. (2000). Not just a matter of time: Field difference and the shaping of electronic media in supporting scientific communication. *Journal of the American Society for Information Science,* 51 (14), 1306-1320.

Lederberg, J. (1993). Communication as the root of scientific progress. *Current Contents,* 1, 5-11.

Lyman, P., & Chodorow, S. (1998). The future of scholarly communication. In *The mirage of continuity: Reconfiguring academic information resources for the 21st century*. Washington, D.C.: CLIR and AAU.

MacDonald, A.H. (1990). Publish and perish: a voyage into the black hole of scholarly communications in the 90's. National Meeting of Vice-Presidents (Academic), Calgary, University of Calgary. 1-20.

McKnight, C. (1993). Electronic journals - past, present...and future? *Aslib Proceedings*, 45, 7-10.

McQuail, Denis (2000). *McQuail's Mass Communication Theory* (fourth edition), London : Sage, pp. 16–34. MAS

Mogge, D. (Ed). (1997). *Directory of electronic journals, newsletters, and academic discussion lists*, 7th ed. Washington, D.C.: Association of Research Libraries. Available at: http://db.arl.org/index.html

Odlyzko, A. M. (1995). Tragic loss or good riddance? The impending demise of traditional scholarly journals. *Notices of the American Mathematical Society*, 42(1), 49-56.

Odlyzko, A. M. (1998). The economic of electronic publishing. *The Journal of Electronic Publishing*, 4(1). Available at: http://www/press/ umich.edu/jep/04-01

Organisation for Economic Co-operation and Development (OECD). (1998). The global research village: How information and communication technologies affect the science system. Washington, DC: OECD Washington Center. Available at: http://www1.oecd.org/dsti/sti/s_t/scs/prod/global.pdf

Parthasarthy, S. (1986). Information communication barriers. *In: National* Conference on Scientific information for Defence, New Delhi, 25-26 Feb. 1936. Conference papers. New Delhi, DESIDOC, S5-1

Peek, R.P., & Pomerantz, J.P. (1998). Electronic scholarly journal publishing. *Annual Review of Information Science and Technology*, 33 : 321-356.

Prasher, R. G. (2003). User education in information and its communication (pp.259-262). New Delhi: Medallion Press.

Roes, H. (1994). Electronic journals: A survey of the literature and the net. *Journal of Information Networking*, 2(3), 169-186.

Price, D.J. de Solla (1963). *Little science, big science.* New York: Columbia University Press.

Prosser, D.C. (2003). Scholarly communication in the 21st century -the impact of new technologies and models. *Serials: the Journal for the Serials Community,* 16(2), 163-167.

Public Library of Science (2005). *Definition of open access.* Available at: http://www.plos.org/oa/definition.html

Ramachandran, R. (2004). The 'free access' debate. *Frontline,* 21 (1).

Regazzi, J. (2004). The shifting sands of open access publishing, a publisher's view. *Serial Review,* 30 (4), 275-280.

Rowlands, I., Nicholas, D., & Huntington, P. (2004). Researchers' attitudes towards new journal publishing models. *Learned publishing,* 17. Available: http://www.alpsp.org/volcont.htm

Senders, J W, (1977). An online scientific journal. *Information Scientist,* 1(1), 3-9.

Shannon, Claude E. & Warren Weaver (1949): *A Mathematical Model of Communication.* Urbana, IL: University of Illinois Press

Strangelove, M. (1993). Electronic journals and newsletters: An introduction (pp. 53-58). In A. Okerson (Ed.), *Directory of Electronic Journals, Newsletters and Academic Discussion Lists* (3rd ed.), Washington, D.C.: Association of Research Libraries.

Suber, P. (2003). *Removing the barriers to research: An introduction to open access for librarians.* Available at: http://www.earlham.edu/~peters /writing/acrl.htm

Suber, P. (2004). *Time line of the open access movement.* Available at: http://www.carlham.edu/~peters/ fos/timeline.htm

Suber, P. (2008). Open Access Overview. Focusing on open access to peer-reviewed research articles and their preprints. Available at: http://www.earlham.edu/~peters/fos/overview.htm

Swan, A., & Brown, S. (2005). *Open access self-archiving: An author study.* Available at: http://cogprints.org/4385/ 01/jisc2.pdf

Clevenger, Theodore Jr. (1991). Can One Not Communicate?: A Conflict of Models, *Communication Studies* 42, 351.

University College London (n.d.). Scholarly communication. Available: http://www.ucl.ac.uk/Library/scholarly-communication/index.shtml

Webster's Third New International Dictionary (1986). Springfield, MA: Merriam-Webster, 460.

Schramm, Wilbur (1954). How Communication Works," in *The Process and Effects of Communication,* ed. Wilbur Schramm (Urbana: University of Illinois Press, pp. 3-26):

3
Information Science – Foundations and Disciplinary Perspective

What is information science? The question, while seemingly simple, begs another more complex one. This chapter presents a skeleton of a systematic and comprehensive knowledge map of the field information science. The map is grounded in the panel discussions. Formulating a knowledge map helps to establish the boundaries of the field and define its main parts. Further, this chapter also deals with inter-disciplinary relation of this field with several other disciplines. However, first of all let us starts this chapter by understanding the connotation of term information in information science.

WHAT IS "INFORMATION" IN INFORMATION SCIENCE?

The concept of information was originated from Latin, maintained throughout the Middle Ages but disappeared as scholastic ontology was superseded by modern science. Since approximately the 16th century the term *information* is used 'to instruct, to furnish with knowledge', whereas the ontological meaning of 'giving form to something' became more and more obsolete. *Information* seemed to lose its connection to the human world, and came to be applied, as a more or less adequate metaphor, to every kind of process through which something is being changed or *in-formed.*

When we are looking for the foundations of a science, we cannot avoid that in the field information science the main concept is not information but - man (= man and woman). As, Winograd and Flores (1986) describes that, information science looks for its subject by considering information to be something *objective* in the *external reality*. Capurro (1991) mention three main epistemological paradigms in our field which are based on a substantialist view of something called *information* as well as on the modern distinction between subject and object. They are:

- the representation paradigm
- the source-channel-receiver paradigm
- the Platonistic paradigm.

According to the *representation paradigm* human beings are knowers or observers of an outside reality. The process of knowledge consists of an assimilation of things through their representations in the mind/brain of the knowing subject. These representations, once processed or codified in our brain, can then be communicated to other minds and/ or stored and processed in machines (computers). Human beings are biological information processors. Information is the codified double of reality. Humans can use information for specific rational purposes, but nothing speaks against the hypothesis that also machines can achieve this level of information processing and use. On this basis information science is concerned with the study of representation, codification and rational use of information.

The *source-channel-receiver paradigm* takes the

phenomenon of human communication as a metaphor to be applied to different levels of reality. When they communicate, human beings, or other kinds of sources and receivers, are said to exchange information. In order for the receiver to understand the meaning of the message sent by the source, a common stock of signs hast to exist. But the exchange of information can be considered only in relationship to the structure of the message.

Under these premisses information science is primarily concerned with the impact of information on the receiver. At the same time, receivers are seekers or users of information in order to solve their problems.

Finally, the *Platonistic paradigm* takes an opposite view to the foregoing. Instead of starting with a knowing subject, it looks for something to be considered as *information in itself*. This is the sphere of human knowledge not as a biological, psychological or sociological process but as objectivized in non-human carriers. We can call it, paradoxically, *materialistic Platonism*. The idealistic version of this paradigm considers knowledge as something objective in itself, independently of any material carrier.

Information science is supposed to study primarily the *world* of *information in itself*, i.e., to contribute to the analysis and construction of it. Information has the same ontological status as the laws of logic with regard to the psychological or biological description of the process of thinking. There remains the problem of the relationship between this *world* and the world of the knowing subject. This is a problem similar to the one posed by the representation paradigm. In its *materialistic* version, information science studies information as far as it is materialized in carriers outside the brain, in the form of documents or of their electronic surrogates. The *idealistic* version considers information as an objective but non-material entity.

All three paradigms have a long tradition in the history of ideas, but they were the object of further developments in modern philosophy particularly with regard to the difference between the knowing subject as a kind of substance or *thing* separated from the objects of knowledge. There are another look of information and that is cognitive viewpoint. Information is treated as directly involving *cognitive processing and understanding.* It results from interaction of two cognitive structures, a "mind" and (broadly) a "text." Information is that which affects or changes the state of a mind. In cases of information services, information is most often conveyed through the medium of a text, document, or record, e.g., what a reader may understands from a text or document. The interpretation by Tague-Sutcliff (1995, pp. 11–12) fits:

Information is an intangible that depends on the conceptualization and the understanding of a human being. Records contain words or pictures (tangibles) absolutely, but they contain information relative only to a user.. . Information is associated with a transaction between text and reader, between a record and user.

DEFINITION OF INFORMATION SCIENCE

The term information science' has been a matter of dispute almost since the term was coined by Chris Hanson of Aslib in 1956. In UK during 1940s the term followed the use of 'information scientist', to describe scientists who specialised in helping their colleagues to find information. (Bottle, 1997). In other words, the original usage did not imply the existence of an information 'science', but simply a set of information practices aimed at scientists. The difficulties with the term became evident when academic programmes in information science began to emerge and when, consequently, teachers and departments began to seek academic respectability by moving from training people in a vocational practice to searching for underlying principles and theories that would provide that respectability. (Wilson, 1981)

Numerous writers (e.g., Debons, 1988; Froelich, 1986; McGarry, 1987; Lancaster, 1994) was on the path to define 'information science' and set out curricula that would constitute a sound basis for a unitary discipline. However, these writers, and others disagree on what constitutes information science and, therefore, the curricula, although overlapping, do not fully agree with one another. Some argue for the inclusion of logic, mathematics, and programming; others for the inclusion of linguistics, philosophy, and economics, and so on.

The impetus for development of information science can be traced to an article almost half a century ago by Vannevar Bush (Bush, 1945) where he mentioned two things: (a) succinctly defined a critical problem that was on the minds of many for a long time, and (b) proposed a solution that was a "technological fix," in tune with time and strategically attractive. The problem was (and in its basic form still is) "the massive task of making more accessible a bewildering store of knowledge." This is the problem of "information explosion," coupled with necessity to provide availability of and accessibility to need-based, accurate, relevant information, acute to this day. His solution was to use the emerging information technology to combat the problem. But he went even further: he proposed a machine named "Memex", incorporating in his words "association of ideas", that will duplicate "mental processes artificially. "Ideas that will govern information science and-artificial intelligence are quite evident. Memex never became a reality, but to this day R&D efforts in a number of fields have similar goals, to address the same problem of "bewildering store of knowledge."

Debates over the "proper" definition of information science, as of any field, are fruitless, and in expectations naive. Information science, as a science and as a profession, is defined by the problems it has addressed and the methods it has used for their solutions over time. Any advances in information science depend on whether the field is indeed progressing in relation to problems addressed and methods used.

Webster routinely defines information science as "the science dealing with the efficient collection, storage, and retrieval of information." It is a general definition of problems addressed by information science. International encyclopedia of information and library science (Routledge, 2003) defines information science as a discipline that investigates the characteristics of information and the nature of the information transfer process, whilst not losing sight of the practical aspects of collecting, collating and evaluating information and organizing the dissemination through appropriate intellectual apparatus and technology.

In the following part we will discuss the concept information science, as looked by different eminent scientists, and has taken from a Critical Delphi study conducted in 2003-2005.

T.D. Wilson, University of Sheffield, UK.

Information science is that set of practices and related disciplinary studies which is concerned with the generation, transmission, organization, storage, retrieval and use of information together with the studies of the user of information.

Elsa Barber, University of Buenos Aires, Argentina

Information Science is the study of the functions, the structure and the transmission of information and the management of information systems. It is the study of data, information, knowledge, and message, as they exist in the collective domain, explores only the mediating aspects, focuses in hi-tech and included user studies.

Prof. Rafael Capurro, **University of Applied Sciences, Stuttgart, Germany**

Information Science in a narrower sense is the study of messages within the context of human communication, which implies the process of meaning offer (i.e., message), meaning selection (i.e., information) and understanding. In a broader sense it is the study of messages in non-human phenomena.

Prof. Charles H. Davis, **Indiana University, USA**

Information science is an interdisciplinary field encompassing all aspects of data from data generation via measurement and observation, through data capture, analysis, representation, organization, evaluation, storage, transformation, presentation, protection, and retention.

Prof. Birger Hjorland, **Royal School of Library and Information Science, Denmark**

Information science is a field studying the documentation of knowledge claims and their representation in primary, secondary and tertiary literatures and information services. Information Science is the study of knowledge dissemination, production and use. Books and documents are selected, represented, described, indexed and so on based on their assumed contribution to knowledge.

Prof. Anthony Debons, **University of Pittsburgh, USA**

Information science is that area of study and practice which attempts to determine the laws and principles pertaining to the analysis, design and evaluation of Data, Information and Knowledge Systems. It is based on the following rationale: All organisms are data, information, and knowledge systems, varying in the degree with which they can process these cognitive/affective functions. Each of these functions are aided and augmented by technology that each species generate, invent, and apply.

Dr. Donald Hawkins, **Information Today, USA**

Information science is an interdisciplinary field concerned with the **theoretical** and **practical** concepts, as well as the technologies, laws, and industry dealing with **knowledge** transfer and the sources, generation, organization, representation, processing, distribution, communication, and uses of information, as well as communications among users and their behavior as they seek to satisfy their information needs.

Prof. Wallace Koehler, **Valdosta State University, USA**

Information science is the totality of the process of communication and understanding, both intra-and inter-personally. As such, it is a broad discipline, ranging from Shannonesque info theory to semiotics and memetics. Information Science is such a broad field that no single meaningful definition is possible unless we seek to limit it and define its other characteristics as something else.

Prof. Charles Oppenheim, **Loughborough University, UK**

Information science is the rational and systematic study of the way information is created, stored, indexed, disseminated and used. It's not to do with knowledge, but with information - the formal recorded types of information in particular. Rationale: information science is to do with the ways human create and process information, so is primarily a social science. However, technological means are an important component, so some of information science falls within that ambit.

Prof. Michael Buckland, **University of California, Berkeley**

Definition. Information science is the field formerly known as "Documentation", and now commonly referred to as "Information Science". My definition would be that it is, broadly, concerned with the creation, dissemination, and utilization of knowledge. Within that broad scope there tend to be two sub-areas: a wide-ranging concern with human and social aspects: information related behavior, organizational and social concerns; and a technical/ engineering concern with the design and evaluation of information systems.

Dennis Nicholson, **Strathclyde University, UK**

Information Science studies information, focusing on the identification, behavior, characteristics, environmental context, use, management, and impact of information in its various forms (i.e., the data - information - knowledge - message continuum), and their instantiations (e.g., electronic data, electronic interactive, human & machine mediated, hardcopy forms etc), on tools and processes for their evaluation, control, transmission, and utilization, and on information futures.

Prof. Paul Sturges, **Loughborough University, UK**

Information science is a name for one of the approaches to information and communication characterized by a background in specialized (scientific and technical) librarianship. The domain exists alongside information systems, informatics, communication studies and various other domains, with which there is surprisingly little linkage given that there is no real barrier separating them.

MODEL OF INFORMATION SCIENCE

Chaim Zins in his study on knowledge map of information science has identify six models of information sciences.

The Hi-Tech Model : Information Science is the study of the mediating aspects of D-I-K-M phenomena as they are implemented in the hi-tech domain.

The Technology Model : Information Science is the study of the mediating aspects of D-I-K-M phenomena as they are implemented in all types of technologies.

The Culture Model : Information Science is the study of the mediating aspects of D-I-K-M phenomena as they are implemented in the cultural domain.

The Human World Model : Information Science is the study of all the aspects of D-I-K-M phenomena as they are implemented in the human realm.

The Living World Model : Information Science is the study of all the aspects of D-I-K-M phenomena as they are implemented in the living world, human and non-human.

The Living & Physical worlds Model : Information Science is the study of all the aspects of D-I-K-M phenomena as they are implemented in all types of biological organisms, human and non-human, and all types of physical objects.

			Explored Phenomena
	Scope	*Domain*	*Data Information Knowledge Message*
Characteristics	**Mediating**	Model (1) **Hi-Tech**	(Focusing on the mediating aspects of D-I-K-M as they are implemented in computer-based technologies)
		Model (2) **Technology**	(Focusing on the mediating aspects of D-I-K-M as they are implemented in all types of technologies)
		Model (3) **Culture/Society**	(Focusing on the mediating aspects of D-I-K-M as they are implemented in human societies)

Inclusive (all aspects)	Model (4) **Human World**	(Focusing on all aspects of D-I-K-M as they are implemented in the human realm)
	Model (5) **Living World**	(Focusing on all aspects of D-I-K-M as they are implemented in the living world)
	Model (6) **Living & Physical Worlds**	(Focusing on all aspects of D-I-K-M as they are implemented in all types of biological organisms, human and non-human, and all types of physical objects)

INFORMATION SCIENCE IN DISCIPLINARY PERSPECTIVE

While defining information science, Borko opines that "Information science is a discipline that investigates the properties and behavior of information, the forces governing the flow of information, and the means of processing information for optimum accessibility and usability. It is concerned with that body of knowledge relating to the origination, collection, organization, storage, retrieval, interpretation, transmission, transformation, and utilization of information. This includes the investigation of information representations in both natural and artificial systems, the use of codes for efficient message transmission, and the study of information processing devices and techniques such as computers and their programming systems. It is an intedisciplinary science derived from and related to such fields as mathematics, logic, linguistics, psychology, computer technology, operations research, the graphic arts, communications, library science, management, and other similar fields. It has both a pure science component, which inquires into the subject without regard to its application, and an applied science component, which develops services and products." Contrary to the above arguments, White and McClain argue that information science is a interface between people and literature. Information science models the world of publication with a practical goal of being able to deliver their content on demand to inquirers.

However, H. Bose mentioned that information science is recognized as a complex multidisciplinary subject ranging computers and telecommunication through cybernetics to psychology, logic and techniques of classification and indexing, and as professional discipline concerned with the accumulation, storage and transfer of recorded knowledge. Similarly, Slamecka explained information science is an interdisciplinary field of study of the nature, properties, control and use of information. Fairthorne explained that the whole group of applied disciplines together with their pertinent fundamental disciplines forming the foundation of information generation, communication and service systems may well be viewed as federation of disciplines or information science. On the other hand, Mansfield critics the arguments and argues that the term 'information' and 'science' are both ambiguous. According to him information science is being used to describe heterogeneous set of activities, so called information science forcing the search for a unifying conceptual framework where none exists.

BOUNDARIES OF INFORMATION SCIENCE

Determining the exact boundaries of information science is not a simple task because of the rapid evolution of the field in the past few decades. Baruchson Arbib's published a classification scheme (http://www.success.co.il/is/2.pdf) reflects the current state of research in the field of information science. Ten key topics have been devised and further divided into subtopics:

1. **Foundations of Information Science (IS) :** history

of information science and librarianship, archival science, history of knowledge formats (manu-scripts, print and digital), information science epis-temology, history of libraries and librarians, library and information science as a profession.

2. Methodology : quantitative and qualitative research, bibliometrics, informatics, bibliography, domain analysis, webometrics.

3. Information/Learning Society : social and cultural aspects of the information society, sociology of knowledge, social communication, electronic learn-ing, information literacy, information science edu-cation, lifelong learning, reading, the application of technology in teaching, reading habits, reading encouragement.

4. Information Technology : communication and com-puter networks, document delivery systems, structure of computerized systems, programming languages, multimedia, information retrieval systems, systems analysis, artificial intelligence, human-computer interaction, information architecture, digital security systems, website construction, networks technolo-gies, knowledge representation, search tools.

5. Data Organization and Retrieval : classification schemes, metadata, indexing, text mining, abstract-ing, knowledge organization, taxonomies, thesauri, ontology, vocabulary control, online searching techniques, reference work, the semantic web.

6. Information Industry Economics and Management: comparative intelligence, databases, digital libraries, information industry market, information manage-ment, information manipulation, knowledge manage-ment, information centres and libraries management, collection management, electronic commerce, influence of websites on marketing.

7. Information Ethics and Law : copyright, digital security, digital divide, censorship, Internet crime, free access to information, information policies, information licensing and fair use, information privacy and ethics, credibility of information.

8. User Studies : human information behaviour, information-seeking behaviour, information needs, reference interview, user-information, scientist-interaction, usability of web information.

9. Diffusion Studies : information dissemination, communication theory, message theory, information centres and libraries, electronic dissemination.

10. Social Information Science : information needs of different cultures, information education, power and ethics, social information banks, social information sections in school and public librar-ies, printed and electronic self-help sources, the social information scientist, community informa-tion, information diffusion in multicultural soci-eties, health information centres, social networks, bibliotherapy.

APPLICATIONS OF INFORMATION SCIENCE

According to ALA encyclopedia of reference services (ALA,1996) there are two applications of information science: logistical and process oriented.

1. Logistical application-Accounting of commodities
   (a) Database creation
   (b) Online information services
2. Process orientation-Human use of commodities
   (a) Management information systems
   (b) Command-control-communication systems
   (c) Decision support system
   (d) Expert system

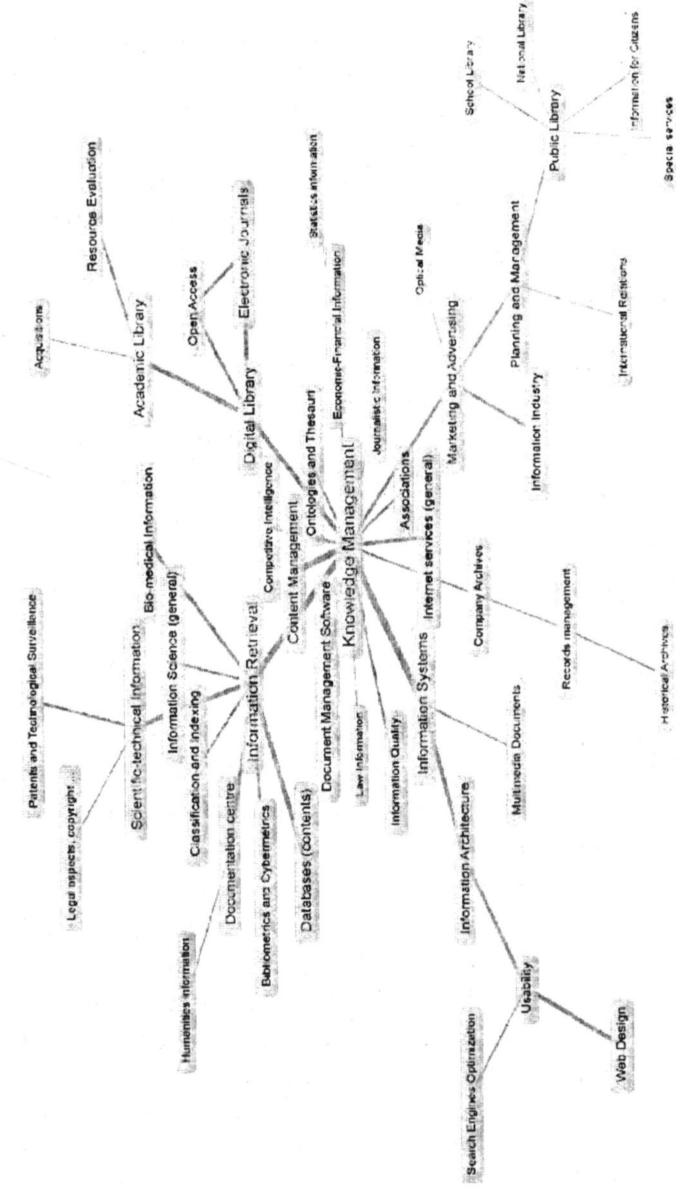

A Network Structure of LIS

Source: Hassan-Montero, Yusef and Herrero-Solana, Víctor (2007).

INTERDISCIPLINARY PERSPECTIVE TO INFORMATION SCIENCE

Ever since its evolution and existence, Information science exhibit three general characteristics. First, the discipline has shared its periphery with many modern fields – i.e. this discipline is highly interdisciplinary in nature, however, the relations with various disciplines are changing. The interdisciplinary evolution is far from over. As Soergel (1998) suggests, information science knows few boundaries, overlaps many disparate fields and draws upon their unique ideas, methods and results. Second, information science is, with may other fields, an active participant in the evolution of information society. Information science has a strong social and human dimension, above and beyond the technology. These characteristics are a framework for understanding the past, present and future of information science. Third, information science is inevitably connected to information technology. A technological imperative is compelling and constraining the evolution of information science, as is the evolution of information society. In the next few parts of this book, we will concentrate on the interdisciplinary relations of information science. Much of what is discussed here is an extension of thoughts presented in Saracevic (1992), where other characteristics of information science are discussed as well.

The interdisciplinary framework of information science has provided depth and breadth to its scope and nature of study. According to Bates (1999) the area information science studies as a meta-field, similar to other information-based professions such as education, communication. The basic problem of understanding information and communication, their manifestations, effects and human information behavior, and the applied problem of "making more accessible the bewildering store of knowledge", particularly including the attempts at technological "fixes," cannot be resolved within any one discipline. This was clear to Bush and Mooers and all the others who thought about the complexities involved. Interdisciplinarity in information science was introduced and is being perpetuated to the present by the very differences in backgrounds of people addressing the described problems. Differences in background were and are many, it makes for both richness of the field and difficulties in communication and education, Clearly not every discipline in the background of people working on the problem made an equally relevant contribution, but the assortment was responsible for sustaining a strong interdisciplinary characteristic of information science. It does not have to be searched for. It is there. Here we will concentrate on interdisciplinary relations with four fields: linguistics, librarianship, mathematics, computer science, cognitive science, and artificial intelligence. Obviously, other fields have also interdisciplinary relations, but these are the most significant and developed ones.

Linguistics

In general the relation between linguistics and information science is clear. There is strong common bond of interest between these two disciplines. While, information science is concerned with all aspects of communication of information, language is the primary medium for the communication of information and linguistics is the study of language as a system for communicating information. Earlier the relationship between these two discipline was loose until the concept like automated indexing, semantic analysis, thesaurus construction, text retrieval process, word-frequency counts, natural language processing, word correction mechanism, Unicode came into the domain of information science. Since science has not provided us with a mean of observing the neural activity of humans, we must select the alternative approach of simulating the intellectual

Domain	Foci	Main Categories (1st division)	Sub-Categories (2nd division)	Sub-Categories*/Examples & Explanations** (3rd division)	Exemplary Fields
Meta-Knowledge	Knowledge on the field of IS itself	1. Foundation	Theory	**B. Disciplines** (e.g., Anthropology (e.g., "culture"), Arts (e.g., "design"), Communication (e.g., "communication", "media", "message"), Computer science (e.g., "computer language"), Economics (e.g., "information economics"), Education (e.g., "learning"), Engineering (e.g., "information technology"), History (e.g., "primary source", "secondary sources", "tertiary source"), Law (e.g., "intellectual property", "copyright"), Linguistics (e.g., "language"), Philosophy (Epistemology (e.g. "knowledge"), Ethics (e.g., "information ethics", "professional ethics"), Political Science (e.g., "democracy"), Psychology (e.g., "cognition"), Research Methodology (e.g., "evaluation", "research", "research methodology"), Semiotics (e.g., "sign"), Sociology ("e.g., "society") **C. Theories**	Theory of IS
			Research	**B. Empirical** **1. Quantitative, 2. Qualitative**	Research Methodology
			Education	academic education and to professional training: theoretical knowledge and practical knowledge.	LIS Education
			History	Historical accounts of the field.	History of IS
Subject-based knowledge	Knowledge on the explored phenomena (i.e., the mediating aspects & conditions of human knowledge)	2. Resources	Issues	quality information (resources), information (resources) quality	Information Quality Information Systems
			Types	Primary resources (i.e., the human originators), secondary resources, tertiary resources	
		Mediating factors – Who? – Mediators: 3. Knowledge Workers	Issues	**A. Personality traits, B. Theoretical knowledge, C. Applied knowledge and practice**	Information Ethics LIS Education
			Types	Taxonomies of professional workers by fields of expertise (e.g., medical informatics), and organizational sector (e.g., librarians, archivists)	
		Mediating factors – What? – Matters: 4. Contents	Issues	Content related issues (e.g., What is a subject?)	
			Types	Taxonomies of structures (e.g., knowledge maps, subject classifications schemes, thesauri), classification systems (e.g., LCC, DDC, UDC, CC, BC), subjects (i.e., Archeology, biology, Computer Science) and the like.	

Why	Motives	**5. Applications**	Issues	Issues related to the development of application oriented systems.	
			Types	Taxonomy of applications (e.g., (information) searching, shopping, socialization and socializing).	
How?	methods	**6. Operations & Processes**	Issues	Issues related to the various operations and processes involved in mediating human knowledge.	
			Types	Taxonomy of operations and processes: documentation, representation, organization, processing, dissemination, publication, storage, manipulation, evaluation, measurement, searching, and retrieving knowledge.	
	means (media)	**7. Technologies**	Issues	Technological related issues (e.g., user-interface design).	
			Types	Taxonomy of knowledge technologies and media: electronic-based technologies (e.g., computer-based information systems, Internet), paper-based and printingbased technologies (e.g., books), communication-based technologies and media (e.g., cellular phones, MP3).	
Where and when?	milieus	**8. Environments**	Issues	Social issues (e.g., Information policy, information accessibility), including ethnic and cultural issues, professional issues related to the settings, as well as legal issues (e.g., Intellectual property, privacy), and ethical issues (e.g., privacy vs. public interests).	Information Ethics Social Informatics
			Types	**A. Ethnic & Cultural environments, B. Settings** (e.g., Education, Health)	
		9.Organizations	Issues	Issues related to the organizational settings (e.g., managing knowledge in business organizations)	
			Types	**A. Organizational Type:** **1. Governmental Sector, 2. Public sector, 3. Private sector, B. Functional type, 1. Memory organizations** **2. Information services**	
10. Users			Issues	User related issues (e.g., user information needs, user behavior, user search strategies)	User Studies Information Behavior
			Types	**A. Individuals** **B. Groups and Communities** **1. Gender-based, 2. Age-based, 3. Culture & ethnicity-based, 4. Need & interest** based (e.g., division by profession)	

operations of the indexer, based on the observable results of these operations and our knowledge about language as a system for communicating information. In information science, content analysis has been largely associated with semantic analysis. In order to perform semantic analysis language has a great role.

Librarianship

Although the discipline librarianship is popularly known as library & information science in present day, these are two different fields in strong interdisciplinary relations, rather than one and the same field, or one being a special case of the other. Similarities are in their sharing of their social role and in their general concern with effective utilization of graphic and other records. But differences in selection and/ or definition of problems addressed, agenda, paradigms, theoretical base, and practical solutions do matter. Thus the conclusion that librarianship and information science while related, are different fields.

Drucker once argue that there are fundamental economic and social changes afoot in which knowledge and information is becoming the base, the prime valuation, for economy and even society as a whole. If we belief that libraries are the storehouse of knowledge and accept Bell's and Drucker's premise that knowledge (and by extension information) is becoming central to the emerging social and economic order, then this has enormous implication for information science, for information retrieval and, of course, for library and information services.

During these days, the relationship between librarianship and information science has become more pronounced and successful in experimentation and development of Online Public Access Catalogs (OPACs) as a information retrieval systems of any library setup.

Mathematics

The very famous Information theory is a branch of applied mathematics and electrical engineering involving the quantification of information. The interdisiclinary relation of mathematics with information science leads to various present state-of-the-art subjects like knowledge systems, improved information retrieval through the deployment of multi-valued logic, appropriate file ordering, effective and efficient retrieval measures, simplified retrieval approaches. Traditionally, informatics, statistics based analysis, citation-based searching, application of Bradford-like distributions to model effective core research literature collection development and usage, biomedical informatics are some of the field where mathematics had a lead role. The development of various models, simulation in information science is due to its relationship with mathematics.

Computer Science

According to the definition of Denning et al, (1989): The discipline of computing is the systematic study of algorithmic processes that describe and transfer information: their theory, analysis, design, efficiency, implementation and application. Further it mentioned that Computer science is about algorithms related to information, while information science is about the very nature of information and their use by humans. The two concerns are not in competition, they are complementary. They lead to different basic and applied agendas.

The influence of computer science on various other field has grown from 1990 onward, and it appears that information science is shifting toward a more technological orientation and more specific areas of expertise (Tang, 2004). Today every discipline relies directly or indirectly on the use of computers. Saracevic (1999) mentioned that the basis of relation between information science and computer science lies in the application of computers and computing in, and the associated products, services and networks. Within last few years this relation also involves research on the evolving digital libraries, with their strong technological base, but also many problems way above any technology.

A number of computer scientist have been involved in R&D on information and its many spin-offs, like symbolisation, structure and transmission of semantic kinds of information. There are several fields of computer science which had no connection with the early evolution of information science, but have addressed information problems similar to those in information science. These include works on expert systems, knowledge bases, hypertext, and human-computer interaction (which is also a strong area in cognitive science). More recently, R&D on digital libraries, Unicode attracting a wide attention of computer scientists from a variety of streams, as well as people from many other disciplines. These areas have a significant informational component, associated with: information representation, its intellectual organization and linkages; information seeking, searching, retrieving and filtering; use, quality, value and impact of information; evaluation of information systems from user and use perspective; and the like - all traditionally addressed in information science.

The technological imperative is forcing for development and application of variety of information services, products, systems and networks. Development of the national and global information infrastructures is bringing not only technological issues to the fore, but many commercial, social, legal and political issues to a head clash. Both fields share concern and uneasiness for development of concept like knowledge commission, electronic highway etc.

Cognitive Science

The field cognitive science share a basic concern about understanding cognitive processes, their realization in the brain, the structure of the mind, and various manifestation of the mind, such as intelligence. The significance of cognitive science lies in interaction of different approaches to these most complex and intriguing problems.

There are two areas in cognitive science of direct interest to information science: artificial intelligence and human-computer interaction. Both of these can be also treated in computer science, but it is better to discuss it under information science, to underscore aspects related to human rather than technological.

Saracevic mentioned that: AI developed two strems: 'strong AI' and 'weak AI.' Strong AI flourished under considerable government subsidies from mid 1950's till the end of 1980's. It addressed both the theoretical and philosophical issues on the nature of intelligence, and the algorithmic issues of making computers behave intelligently. While it came up with many innovations, some revolutionary, related to computer programming, it also engaged philosophers and many others in some of the most spirited intellectual controversies of the second half of this century. But with waning support and limited successes in making computers truly intelligent, strong AI lost its flourish. Weak AI had more limited ambitions, confining itself to 'the art of making computers do smart things' (Waldrop, 1987). Weak AI enjoyed great pragmatic success; much of today's computing follows in its footsteps. Many AI workers migrated to the problems related to information, and in the process they are transforming R&D efforts, including those in digital libraries. Information science heavily borrowed from both theoretical and experimental ideas in AI.

Artificial Intelligence

Artificial Intelligence (AI) is the science and engineering of making intelligent machines, especially intelligent computer programs. It is related to the similar task of using computers to understand human intelligence. The term was first coined by John McCanthy (regarded as Father of AI) in the year 1956 at Darmouth Conference. The subject AI, typically studied as a research area within Computer Science, is multidisciplinary in nature. AI study aims at achieving a good understanding of the nature of intelligence and building intelligent agents which are computational systems demonstrating intelligent behavior. Although, this subject has been developed over more than 50 years, its implication is more in present day context. The topics studied in AI are quite broad, ranging from knowledge representation and reasoning, knowledge-based systems, automatic programming, computer vision, expert systems, intelligent computer-assisted instruction, data mining, natural language processing, speech recognition, image processing, robotics, intelligent information systems. and planning and decision support.

Artificial intelligence has both short term and long term effects on information retrieval. In the short term, it would modify the results of a current search during a query to meet the user's current needs. In the long term, it would modify the document representations to improve responses.

Numerous successful AI systems have been deployed in real-life applications in engineering, finance, science, health care, education, and service sectors. AI research has also significantly impacted the subject area of Library and Information Science, helping to develop smart Web search engines, personalized news filters, and knowledge-sharing and indexing systems. Intelligent library systems utilize artificial intelligence technologies to provide knowledge-based services to library patrons and staff.

Business

The importance of information in society is constantly on the rise, and many are involved in its various aspects, with a large number of studies, initiatives and businesses dedicated to information-related areas. In the chapter 'Marketing of Information' we have tried to discuss how economics and business discipline influence the field information science.

CONCLUSION

This chapter has presented an overview of information science and its relationship with various disciplines. We have also explained various models and boundaries of information science here. Although, Saracevic explained 'Information Science is interdisciplinary in nature', he warns against the dan-ger of 'losing the field' and its possible division into two isolated areas - an information science researching techno-logical systems, which is practised mainly by computer professionals, and an information science that focuses on the information user. In his opinion both areas should be covered by the one field (Saracevic, 1999).

REFERENCES

Bates, M.J. (1999). The Invisible Substrate of Information Science, *Journal of the American Society for Information Science* 50(12), 1043–50.

Borko, H. (1968). Information science: What is it? *American Documentation,* 19(1), 3–5.

Bose,H. (1986). Information Science: principles and practice New York: Envoy press.

Bottle, R.T. (1997). 'Information science', in: John Feather and Paul Sturges, editors. *International encyclopedia of information and library science.* London: Routledge.

Bush, V. (1945). As we may think. *Atlantic Monthly,* 176(1), 101-108.

Capurro, Rafael (1991). Foundation of information science: Review and perspective. International Conference on Conceptions of Library and Information Science, University of Tampere, Tampere, Finland, 26-28 August 1991.

Debons, A. (Ed.). (1974). Information science, search for identity. *Proceedings of the 1972 NATO Advanced Study Institute in Information Science held at Seven Springs, Champion, Pennsylvania, 12-20 August, 1972* . New York, NY: Marcel Dekker.

Debons, A., Horne, E., & Cronenweth, S. (1988). Information science: An integrated view. New York: G.K. Hall.

Denning, P.J. et al (1989). Computing as a discipline. *Communication of the ACM,* 32, (1), 9-23.

Fairthorne,R.A. The scope and aims of information sciences and technologies. In Mikhailov, A.I and others; Ed. On theoretical problems of informatrics, pp25-31.

Froehlich, T. J. (1986). Challenges to curriculum development in information science. *Education for Information, 4* (4), 265-289.

Hassan-Montero, Yusef and Herrero-Solana, Víctor (2007). Visualizing Library and Information Science from the practitioner's perspective. 11th International Conference of the International Society for Scientometrics and Informetrics June 25-27, 2007, Madrid (Spain)

Lancaster, F. W. (1994). The curriculum of information science in developed and developing countries. *Libri,* 44 (3), 201-205.

Mansfield, Una (1987). The wider scope of information research, (Current trends in information: research and theory, Bill Katz and Robin Kinder eds.) New York: Haworth, p.64

Saracevic, Tefko (1995). Interdisciplinary nature of information science. *Ciência da Informação* 24(1).

Saracevic, Tefko (1999). Information Science, *Journal of the American Society for Information Science.* 50(12),1051–1063

Soergel, Dagobert (1998). An Information Science Manifesto, *Bulletin of the American Society for Information Science and Technology,* 24(2), 10–12.

Slamecka,V. (1965). Information Science Generally and Specifically

Southeastern librarian.15,15-18

Soergel, D. (1998). An information science manifesto. Bulletin of the American Society for Information Science, (Jan/Dec), 11-12.

Tague-Sutcliffe, J. (1995). Measuring information: The information services perspective. San Diego, CA: Academic Press

Tang, R. (2004). Evolution of the Interdisciplinary Characteristics of Information and Library Science, *Proceedings of the American Society for Information Science and Technology* 41(1): 54–63.

Waldrop, N.M. (1987). *Man-made minds: The promise of artificial intelligence.* New York: Walker.

Wersig, G. (1993). Information science: the study of postmodern knowledge usage, *Information processing and management* 29, 229-239.

Wilson,T.D. (1981). Sociological aspects of information science *INT Forum Information Documentation* 6, 13-18

Winograd, T., Flores, F. (1986). Understanding Computers and Cognition: A New Foundation for Design. New Jersey: New Jersey.

Zins, Chaim (2007). Knowledge Map of Information Science. *Journal of the American Society for Information Science And Technology,* 58(4), 526–535

4
Information Science From System Perspective

The term 'system' derived from the Greek word 'systema', means an organized relationship among functional units or components. The basic definition of a system is an orderly grouping of independent components linked together according to a plan to achieve specific objectives. Ackoff and Emery (1972) defined a system as 'a set of interrelated elements each of which is related directly or indirectly to every other element, and no subject of which is interrelated to any other subject'. Any system has some basic characteristics:

(a) Organization : Organization implies structure and order of components that help to achieve objectives. A computer system, for example, is designed around input/output device, a central processing units and one or more storage.

(b) Interaction : Interaction refers to the manner in which each components functions with other components of the system. In an information system, the event world must interaction with motor/control system with input/ acquisition system.

(c) Interdependence : Interdependence refers dependence of one organ with other to perform composite function. Interdependent elements are linked together to coordination overall plan.

(d) Integration : Integration refers to the holism of systems. It means that parts of the system works together within the system even though each parts performs a unique function. A successful integration typically produces a synergic effect.

(e) Central objective : It means that although each units of a system function independently, the system have an overall central objective for which each unit function uniquely.

C.W. Churchman, a philosopher and professor of business administration has identified following characteristics of a system:

(i) It is teleological (purposeful)

(ii) One can determine its performance

(iii) It has user or users

(iv) It has parts (components) that in an of themselves have purpose.

(v) It is embedded in an environment.

(vi) It includes a decision maker who is internal to the system and who can change the performance of the parts.

(vii) There is a designer who is concerned with the structure of the system and whose conceptualization of the system can direct the actions of the decision maker and ultimately affect the end result of the actions of the entire system.

(viii) The designer's purpose is to change a system so as to maximize its value to the user.

(ix) The designer ensures that the system is stable to the extent that he or she knows its structure and functions.

ELEMENTS OF A SYSTEM

The common prime elements of any system are:

(i) Event world/Environment - every system function on some environment.

(ii) Input/ Ingestor/ Internal or Input transducer - through which system receives matter and energy.

(iii) Distributor/Transmitter/Channel - through which system distribute the converted matter/energy or input matter/energy to other unit.

(iv) Encoder/Decoder/Converter/ Processor - Convert one form of input into another form so that it can be used by system.

(v) Control/Motor - the main unit of a system which control the whole affairs.

(vi) Storage/Memory - unit that store or keep matter/ energy for further use.

(vii) Feedback - through which system understand the system need accordingly change, if desire.

(viii) Output/output transducer- through which system put out processed information for the system or excrete unused matter/energy.

(ix) Interface - through which it interact with outer world.

SYSTEM THEORY

In order to know what a system is how it works is general system theory. According to Churchman, system theory attempts to uncover some general principles related to system in the broadest sense, and then to identify the role of the various discipline contribute to this understanding.

Kenneth E Boulding (1968), propounder of general system theory, explain that "the objectives of general system theory can be set out with varying degrees of ambition and confidence. A low level of ambition but with a high degree of confidence it aims to point out similarities in the theoretical constructions of different disciplines, where these exist, and to develop theoretical models having applicability to at least two different fields of study. At a higher level of ambition, but with perhaps a lower degree of confidence it hopes to develop something like a spectrum of theories - a system which may perform the function of a gestalt in theoretical construction.

Machlup and Mansfield (1983) in their study identified following characteristics in system theory. They are:

1. There is no general agreement as to the scope of system theory.
2. System theory is primarily mathematical
3. System theory is not a theory of concrete systems but a theory of models. It does not accept responsibility for the accuracy or relevance of these models.
4. System theory contributes to the other sciences by generating a set of models for any well-defined system, but does not specify which model is best for a particular system.
5. System theory is reductionistic. Reductionism refers to attempt to isolate specific variables that influence a phenomenon for study.
6. System theory can provide the basis for organizing the social sciences.
7. While general system theory deals with the most fundamental, abstract and general aspects if system, system theory deals with more specific questions about more well-defined kinds of system.

SYSTEM PERSPECTIVE

Taking into account all of the behaviors of a system as a whole in the context of its environment is the systems perspective. While the concept of system itself is a more general notion that indicates separation of part of the universe from the rest, the idea of a systems perspective is to use a non-reductionist approach to the task of describing the properties of the system itself.

In the systems perspective, once one has identified the system as a separate part of the universe, one is not allowed to progressively decompose the system into isolated parts. Instead, one is obligated to describe the system as a whole. If one uses separation into parts, as part of the description of the system properties, this is only part of a complete description of the behavior of the whole, which must include a description of the relationships between these parts and any additional information needed to describe the behavior of the entire system.

System analysis and design are the application of the systems approach to problem solving, generally using its elements. In fact, system analysis a comprehensive management techniques for solving complex problems and thereby increase the efficiency and effectiveness of a system. System analysis have certain objective:

(a) It can provide the decision making ingredients necessary in the consideration of conversion from one system to another, whether be from manual to machine.

(b) Facilitates compatibility with system and their components.

(c) Permits to clarify job, streamline existing methods, eliminate unnecessary work, plan new techniques and to collect cost effective information.

(d) Facilitate better communication with top management.

(e) Continue to improve productivity so that cost is reduced.

TYPES OF SYSTEM

Ackoff and Emery explain following categories of system.

(a) Abstract System : Abstract system means a system in where all its elements are explainable concepts. One can clearly connote the boundaries of such concepts. Just like mathematical system, written or spoken language system where number, words are conceptual in nature.

(b) Concrete system : As again abstract system, in concrete system at least two elements are tangible that exists in space and time. A human being is a concrete system. The numeral and letter are also abstract system by which we represent abstract mathematical concepts. There are various types of abstract system.

(i) ***Purposeful system*** : According to McCormick abd Sabder (182) a purposeful system can change its goals in a constant environment. This type of system adapts the behavious in where it occurs. Just like living system adapt the environment where they survive.

(ii) ***Closed system*** : In this type of concrete system, the boundaries are impermeable to the transmission of matter, energy or data, both into the system from the environment and from the environment to the system. The biosphere of earth is an example of closed system.

(iii) ***Open system*** : As against closed system, its boundaries are open to receive matter, energy, data from outside environment. Any living system is open system because it receives matter and energy from outside world and also returns what are unused.

REFERENCES

Ackoff, Russell L., and Emergy, Fred E. (1972). *On purposeful systems.* Chicago: Aldine-Atherton, 18.

Boulding, Kenneth E. (1968). General systems theory – The skeleton of science. *In: Modern System Research for the Behavioural Scientist,* edited by W. Buckley, Chicago: Aldine, 3-10.

Machlup, Fritz and Mansfield, Una. (1983). The study of information. New York, John Wiley & Sons.

McCormik, E.J. and Sanders, M.S. (1982). Human factors in Engineering and design. 5th ed. New York, McGraw-Hill.

Churchman, C.W. (1971). The design of inquiring system: Basic concepts of systems and organization. New York, Basic Books.

5
Management Information System

"It is well for us to realize that the great increase in knowledge in the world does not necessarily make us wiser or better. We must know how to use that knowledge properly before we rush ahead in our powerful car. We must have some idea of what the aim and object of life should be." — **Mahatma Gandhi**

During last few decades information system has been studied either through general system theory or by system models. C.W. Churchman's Inquiry Systems is an example of general system theory and Miller's living system model and Debons EARTPUT model are some of example of system model. Additionally, there have also some components oriented models which represent statements on the nature and function of components (subsystems) of information system. Yovit's model, Samuelson's model, Heilprin's model are some of the example of such category. However, in the following three consecutive chapters we are looking for function oriented models which are very popular in these days. They are Management Information System, Expert System and Decision Support System. Because of their heavy emphasis to achieve the functions desired and because of their importance to the interests of information scientists, these models deserve our attention. Before discussing Management Information System, let us first understand each terms associate with this whole concept and the connotation of these terms in MIS perspective.

CONCEPTUAL BACKGROUND OF MIS

Management

During last few decades organization have grown both in size and complexity. Expanded programme, greater service responsibility, timely reporting, research commitments requires proper planning, controlling and monitoring. Management involves planning, controlling and monitoring, and decision making. Among these elements, planning, as Kumar (1989) mentioned, consists of five sequential and interactive steps. These are: (a) selecting objectives; (b) identification of the activities which are required to achieve the stipulated objectives; (c) detailing the resources - including the various skills - required to undertake the activities; (d) determining the duration of each activity to be performed; and defining the sequence of the activities. Through the process of controlling and monitoring any organization establish standards of performance in order to reach the objective; these measure actual performance against the set standards; and keep actions on course by correcting deviations as they appear (mid-course corrections) (Murdick and Ross, 1975). Decision making is the process of selecting the most desirable or optimum alternative to solve a problem or achieve an objective. The quality and soundness of managerial decisions is largely contingent upon the information available to the decision-maker. Gorry and Scott Morton (1971) classified decision making on three levels of a continuum: *Strategic* decisions are future-oriented because of uncertainty. They are part of the planning activity. *Tactical* decision making combines planning activities with controlling. It is for short-term activities and associated allocation of resources to them to achieve the objectives. *Technical* decision making is a process of ensuring efficient and effective implementation of specific tasks.

Information

Information is a set of classified and interpreted data used in decision making. It has also been defined as 'some tangible or intangible entity which serves to reduce uncertainty about future state or events' (Lucas, 1978). Simply, information supports in decisions, decisions trigger actions. And finally actions affect the achievements or performance of the organization. If we can measure the differences in performance, we can trace the impact of information, provided that the measurements are carefully performed, the relationships among variables are well defined, and possible effects of irrelevant factors are isolated. The measured difference in performance due to informational factors is called the *realistic value* or *revealed value* of information. In any organization the information can be used for various purposes,

- strategic planning
- delivering increased productivity
- reducing service cycles
- reducing product development cycles
- reducing marketing life cycles
- increasing the understanding of customers' needs
- facilitating business and process re-engineering

For centuries, information has been accumulating at an exponential rate. This explosion of information provides exciting possibilities for analysing and cross tabulating data for generating new ideas for improving the world. The challenge is, on the other hand, to develop efficient ways to sort, store and distribute these vast amounts of information.

System

Hopkins defines system as "a set of elements forming an activity or a procedure/scheme seeking a common goal or goals by operating on data and/or energy and/or matter in a time reference to yield information and/or energy and/or matter." Modern management is based upon a systems approach and the systems approach views an organization as a set of interrelated sub-systems in which variables are mutually dependent. The interaction between different sub-system of the organization depends upon integration, communication and decision making. While, integration ensures that different sub-systems work towards the common goal, coordination and integration ensure smooth functioning in the organization, particularly as organizations become large and increasingly complex. Communication integrates different sub-systems at different levels in an organization. So, a system can be perceived as having:

- some components, functions and the processes performed by these various components;
- relationships among the components that uniquely bind them together into a conceptual assembly which is called a system; and
- an organizing principle that gives it a purpose (Albrecht, 1983).

The systems approach provides a total view of the organization. It enables analysis of an organization in a scientific manner, so that operating management systems can be developed and an appropriate MIS designed (Murdick and Ross, 1975).

Combing these all terms now we see what then MIS is? As Davis & Olson mentioned Management Information System (MIS) is: "An integrated user-machine system for providing information to support operations, management and decision making functions in an organization. The system utilizes computerized and manual procedures; models for analysis, planning, control and decision making; and a database." It is indeed a conveyor belt for appropriate high quality information from its generation to its users.

In order to make decision, prepare plans, and controls activities, information is essential. Every organization obtained information from two major sources namely: formal and informal sources such as face-to-face conversations e.g. telephone calls, social contacts and so on.

Planning and decision making have primarily been management tasks that occur at every level of management. Although, the type of planning and decision making differs, it cut across all levels. The emergence of MIS has led to new vistas in organizations especially for their information management needs.

There is often confusion exists between MIS and Information Management System (IMS). Information management system basically helps to manage information, better referred to data as in content. They provide a basis for managing resources available in various section, like acquisition, circulation etc. Whereas, MIS is basically concerned with processing data into information for different levels of managers, which is then communicated to the various Departments in an organization for appropriate decision-making. MIS facilitates managerial functioning. Management information is an important input at every level in the organization for decision making, planning, organizing, implementing, and monitoring and controlling.

CHARACTERISTICS OF MIS

- Management-oriented: Effective MIS should start its journey from appraisal of management needs, mission and goal of the business organization.
- Management directed: When MIS is management-

oriented, it should be directed by the management because it is the management who tells their needs and requirements more effectively than anybody else.

- Integrated: It means a comprehensive or complete view of all the sub systems in the organization of a company.
- Common data flows: The integration of different sub systems will lead to a common data flow which will further help in avoiding duplicacy and redundancy in data collection, storage and processing.
- Heavy planning-element: The preparation of MIS is not a one or two day exercise. It usually takes 3 to 5 years and sometimes a much longer period.
- Sub System concept: When a problem is seen in two sub parts, then the better solution to the problem is possible. Although MIS is viewed as a single entity but for its effective use, it should be broken down in small parts or subsystems so that more attention and insight is paid to each sub system.
- Common database: For all the levels of manager a common database is used.
- Computerized.
- User friendly/Flexibility

STRUCTURE OF MIS

The common structure of an MIS four levels pyramidal, with four levels of information resources. The levels of information need depend upon the structure of the organization. The top level manger need of such information which helps them in strategic planning and policy making. The second level of information resources aid tactical planning and decision making for management control. The third level supports day-to-day operations and control. The bottom level consists of information for transaction processing (TP). It then follows that since decision making is specific to hierarchical levels in an organization, the information requirements at each level vary accordingly. Generally, MIS serves the information need of middle level managers of an organization by providing reports, it also serve as an important tool for all level of managers. MIS serves managers interested only in weekly, monthly and yearly results, not the day to day activities. MIS takes in high volume transaction data and simple models from TPS as input and process them using simple routines such as summaries and comparisons as opposed to sophisticated mathematical tools and compress their findings in the form of pre-specified long reports to support the business decision making requirements in regular schedules. MIS is usually inflexible and is not concerned with external environment.

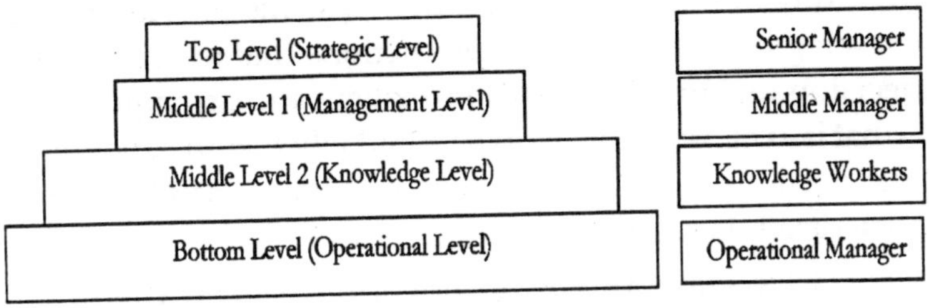

By providing the required information, an MIS can help interrelate, coordinate and integrate different sub-systems within an organization, thus facilitating and increasing coordinated working of the sub-systems, with consequent synergism.

CLASSIFICATION OF MANAGEMENT INFORMATION SYSTEMS

There are various types of management information systems. Mason and Swanson (1981) describe four categories of management information systems: (1) databank information system, (2) predictive information system, (3) decision-making information system, and (4) decision-taking information system. The classification is based on the level of support that the information system provides in the process of decision making.

1. Databank Information System : The responsibility of this information system is to observe, classify, and store any item of data which might be potentially useful to the decision maker. The information provided by the databank is merely suggestive, due to that the decision-maker has to determine contextually the implication of such information keeping in mind the cause and effect relationships. MIS designs based on the databank information system are better suited for unstructured decisions.

2. Predictive Information System : This system moves beyond pure data collection and the determination of trends over time. Predictive information systems provide for the drawing of inferences and predictions that are relevant to decision making. The decision-maker can also enquire as to 'what if a certain action is taken?' and whether the underlying assumptions are true. This type of MIS is useful for semi-structured decisions.

3. Decision-Making Information System : This system goes one step further in the process of decision making and incorporates the value system of the organization or its criteria for choosing among alternatives. provide expert advice to the decision-maker either in the form of a single recommended course of action or as criteria for choice, given the value system prevailing in the organization. This type of information systems are suitable for structured decisions.

4. Decision-Taking Information System : Examples of decision-taking information systems are not usually found in an extension organization. This is a decision system in which the information system and the decision maker are one and the same. Management is so confident in the assumptions incorporated in the system that it basically relegates its power to initiate action to the system itself.

Airplanes carry automatic pilot systems, which are an example of a decision-taking system. Once activated, the system itself keeps the plane on course and at the proper speed and altitude (according to parameters determined by the pilot). Another example of decision-taking information systems is found in modem factory production. In automobile production, continuous inventories of parts are maintained by computer as cars move down an assembly line. Orders are placed automatically by the computer when additional parts are needed. This is done without the intervention of a manager.

The choice of an appropriate MIS category primarily depends on the nature of the decisions it supports. While unstructured decisions may use MIS-category (i), the highly structured ones, such as production schedules in an industry, may use MIS-category (iv). Further, Banerjee and Sachdeva (1995) observe that "as the deep structure of the decision problem becomes more and more understood, we may move to higher level of MIS i.e., from MIS-category (i) to MIS-category (ii); and MIS-category (ii) to MIS-category (iii); and so on."

STEPS OF MIS DEVELOPMENT

Murdick and Ross, (1975) describe seven steps in the MIS process. They are:

1. First establish management information needs and formulate broad systems objectives so as to delineate important decision areas (e.g., general management, financial management or human resources management). Within these decision areas there will be factors relevant to the management decision areas, e.g., general management will be concerned about its relationship with the managing board, institute-client relationships and information to be provided to the staff. This will then lead the design team to ask what

information units will be needed to monitor the identified factors of concern. Positions or managers needing information for decision making will be identified.

2. Develop a general description of a possible MIS as a coarse design. This design will have to be further refined by more precise specifications. For efficient management of information processing, the MIS should be based on a few databases related to different sub-systems of the organization.
3. Once the information units needed have been determined and a systems design developed, decide how information will be collected. Positions will be allocated responsibility for generating and packaging the information.
4. Develop a network showing information flows.
5. Test the system until it meets the operational requirements, considering the specifications stipulated for performance and the specified organizational constraints.
6. Re-check that all the critical data pertaining to various sub-systems and for the organization as a whole are fully captured. Ensure that information is generated in a timely manner.
7. Monitor actual implementation of the MIS and its functioning from time to time.

Strategies for determining MIS design

Six strategies for determining MIS design have been suggested by Blumenthal (1969):

a. Organization-chart approach : Through this approach, the MIS is designed on the basis of functional areas of the organization, such as acquisition, processing, service, R&D, extension etc. These functional areas define current organizational boundaries and structure.

b. Integrate-later approach : This approach does not conform to any specified formats as part of an overall design. There is no notion of how the MIS will evolve in the organization. Such an MIS becomes difficult to integrate. In today's environment - where managers demand quick and repeated access to information from across sub-systems - the integrate-later approach is becoming less and less popular.

c. Data-collection approach : This approach involves collection of all data which might be relevant to MIS design. The collected data are then classified. This classification influences the way the data can be exploited usefully at a later stage. The classification therefore needs to be done extremely carefully.

d. Database approach : In this approach all the relevant and detailed information of the organization are stored and maintained in a database. The database approach is more and more accepted for two main reasons: first, because of data independence it allows for easier system development, even without attempting a complete MIS; and, second, it provides management with immediate access to information required.

e. Top-down approach : The top-down approach involves defining the information needs for successive layers of management. If information required at the top remains relatively stable in terms of level of detail, content and frequency, the system could fulfill MIS requirements (Zani, 1970). The usefulness of this approach depends on the nature of the organization. It can be suitable for those organizations where there is a difference in the type of information required at the various levels.

f. Total-system approach : In this approach the interrelationships of the basic information are defined prior to implementation. Data collection, storage and processing are designed and done within the framework of the total system. This approach can be successfully implemented in organizations which are developing.

BENEFITS OF MIS

The field of MIS can deliver a great benefits to businesses, governments, scientists, universities, students, nonprofits and all other entities. Following are some of the major benefits of MIS

Implementing MBO (Management by Objectives)

MBO is a management process by which managers and subordinates agree upon a series of objectives for the subordinate to attempt to achieve within a set time frame. While MIS systems are extremely useful in generating statistical reports and data analysis they can also be of use as a Management by Objectives (MBO) tool.

Strategy Support

Computers cannot create business strategies by themselves they can assist management in understanding the effects of their strategies, and help enable effective decision-making. A computerized MIS systems can handle various hypothetical scenarios that answer a range of 'what if' questions regarding alterations in strategy. For instance, MIS systems can provide predictions about the effect on potential users that an alteration in timing would have on a library opening hours.

Core Competencies

Every market leading enterprise have at least one core competency – through which they perform better than their competitors. By building an exceptional management information system into the enterprise it is possible to push out ahead of the competition. MIS systems provide the tools necessary to gain a better understanding of the market as well as a better understanding of the enterprise itself.

Generates competitive advantages

Businesses succeed or fail based on how they face competitive challenges. MIS, if implemented properly, provides a wealth of information to allow management to construct effective plans to meet, and beat, their competition.

Enhance Supply Chain Management

Improved reporting of business processes leads inevitably to a more streamlined production process. With better information on the production process comes the ability to improve the management of the supply chain, including everything from the sourcing of materials to the manufacturing and distribution of the finished product.

Fast reaction to market changes

As a corollary to improved supply chain management comes an improved ability to react to changes in the market. Better MIS systems enable an enterprise to react more quickly to their environment, enabling them to push out ahead of the competition and produce a better service and a larger piece of the pie.

Data Processing

Not only do MIS systems allow for the collation of vast amounts of business data, but they also provide a valuable time saving benefit to the workforce. Where in the past business information had to be manually processed for filing and analysis it can now be entered quickly and easily onto a computer by a data processor, allowing for faster decision making and quicker reflexes for the enterprise as a whole.

Further information about MIS can be found at the Bentley College Journal of MIS and the US Treasury's MIS handbook, and an example of an organisational MIS division can be found at the Department of Social Services for the state of Connecticut.

LIMITATIONS

1. Highly sensitive and requires constant monitoring: Change in management, either staff or process, effect on the working and monitoring of certain organization practices including MIS systems. Since MIS is a critical component of an organization's risk management strategy and allied systems, constant monitoring is necessary to ensure its effectiveness. Quality of inputs into MIS needs to be monitored; otherwise consistency in the quality of data and information generated gets effected. Managers are not able to direct business, operational and decision-making activities with the requisite flexibility.

2. Inability of many system designers to identify information needs for managers : It is very difficult to determine the information needs for managers. Because managers, by the nature of some of their decisions, cannot determine their own information needs. System designers, not being sure what information the managers actually require, go ahead and design systems they hope will satisfy the managers. Sometimes systems designers are able to determine the information needs of the operating management and they try to apply those needs to all the other management levels, which is of little use.

3. Lack of flexibility to update itself : Some MISs fail the test of time when the environment they were designed for changes. Making changes quickly to reflect fluctuating business operations may not be possible depending on the MIS style and functionality. Any MIS requires a degree of flexibility to meet changing and diverse information needs of managers.

4. The expense to create and implement an MIS : MIS implementation can be very expensive for companies looking to manage their operations more effectively. The cost of this followed by the installation costs can be extremely expensive for large companies.

5. Constant training required : In order to implement MIS properly there is constant need of training to the users of the organization. Lack of training and appreciation to the users of information and the generator of data, leads to failure of MIS.

6. Poor implementation program : Another important reasons for failure of MIS is lack of proper implementation programs. When considering implementation, a number of issues are involved, such as how should MIS be implemented? Also connected with the implementation program is the fact that there is a tendency for many organizations to try to implement MIS through the same techniques and people as used for data processing.

7. Capturing wrong or incomplete information : MIS information analysts must make many information, some of which hold while others do not. False information often lead to improperly defined system objectives.

CRITERIA TO JUDGE EFFECTIVE MIS

Crowe and Avison (1982) suggested five criteria for an MIS:

Relevance : Information should be relevant to the individual decision-makers at their level of management.

Management by exception : Managers should get precise information pertaining to factors critical to their decision making.

Accuracy : The database from which information is extracted should be up-to-date, contextually relevant and validated.

Timeliness : The information should be provided at the time required.

Adaptability : The information system should have an in-built capability for re-design so that it can suitably adapt to environmental changes and changing information requirements.

MIS IN LIBRARIES

In the past few years libraries have grown both in size and complexity. Exploring new areas, greater service responsibility, service commitment towards clients requires planning and coordination to maintain a smooth operation and a continuous growth pattern. In order to develop new plans and its implication there is always needs of information. Information is seen as one of the most important elements for day-to-day running of activities for decision making. Management Information System (MIS) is generally thought of as an integrated user-machine providing information to support operations, management and decision making to effectively function in an organization.

Debons and Montgomery simply define MIS as a "set of formalized rules and procedures designed and maintained and used by people with the help of information processing technology for the purpose of providing different level of information to fulfill management needs. A MIS is a single source from which the manager can obtain specific information. A Library System is an organisation with an organisational structure, where different level of information is required for the purpose of management of the system. MIS in libraries can provide the relevant information for different level of librarians for effective management of the libraries and decision making".

Planning is an essential part of management of any system, including in a library and information system. For the purpose of planning, the top librarian require relevant information, and for this purpose the information required is provided by the Management Information Systems.

A well integrated MIS can also assist staff with the daily decision making process; to maintain better accountability and control of resources; to monitor budget allocations; to improve overall library effectiveness by focusing on outcomes; to generate internal and external reports; to improve long-term planning; and to facilitate performance measures activities.

The emergence of MIS has led to new vistas in libraries especially for their information management needs. Today, MIS has become the life blood of management in all libraries and information centers. MIS binds together the various elements of a library's units (reference, circulation, audio-visuals, reprography etc.) with one another and with the library's objective of serving patrons. The eventual benefits of a MIS in the library setting as explained by Amos Lakos are

- **Assist Managers and Staff in their Daily Decision-Making Process :** The increased quality of available information can make decisions more effective.
- **Maintain Better Accountability and Control on Resources :** a MIS gives better real-time information for resource management, and allow for more assured accountability.
- **Monitor and Control Resource Allocations :** an equitable allocation of budgets, especially material budget allocations, is always a difficult exercise. A well-organized MIS may improve the process, both for reliable analysis and for the approval process.
- **Improve Overall Library Effectiveness :** paying attention to outcomes, to improved quality of work and service, is important. Better analysis of client needs, better allocations of resources and services, better management decisions should improve effectiveness over time.
- **Generate Internal and External Reports :** Any library requires to produce a large number of reports, both internally and for external agencies. Libraries invest a large amount of staff resources in collecting,

organizing, filing, sending and receiving these reports. A MIS automates most of these activities and execute them efficiently. These tools will also enhance comparative analysis between libraries.

- **Improve Long Term Planning :** a MIS should be incorporated into the planning process - or be the catalyst to enable planning where it is not present or not yet institutionalized.
- **Facilitate Performance Measures Activities :** a MIS would help with other qualitative performance measure activities by providing reliable information and tools.

Charles McClure recognized the need for systematic application of Management Information Systems in libraries many years ago. However, systematic application of some kind of MIS in the library environment has been and remains rare. One of the common reasons for the scarcity of any MIS infrastructure in libraries is lack of resources allocated for achieving this goal. It became clear that assessment activities were fragmented, duplicated and done in isolation. Most assessment activities such as surveys, analysis of surveys, gathering of data, etc, are done either on a project basis or are not centralized. This meant that analysis is haphazard and follow-through based on information was either non-existent or out of context. Other difficulties for implementing MIS in libraries are: Lack of Executive Leadership, Lack of Technical Skills, Insufficient Planning, Lack of System Thinking, and certainly Resistance to Change.

CONCLUSION

This chapter argues that management information systems are the backbone of any organization including library and information centres. Therefore, manager of the organization must be knowledgeable about the effectiveness and problems associated with the use of MIS's. Knowledge of components of MIS's, effect on accountability and ways to preserve, store and file large amounts of information in computers are important for effective MIS implementation.

REFERENCES

Albrecht, K. (1983). A new systems view of the organization. *in: Organization Development.* Englewood Cliffs, NJ: Prentice-Hall.

Banerjee, U. K., & Sachdeva, R. K. (1995). *Management information system: A new frame work.* New Delhi: Vikas Publishing House.

Blumenthal, S.C. (1969). *Management Information System: A Framework for Planning and Control.* Englewood Cliffs, NJ: Prentice-Hall.

Burch, J.G., Jr., & Strater, F.R., Jr. (1979). *Information Systems: Theory and Practice.* New York, NY: John Wiley.

Crowe, T., & Avison, D.E. (1982). *Management Information from Databases.* London: Macmillan.

Davis, G.B., & Olson, M.H. (1984). *Management Information Systems: Conceptual Foundations, Structure and Development.* 2nd ed. New York, NY: McGraw-Hill.

Gorry, G., & Scott Morton, M.S. (1971). A framework for management information systems. *Sloan Management Review,* Fall.

Hopkins, R.C. (1960). *A systematic Procedure for System Development:Systems Philosophy.* Englewood Cliffs, NJ: Prentice-Hall

Kumar, H. (1989). *Management Information Systems: A Conceptual and Empirical Approach.* New Delhi: Ashish Publishing House.

Lakos, Amos. (1997). Library Management Information Systems in the Client Server Environment – A Proposed New Model. 2nd Northumbria Conference, Longhirst Hall, September.

Lucas, H.C., Jr. (1978). *Information Systems Concepts for Management.* New York, NY: McGraw-Hill.

Mason, R. D., & Swanson, B. E. (1981). *Measurements for management decision.* Reading, MA: Addison-Wesley.

Murdick, R.G., & Ross, J.E. (1975). *Information Systems for Modern Management*. Englewood Cliffs, NJ: Prentice-Hall.

Olorunsola, Richard (1997). MIS in Nigerian Universities. *ASLIB Proceedings*, 49(5), 113-116

Zani, W.M. (1970). Blueprint for management information system. *Harvard Business Review*, November-December.

6

Expert System

An expert is a man who has made all the mistakes which can be made, in a narrow field. **- Niels Bohr**

The post-industrial society has been characterized by huge production of information. This enormous quantity of information leads to information explosion in one hand but caused two major problems on the other. The first one was related to the storage of information, which computer experts overcome easily by developing various types of high efficient storage devices. But the second problem was associated with retrieval of this huge storage. With the exponential growth of information in every minute, it becomes a great challenge to the information providers to provide right information to the right people at right time. The obvious questions arise were:

- How to approach to the system to retrieve the relevant information?
- How to conduct search or what may be strategy to search? and;
- How to negotiate for ramification of queries once formulated?

Among various alternatives, one probable solution came to mind to the information scientists was if we can develop a system which gives expert assistance to the every user in their problems, the problem become nominal. In this sequence expert system developed. Before discussing the Expert System in detail, let us take two of its associate terms: experts and system.

Expert : The dictionary meaning of an 'Expert' is someone who has skill and expertise in the area of concern.

System : A group of inter-related element, comprising a unified whole, that interact regularly to perform a common task or to achieve a common goal.

So, expert system can be explained as a system designed for solving problems in particular application area. One can draw inference from a stored knowledge base that was developed by recording and structuring human expertise through an individual commonly called knowledge engineer. A knowledge engineer interviews experts in a certain domain and tries to embody their knowledge in a computer for carrying out some task. The expert systems are limited to specific domain or area and they are drawing conclusions and references in the form of advice or problem solution. It is source of useful application of artificial intelligence. Due to increasing complexities of problem structure, expert system uses computer as tool to establish a system that use human knowledge and reasoning techniques to solve problem. Basically, expert systems are software that aims to provide expert consultancy or advice or assistance. Based on a review of major models of human intelligence, Cook et al. (1998) mentioned that the following ten factors are most pertinent to expert system research:

1. Acquisition : the ability to acquire new knowledge.

2. Automatization : the ability to refine procedures for dealing with a novel situation into an efficient functional form.

3. Comprehension : the ability to know, understand,

cognize and deal with novel problems.

4. Memory management : the ability to represent knowledge in memory, to map knowledge on to that memory representation, and to access the knowledge in memory.

5. Metacontro : the ability to control various processes in intelligent behaviour.

6. Numeric ability : the ability to perform arithmetic operations.

7. Reasoning : the ability to use problem-solving knowledge.

8. Social competence : the ability to interact with and understand other people, machines or programs.

9. Verbal perception : the ability to recognize natural language.

10. Visual perception : the ability to recognize visual images.

DEFINING EXPERT SYSTEM

According to Tom Schwartz "an expert system is a computer program conceived to stimulate some forms of human reasoning (by the intermediary of an inference engine) and capable to manage an important quantity of specialized knowledge". On the other hand, Turban and Aronson, (2001) explained expert system as a system that uses human knowledge captured in a computer to solve problems that ordinarily require human expertise. Similarly, Feigenbaum described expert system as an intelligent computer program that uses knowledge and inference procedure to solve problems that was difficult enough to acquire significant human expertise for the solutions. Usually, subject experts are interviewed by the software developers to determine the steps the expert would use to make a particular decision. Sometimes, experts are followed by not-taking observers as the experts go about formulating decisions. This often reveals that the experts was not aware of all the steps and question used.

More often, the two terms, expert systems (ES) and knowledge-based systems (KBS), are used synonymously. Taken together, they represent the most widespread type of AI application. The area of human intellectual endeavor to be captured in an expert system is called the *task domain*. *Task* refers to some goal-oriented, problem-solving activity. *Domain* refers to the area within which the task is being performed. Typical tasks are diagnosis, planning, scheduling, configuration and design.

Overall, an expert system is a computer application that solves complicated problems that would otherwise require extensive human expertise. To do so, it stimulates the human reasoning process by applying specific knowledge and interfaces. These capacities for reasoning and management allow the system to target a small number of relevant hypotheses in the mass of potential diagnoses and being able to find a satisfactory diagnostic conclusion. Often, the term expert systems is reserved for programs whose knowledge base contains the knowledge used by human experts, in contrast to knowledge gathered from textbooks or non-experts.

WHY EXPERT SYSTEM

Human beings are the best decision maker in the universe. However, expert systems are necessitated by the limitations associated with conventional human decision-making processes, including:

1. Human expertise is not easily accessible.
2. Humans get tired from physical or mental workload.
3. The common habit a human is to forget. He can forget crucial details of a problem.
4. Humans are inconsistent or biased in their day-to-day decisions.

5. Humans have limited working memory and unable to process complex, large amount data.
6. The capacity to retain and access of store data differs from human to human.
7. Humans can deliberately avoid decision responsibilities.
8. Humans lie, hide, and die. He may also retire or transferred from his job.

CHARACTERISTICS OF AN EXPERT SYSTEM

Branchman identify some basic characteristics of an expert system that are essential to accomplish the task:

1. Expertise : The system should be able to perform in the same way as an expert human does.

2. Symbol manipulation : The system should be able to reason by manipulating various underlying symbols.

3. Intelligence : The system should exhibit an intelligent behaviour

4. Complexity : The system should be able to deal with complex problem

5. Reformulation : The system should accept a problem stated in any manner and then should be able to convert it according to the system requirement.

6. Reasoning about self : The system should be able to justify its own decision; and

7. Type of task : The system should be designed on accordance with the problem to be solved or the task to be performed.

On the other hand, Forsyth explained the expert systems have the following characteristics:

- Limited to a specific domain of expertise.
- Able to reason with uncertain data.
- Able to explain itself in a sensible way.

- Delivering advice as output.
- Designed to grow incrementally.
- Having a clear separation of knowledge and inference mechanism.
- Typically (not necessarily) rule-based.
- Always restricted to a narrow domain of expertise.
- The expertise is acquired and codified during lengthy' interviews with one or .more experts in the relevant domain.
- The expertise is codified as a collection of facts and rules, which together constitutes the knowledge base.
- The rules may be held as discrete production rules, or as a semantic network, or occasionally in some other way.

Most usually, the literature defines expert systems by seven ideal characteristics: (i) ES can solve very difficult problems as well as or even better than human experts. (ii) ES reason using what the experts consider to be effective heuristics, and they interact with humans in appropriate ways, including natural language. (iii) They manipulate and reason about symbolic descriptions. (iv) They can function with data which contain errors, using rules which can handle uncertainty. (v) They can contemplate multiple, competing hypotheses simultaneously. (vi) They can justify why they are asking a question. (vii) ES can justify their conclusions.

FEATURES OF EXPERT SYSTEM

- The expert system is always and instantly available;
- Skills of several experts can be combined;
- It is logical, objective and consistent;
- It does not forget or never make mistake in calculation;
- It is directly and instantly available for consultation.
- Access is not limited by time and location;

- It is useful in training progarmes; and
- When faced with an universal situation-human experts develop entirely new, original approaches, and human experts are far flexible than computer.

COMPONENTS OF EXPERT SYSTEM

Every expert system consists of three principal parts: the knowledge base; the reasoning, or inference, engine and the user interface.

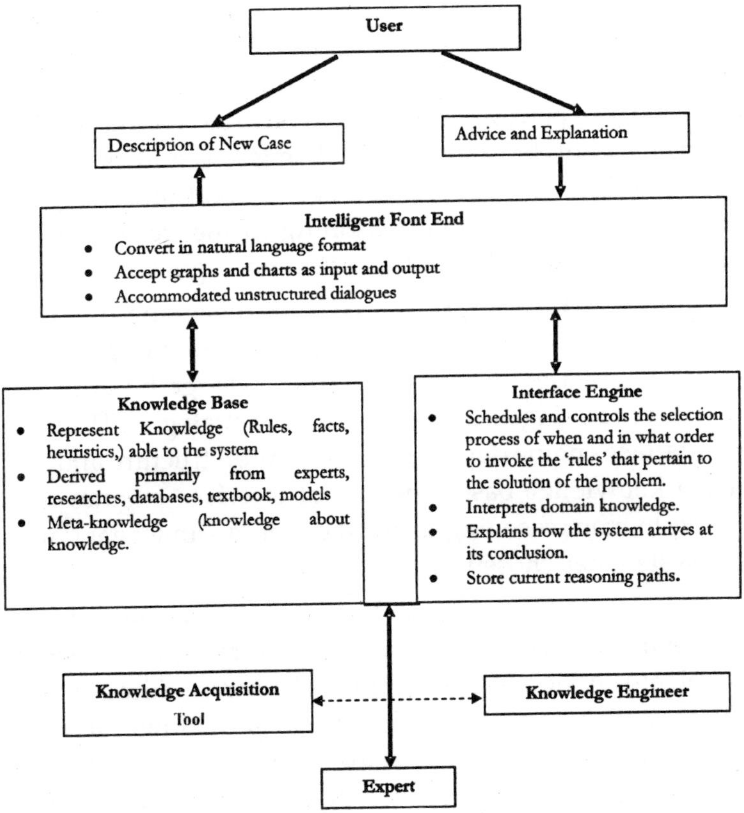

Major parts of an Expert System

1. Knowledge Base : Knowledge base is the most important element of expert since it holds problem - solving knowledge. The power of expert systems resides in the specific, high-quality knowledge they contain about task domains. The expertise knowledge of a particular domain stores in knowledge base. It consists of rules, facts, frames, scripts, decision tree, relationship and semantic net. The *knowledge base* of expert systems contains both factual and heuristic knowledge. *Factual knowledge* is that knowledge of the task domain that is widely shared, typically found in textbooks or journals, and commonly agreed upon by those knowledgeable in the particular field. *Heuristic knowledge* is the less rigorous, more experiential, more judgmental knowledge of performance. In contrast to factual knowledge, heuristic knowledge is rarely discussed, and is largely individualistic. It is the knowledge of good practice, good judgment, and plausible reasoning in the field. It is the knowledge that underlies the "art of good guessing."

2. Interface engines : The inference engine is the program that locates the appropriate knowledge in the knowledge base, and infers new knowledge by applying logical processing and problem-solving strategies. The form of interface engine depends in the nature, structure and size if the knowledge base. The aim of interface engines is to mimic human reasoning so that the user can understand why the system has chosen the steps it has.

3. The User Interface : The user interface is the means of communication between a user and the expert systems problem-solving processes. It provides communication with the user both in accepting input and providing output. A good expert system is not very useful unless it has an effective interface. It has to be able to accept the queries or instructions in a form that the user enters and translate them into working instructions for the rest of the system. It also has to be able to translate the answers, produced by the system, into a form that the user can understand. Careful attention should be given to the screen design in order to make the expert system appear 'friendly' to the user.

In addition to these main components, an expert system could have:

4. Explanation module : Explanation capability, which shows the line of reasoning leading to one conclusion and informs the user why a particular facts is needed.

5. Global Database : It is the section of the program that keeps track of the problem by storing data, facts obtained from external sources. It offers link with other system and will support the main expert system and will have interaction with outside world, such as Database Management System and Spreadsheet.

6. Knowledge Domain : A knowledge maintenance module to update the knowledge base.

TYPES OF EXPERT SYSTEM

Sekari, Srinath and Veluchamy classified expert systems into different categories as stated below:

1. Interpretation Systems : This includes analysis of intelligence by way of surveillance, understanding of speech, image analysis etc. Meanings are expressed symbolically and situations described as a result of observation.

2. Prediction Systems : These systems infer liable consequences of given situations, such as economic and weather forecasting, demographic prediction, crop estimation and military etc.

3. Diagnostic Systems : These systems analyze the organizations' performance and diagnose the failure even in the medical field.

4. Design Systems : These systems develop circuit layout and building design etc.

5. Planning Systems : These systems help in automatic planning in project management, routing, communication, military operation etc.

6. Instruction Systems : These systems are otherwise called 'Education and Training systems' which incorporate diagnosing and debugging of sub-system. These systems diagnose the weakness in the students' knowledge and identify appropriate remedies and also plan a tutorial interaction to deliver remedial knowledge to the student.

7. Model-Based Systems : Here the knowledge is based on human expertise and is represented as rules with which a model is designed as to understand the system and then used to identify the course of the equipments failure.

DEVELOPING EXPERT SYSTEM

Building an expert system is known as *knowledge engineering* and its practitioners are called *knowledge engineers.* A knowledge engineer is a computer scientist who knows how to design and implement programs that incorporate artificial intelligence techniques. The knowledge engineer must confirm that the computer has all the knowledge needed to solve a problem.

Presently, there are two ways to build an expert system. It can be built either from scratch, or built using a piece of development software known as a "tool" or a "shell." Before we discuss these tools, let's briefly discuss what knowledge engineers do. A knowledge engineer interviews and observes a human expert or a group of experts and learns what the experts know, and how they reason with their knowledge. The engineer then translates the knowledge into a computer-usable language, and designs an inference engine, a reasoning structure, that uses the knowledge appropriately. This is called *knowledge representation*. Knowledge engineers also determines how to integrate the use of uncertain knowledge in the reasoning process, and what kinds of explanation would be useful to the end user. Through *Knowledge representation,* knowledge has been formalized and organized. One widely used representation is the *rules.* A rule consists of an IF part and a THEN part (also called a *condition* and an *action*). The IF part lists a set of conditions in some logical combination. The piece of knowledge represented by the production rule is relevant to the line of reasoning being developed if the IF part of the rule is satisfied; consequently, the THEN part can be concluded, or its problem-solving action taken. Expert systems whose knowledge is represented in rule form are called *rule-based systems.*

Another widely used representation, called the *unit* (also known as *frame, schema,* or *list structure*) is based upon a more passive view of knowledge. The unit is an assemblage of associated symbolic knowledge about an entity to be represented. Typically, a unit consists of a list of properties of the entity and associated values for those properties. Since every task domain consists of many entities that stand in various relations, the properties can also be used to specify relations, and the values of these properties are the names of other units that are linked according to the relations. One unit can also represent knowledge that is a "special case" of another unit, or some units can be "parts of" another unit.

The *problem-solving model,* or *paradigm,* organizes and controls the steps taken to solve the problem. One common but powerful paradigm involves chaining of IF-THEN rules to form a line of reasoning. If the chaining starts from a set of conditions and moves toward some conclusion, the method is called *forward chaining.* If the conclusion is known (for example, a goal to be achieved) but the path to that conclusion is not known, then reasoning backwards is called for, and the method is *backward chaining.* These problem-solving methods are built into program modules called *inference engines* or *inference procedures* that manipulate and use knowledge in the knowledge base to form a line of reasoning.

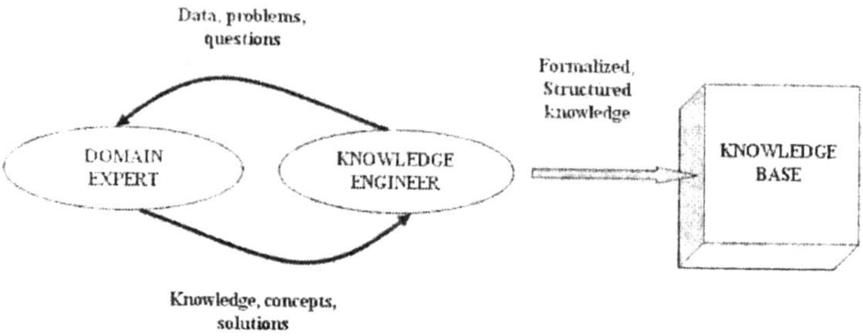

Source: Aziz: http://www.generation5.org/content/2005/PDAMum.asp

Next, the inference engine and facilities for representing knowledge and for explaining are programmed, and the domain knowledge is entered into the program piece by piece. It may be that the inference engine is not just right; the form of knowledge representation is awkward for the kind of knowledge needed for the task; and the expert might decide the pieces of knowledge are wrong. All these are discovered and modified as the expert system gradually gains competence.

MYCIN is one of the well-known expert systems in the field of medicine that was built in mid 1970s. This provides consultative advice on diagnosis and the treatment for infectious blood diseases. Mycin facilitates high level performance of selecting antibiotic therapy for Bacteremia (infectious blood disease) Apart from this, there are expert systems on various aspects such as financial forecasting, schedule routes for delivery vehicles, analysis of structures of chemical compounds and planning of actions sequentially etc. Some expert systems are designed to take the place of human experts while others are designed to aid them.

There are many well known **advantages** to using computerised tools and expert systems:

- reduction of missing data,
- better collection of data,
- no omission of questions,
- no data transcription,
- broader coverage of diagnoses

Tools

In order to develop expert systems for various operation of libraries, two programming language, such as LISP and PROLOG, mostly was used. List Programming (LISP) is a tool for process lists. This is used for manipulating symbolic representation of items called atoms. LISP programs are composed of atoms, group of atoms (lists), and group of lists (expressions). Programming logic (PROLOG) is used for interpreting logical structures. PROLOG programs are composed of facts and rules. In addition, there is another program call expert system shell, that contains an interface engine. Programming in LISP and PROLOG takes time and resulting expert system become more finely tailored to suit librarians' need. Whereas, expert system shell may be better to choose to speed development and it is easy to handle. However, the flexibilities are not as good as like LIPS or PROLOG.

Expert Systems can be developed by writing programs using certain programming languages, such as, Fortran, Pascal, C++, Visual Basic and dbase. Most of the expert system, however, are developed via specialized software toll called shells. There are expert systems shells, which are ready made software packages, which facilitate designing of expert system without writing complicated programs. They provide the inference engine and user interface commands - backward chaining, forward chaining, or both. It has the facility to construct the rules in spoken English language and has a built in editor.

LIBRARY EXPERT SYSTEMS

With the development of powerful and affordable computers, librarians tries to develop and implement expert systems to improve services and accomplish tasks that previously had to be performed by librarians by own. Ford, suggested some expert system that can be developed for professional tasks in both traditional and non-traditional library and information services and management tasks. Here we will discuss some of the expert system in the major division of librarianship: technical services, public services and administration.

In Technical Services

More effort has been expanded in developing expert system for various technical services like classification, cataloguing and collection development.

a. Classification : Although the classification profess involves application of logic and mental judgment, it is difficult to capture in an expert system. In fact in classification there are no strict rules available, and the relationship between objects and classes are often ambiguous. A classifier used to choose class number by understanding the titles, table of contents or indexes. The question is how does one program of an expert system can understand new titles, subjects, non-representative titles, and synonymous terms which are not available in knowledge base. In subject specific libraries, like medicine, where a broad spectrum of human understanding is represented, classifying such documents through expert system requires equally broad knowledge base. However, these system is suitable for such domain where a precisely controlled vocabulary is available.

In 1986, Paul Burton conducted an exploratory research at the University of Strathclyde in the United Kingdom, aiming to assess the merits of various ways of know-ledge representation and to assess the suitability of ES in classification. The re-search resulted in a prototype ES that was able to advise a Dewey classification number based on the information provided by the user, to justify the reasoning and to explain why the ES asked certain questions.

CUTT-x, an ES for automatic assignment of Cutter numbers (Savic, 1996) was developed using Microsoft ACCESS relational database in the MS-Windows personal computer based environment. On evaluation, it was found that the system per-formed well for the International Civil Aviation Organisation Library. Savic noted that libraries require more complex cuttering and therefore would require a more complex CUTT-x system.

ShelfPro, developed by Drabenstott, Riester and Dede (1992) addresses shelflisting. Shelflisting is concerned with assigning a book number, as opposed to the class mark portion of the call number, to an item.

Cosgrove and Weimann (1992) describes how the n-Cube expert system development tool can assist in item classification using the Universal Decimal Classification (UDC) standard. The n-Cube makes use of a tree classification structure with associated rules and default inheritance features. Any information known about a particular classification is a combination of the defaults known about that class, as well as the defaults associated with any of its parent classes. As a result, many of the problems associated with simple rule-based systems are overcome.

Pekka Valkonena and Olli Nykänen developed prototype IPC expert system for paten classification, generated in Finland on a Macintosh personal computer.

b. Cataloguing : Implementing expert system for Cataloguing is comparatively easy because of the fact that the job of cataloguing is based on certain rules that are available in various codes. There rules can be adapted in developing expert system. In most cases AACR-II has been used by using nearly 2000 rules. For example, Roy Chand developed a cataloguing expert system based on the rules of AACR-II. However, he mentioned that its usefulness was limited because the system had not means of interpreting rules as he said that "cataloguing problems today are too widespread for employing expert system. In fact, the expertise of the cataloguer lies not only in knowing when to use what rules, but also in knowing when to draw on personal experience. Due to that better inference engine is essential to implement AACR-II rules.

There are two well known expert system is available in cataloguing: MAPPER and CATALYST (developed by Gibb and Sharif (1988) using the shell ESP Advisor). While, Mapper is for cataloguing of based on AACR-II, developed by University of California, Los Angeles, Catalyst an advice expert system to choose and form of access point.

MacCat, like MAPPER, developed at the University of California, Los Angeles by Maccaferri used Apple's Hypercard environment. MacCat is intended for establishing headings, together with their MARC field and sub-field codes. Since MacCat is implemented on the Apple Macintosh, full advantage is taken of the mouse and icons for entering data. This makes it more flexible than ear-lier systems that force the user to proceed through chains of menus one step at a time. Another system which makes extensive use of windows was designed by Piotr Murasik, of Gdansk University in Poland, called APEX (Access Point EXpert). Written in PROLOG, it was completed in early 1991. Like MacCat, users are allowed short cuts so that they do not have to go through the entire cataloguing procedure to provide a bibliographic record.

There are some other expert system have been developed to create MARC records. MITINET is such an example to convert records in MARC format. It allows cataloguers to enter information through prompting and the system output the records in MARC format.

National Agricultural Library (NAL) developed CatTutor, a hypertext prototype tutorial for training cataloguers to provide descriptive cataloguing of computer files. Included in the program are portions of the AACR2, the MARC format for computer files, a glossary, five illustrative bibliographic records accompanied by instructional text, quizzes, and a mastery test. Evaluators were enthusiastic about computer-assisted training and the ma-chine-readable versions of the AACR2 and MARC format was integrated in the pro-gram. It was felt, however, that the pro-gram must be redesigned to create different paths for different levels of expertise of the users, or it must be directed at a single type of user (Thomas, 1992).

Hjerppe, Olander and Marklund (1985, 1989) conducted the well-known ESSCAPE (Expert System for Simple Choice of Access Points for Entries) Project in Sweden, which resulted in the creation of two ES - ESSCAPE/EMYCIN and ESSCAPE /Expert-Trees. Rather than producing systems for practical use, the aim was to discover issues entailed in the creation of the knowledge base..

Weibel, Oskins and Vizine-Goetz (1989). They built a prototype rule-based ES at OCLC known as "the OCLC Automated Title Page Cataloguing Project" to auto-mate descriptive cataloguing from title pages. The system used OCR techniques and their study reports a success rate of 75% in identifying and interpreting bibliographic data on title pages using visual and linguistic characteristics codified in only 16 rules.

c. Collection Development : As the selection of new materials as well as discard of old materials, two possible responses are possible, i.e. either yes or no, it is easier to develop an expert system in such process. There has been one successful expert system exists in collection development job. The Applied Physics Library developed an expert system to process gifts. The system helps librarians to determine which gifts to keep. As for general academic libraries, developing expert system for collection development is bit difficult. Because the subject areas are varied, the system need to decide on materials in various disciplines. Mark Johnston developed an expert system which help librarians to decide does the material support institutional programmes. By asking relevant subject experts about the degree to which the material supports institutional programmes. Using PROLOG program, system process responses and help in determining whether or not the material should be added to the collection.

Journal Expert Selector (JES) was developed by Roy Rada (1987), editor of *Index Medicus*, and colleagues to capture the expertise of human journal selectors at the National Library of Medicine who were making decisions as to which journals should be indexed in *Index Medicus*. The main criteria of JES included (1) composition of the journal, (2) producers of the journal, (3) information in articles, and (4) authors of articles.

The Bibliographer's Workstation, develop-ed by Meador and Cline (1992) at South-west Missouri State University, represents the use of a hypertext tool rather than an ES. The system models the four-step collection decision process; identification of material, evaluation, selection (or rejection), and acquisition. Each stage relies on different sets of data. The data are organised into four groups; (1) bibliographic data, such as the library's local OPAC; (2) critical and contextual data, such as collection development policies and accreditation standards; (3) financial data, such as the library's materials budget allocations; and (4) commercial data, such as vendor databases.

Public Services

Expert system for reference and information retrieval has been developed for assisting patrons in locating materials and information, answering specific reference questions. For online searching expert system choose appropriate database and delivery best results.

a. Reference Services : One of the earliest systems developed to answer routine enquiries was REFLES1 (Reference Librarian Enhancement Sys-tem) developed at the University of California, Los Angeles (UCLA) in the late 1970s (Bivins and Palmer, 1980). It was a microcomputer-based system for in-house data files of information about library facilities, services and operations, and also gave details of specific types of library materials along with some 'how to use' comments on the catalogue, abstracting and services. An enhanced version of REFLES1, called REFLINK, was subsequently produced at Linkoping University in Sweden (Bivins and Eriksson, 1982).

A prototype reference system, DISTREF, for students taking courses by distance learning offered by Charles Sturt Univer-sity in Australia was designed to provide assistance in the choice of search terms by using 'discipline maps' (McDonald and Weckert, 1990). DISTREF is an ES which is intended to link with a union catalogue on CD-ROM of the holdings of a wide range of libraries in New South Wales.

The Workstation for Information Seekers planned by Micco and Smith (1989) is in-tended to provide access to a thesauri of terms on maps. The system is used for searching reference works which would be stored, along with the thesauri and catalogues of various collections, on a CD-ROM jukebox. Search strategies employing ES techniques, including user model-ling are used to narrow the search space.

In Johnsson Library of Government Documents of

Standford university developed the Government Document Reference Aid (GDRA) to help patrons in identify and locating international, federal, state and local government documents. This expert system prompts the user for the type of information needed and display materials that contain it.

There are also some well know expert system exists in reference services. National Agricultural Library developed ANSWERMAN whose knowledge base contains facts documents from agriculture. It provides links to well popular database of agriculture, AGRICOLA. Other popular expert system is POINTER (developed at the State University of New York at Buffalo). In order to provide referral service prototype micro-computer based expert system PLEXUS is also used. In order to provide online assistance during online database search, TOMSEARCH is very popular.

Online Reference for Expertise in Opera (ORFEO) recommends sources to answer questions about opera. It contains a know-ledge base developed from one major bibliography of 700 items, plus some items added by Gerber (1992). This system is based on the "given (the information known by the client) and wanted (the in-formation required by the client)" notion of reference theory and is purely a prototype. Another subject specific reference ES was AquaRef. It was designed by the U.S. National Agricultural Library to give assistance with a limited range of frequently asked reference questions about aquaculture (Haufman, 1989). AquaRef was design-ed as a result of experiences with an earlier ES Answerman (Waters, 1986).

Sourcefinder (SOFI) is an ES consisting of a database of annotated reference sources, using the Nota Bene software, which serves as a support for reference services at the reference desk of the Main Library at Ohio State University (Stalker, 1996). SOFI is used by new reference librarians as a training aid, by experienced librarians in unfamiliar subject areas and has the potential to be when reference librarians are unavailable.

b. Information Services : Marcus and Reintjes (1981) developed the Connector for Networked Information Transfer (CONIT) to aid end-user searching in overcoming the complexity and diversity of online search systems. CONIT gave user-friendly access to several hosts by means of a simple common-command language. CONIT also included some limited facilities for reformulating searches, such as automatically rerunning a search with exact terms only when too many references were retrieved. Another system, EXPERT took a more active role in the search process, by suggesting suitable databases and prompting the user for terms and synonyms before translating them into Boolean search statements (Marcus, 1981).

The Composite Document Expert/Extended/Effective Retrieval (CODER) system, another distributed ES was developed by Fox (1987) as a test bed for analysis, filing, and retrieving documents with widely differing contents and structures, such as those generated within electronic mailing systems. CODER was unique in that it could be distributed over several machines and included a temporal reasoning expert to identify, parse, and represent query expressions relating to dates. CODER used m-Prolog to build a complex, multi-tiered system for document retrieval. Subsequently, Lucarella and Morara (1991) have attempted to extend the representative power of Prolog by building with it a document retrieval sys-tem, FIRST (Fuzzy Information Retrieval SysTem), which uses fuzzy instead of Boolean logic.

c. Indexing : FASIT (Dillon and Gray, 1983) was one of the first systems to incorporate syntactic knowledge for automatic indexing purposes. The system uses 161 predefined concept forms built around desired combinations of syntactic categories. These concept forms are specified in such a way as to be able to accommodate any unresolved ambiguities present in the text once it has passed through the syntactic categoriser.

The MedIndex system (Humphrey, 1989) assist indexers to select the most appropriate indexing terms from MeSH, the National Library of Medicine's computerised thesaurus. The system provides prescriptive aids, such as enforcing the rule of specificity, which is common to most manual indexing systems, as well as suggestive aids, such as prompting users to fill slots in the frame structures.

Carande (1989) wished to demonstrate to other library staff that a series of subject-specific ES could extend the expertise of reference librarians well beyond their specific bibliographic knowledge. He developed INDEXES using the demonstration version of EXSYS that allowed a maxi-mum of 25 production rules but did not govern the number of sources that could be recommended. This limited prototype assigned probability weightings to possible sources based on their suitability.

Index Expert designed by Bailey, et al. (1989) used frames to represent the bibliographic records of reference sources. The hierarchical structure of the frames, allow for efficient representation and maintenance of the knowledge base, which is written in Turbo Prolog, using the Know-ledge Base Management system. This allows the use of a fully featured editor to update and to change the knowledge base, which could be reloaded into the system for error checking. Table 7 gives a summary of systems developed for indexing.

Administration

Several attempts have been made to develop expert system for business, little have been for library management. Here we are specify some of the areas where there are some development occurred.

a. Acquisition : The first system is the Monographic Acquisitions Consultant (MAC) which was designed to eliminate the discretionary component in monographic vendor selection, replacing it with a more quantitative decision-making model. The MAC uses the macro capabilities of the spreadsheet Lotus 1-2-3 to allow it to act like an inference engine. The system was also developed to support the library's philosophy of using multiple vendors for monographic ordering (Zager and Smadi, 1992). Zager encountered the classic problem of the expert not always being able to articulate her reasons for making a selection or the factors considered. Hardware problems and the constant need to maintain the know-ledge base have precluded the system from being used in production.

The second ES developed at Pennsylvania State University by Lynne Branche Brown (1993) determines whether a title requested for order would be received on any of the extensive approval plans maintained by the library. The receipt of books on approval plans is determined by a set of rules called the plan profile, which could be incorporated into an ES. Once again in this system, the need for continuous maintenance was evident. The system must be updated as changes are made in each pro-file, as, for example, when publishers are added or deleted (Hawks, 1994). Table 8 gives a summary of ES systems developed for acquisitions.

b. Budgeting : During preparation of budget the administrator always determine what items to cut and by how much. Due to financial crunch, cutting serial budget is very common for all libraries. An expert system could be helpful in assisting the administrator in taking these decision.

The Bibliographer's Workstation, develop-ed by Meador and Cline (1992) at South-west Missouri State University, represents the use of a hypertext tool rather than an ES. The system models the four-step collection decision process; identification of material, evaluation, selection (or rejection), and acquisition. Each stage relies on different sets of data. The data are organised into four groups; (1) bibliographic data, such as the library's local OPAC; (2)

critical and contextual data, such as collection development policies and accreditation standards; (3) financial data, such as the library's materials budget allocations; and (4) commercial data, such as vendor databases.

c. Planning : Using information from traffic patterns and materials usage, an effective expert system for planning can be possible to prepare. The system then help administrator to determine the proper location circulation desk from which most effective access is possible, putting OPAC terminal on what place will not create any obstacles etc.

ADVANTAGES

The general advantage of an expert system as suggest by Morris' are listed below:

1. Experts can be freed from routine tasks and made available for more exciting, creative and demanding work.
2. Expertise can be pooled when more than one expert contributes to the system development. The pooling exercise can assist in the refinement of the procedures and help to make them more consistent.
3. Knowledge can be safeguarded, developed and distributed. Enormous sums of money are spent on training individuals, yet all their knowledge and expertise is lost when they die or leave the company. Expert systems offer a way of capturing this expertise and knowledge and at the same time making it available to other people.
4. Expertise can be available. Since expert systems provide explanations for advice given they can be used 24 hours a day without the presence of the expert.
5. Expert systems can be used for training purposes. The-problem-solving and explanation capabilities of expert

systems are particularly useful in training. situations. Training can also be distributed throughout ' a company and done on an individual basis at times suited to the employee.

6. Expert systems can provide a standardized approach to problem solving.
7. The development of an expert system offers the expert with an opportunity to critically assess and improve his problem-solving behaviour.
8. The performance of non-experts can be improved over a period of time and they may eventually even reach expert status.
9. In many situations, expert systems can provide solutions to problems far more quickly than a human expert.
10. Expert systems have the potential for saving companies a vast amount of money, thus increasing profits.

LIMITATIONS

Like every system, expert system have some limitation. Few of them are:

1. The very first problem associate with knowledge acquisition, it is not very easy task to develop complete, consistent and correct knowledge base. Experts are mostly poor in expressing their knowledge as required format. Similarly, knowledge engineers may not know what they are looking for.
2. Verification and validation of knowledge store in another problem. The knowledge may be inaccurate, incomplete, and non-relevant with a problem.
3. Experts knowledge are very domain specific and can not be generalize this knowledge for common case. So, a new expert system is required for each problem.

4. Another problem associate with the brittleness of the system and as result user may not know the limitations of the system. This is mostly occurred due to limitation of the software that are used to develop an expert system. The limitation of software effect the functioning of the system.
5. Experts system lacks meta-knowledge, so they can not reason about their limitations or the effect of this on the decision that are made.

REFERENCES

Bailey, Charles W., et al. (1989). The index ex-pert system: a knowledge-based system to assist users in index selection. *Reference Services Review*, 17(4), 19 - 28.

Bivins, K. T. and L. Eriksson. (1982). RE-FLINK: a microcomputer information re-trieval and evaluation system. *Information Processing and Management*, 18(3), 111 - 116.

Bivins, K. T. and R. C. Palmer. (1980). REFLES: an individual microcomputer system for fact retrieval. *Online Review*,.4(4), 357 - 365.

Branchman, R.J. (1979). *On the epistemological status of semantic networks*. In Associative Networks: Representation and Use of Knowledge by Computers, N. V. Findler (ed.), pp. 3-50. New York, Academic Press.

Brown, Lynne C. Branche. (1993). An expert system for predicting approval plan receipts. *Library Acquisitions: Practice & Theory*, 17, 156-162.

Carande, R. (1989). Reference advisory system (RAS): some practical issues. *Reference Services Review*, 17, 87 - 90.

Cosgrove, S. J. and J. M. Weimann. (1992). Ex-pert system technology applied to item classification. *Library Hi Tech*, 10, 34.

Dillon, M. and A.S. Gray. (1983). FASIT: a fully automatic syntactically based index-ing system. *Journal of the American Society for Information Science*, .34(.2), 99 - 108.

Drabenstott, Karen Markey; Leslie C. Riester and Bonnie A. Dede. (1992). Shelflisting using expert systems. In: *Classification Research for Knowledge Representation and Organization.* Amsterdam : Elsevier, pp. 199- 207.

Forsyth, R. Ed., (1984). Expert Systems: Principles and Cases Studies. New York : Chapman & Hall.

Fox, Edward A. (1987). Development of the CODER system: a test bed for artificial intelligence methods in information retrieval. *Information Processing and Manage-ment,* 23(4), 341 - 366.

Gibb, Forbes and Carolyn Sharif. (1988). CA-TALYST : an expert assistant for cataloguing. *Program* 22(1), 62 - 71.

Haufman, Deborah (1989). AquaRef : an expert advisory system for reference support. *The Reference Librarian,* 23, 113 - 133.

Hawks, Carol Pitts (1994). Expert systems in technical services and collection manage-ment. *Information Technology and Libra-ries,* 13(3), 203 - 212.

Hjerppe, Roland; Birgitta Olander and Kari Marklund (1985). Project ESSCAPE - expert system for simple choice of access points for entries : applications of artificial intelligence in cataloguing. *Paper presen-ted at 51st International Federation of library Association (IFLA) General Confe-rence;* 18-24 August, 1985; Chicago, Illinois.

Humphrey, Susanne M. (1989). A knowledge-based expert system for computer-assisted indexing. *IEEE Expert,* 4(3), 25 - 38.

Cook, John A.; Whittaker, Dale; Thieme, Ronald H.; Smith, Owen R. and Salvendy, Gavriel (1988). Human Intelligence Models and their Implications for Expert System Structure and Research, *Behaviour and Information Technology,* 7(October-December), 424-425.

Lucarella, D. and Morara, R. (1991). FIRST : Fuzzy Information Retrieval System. *Journal of Information Science,* 17(2), 8-91.

McDonald, Craig and Weckert, John. (1990). DISTREF: a prototype distance referral system. In: McDonald, Craig and Weckert, J, (ed.). *Libraries and Expert Systems.* London : Taylor Graham, pp. 28 - 37.

Meador, John M. and Cline, Lynn. (1992). Displaying and utilising selection tools in a user-friendly electronic environment. *Library Acquisitions: Practice and Theory*, 16, 290 - 294.

Meador, John M. and Cline, Lynn. (1992). Displaying and utilising selection tools in a user-friendly electronic environment. *Library Acquisitions: Practice and Theory*, 16, 290 - 294.

Micco, Mary H. and Smith, Irma. (1989). Designing a workstation for information seekers. *The Reference Librarian*, 23, 135-152.

Morris, Anne. (1992). Overview of Expert Systems. In The application of expert systems in libraries and information centres, edited by Morris, A, London: Bowker-Saur, p.3-4.

Rada, Roy, et al. (1987). Computerised guides to journal selection. *Information Techno-logy and Libraries*, 6, 180.

Cosgrove, S.J. and Weimann, J.M. (1992). Expert system technology applied to item classification", Library Hi Tech, 10(1/2), 33 - 40

Savic, Dobrica. 1994. Designing an expeı t system for classification of office docu-ments - a case study of CLOD-x. *ARMA Quarterly*, 28(3).

Sekari, G.Gnana et al. Expert System-An Innovative Tool for Managing Indian Traditional Medical Knowledge. Available at: *www.icml9.org/program/track7/public/documents/G-133438.doc*

Stalker, J. C. (1996). Why reference librarians won't disappear: a study of success in identifying answering sources for reference questions. *Research Quarterly*, 35(4), 489 - 503.

Thomas, Sarah E. (1992) CatTutor : a ptoto-typical hypertext tutorial for catalogers. *Library Resources and Technical Services*, 36(4), 505 - 515.

Turban, E., and Aronson, J.E., (2001). Decision support systems and intelligent systems, Sixth edition, Prentice Hall.

Valkonen, Pekka and Nykanen , Olli. 1991. An expert system for patent classification. *World Patent Information*, 13(3), 143-148.

Waters, Samuel T. (1986). Answerman, the expert information specialist: an expert system for retrieval of information from library reference books. *Information Technology and Libraries,* 204-212.

Weibel, Stuart; M. Oskins and Diane Vizine-Goetz. (1989). Automatic title page cataloguing: a feasibility study. *Information Processing and Management,* 25(2), 187-203.

Zager, Pam and Smadi, Omar. (1992). A know-ledge-based expert systems application in library acquisitions : monographs. *Library Acquisitions : Practice & Theory,* 16, 148.

7
Decision Support System

Imagination is more important than knowledge .

- Albert Einstein

DEFINING DECISION SUPPORT SYSTEM

Human being is unique from any other animals because of our ability to take decision. Human decisions came out of the mental or cognitive process to choose a course of action among alternatives. Although, it is one of the greatest strength of human beings of taking decision, it is, however, based on intuitive strategies as opposed to normative rules. These intuitive strategies are referred to as heuristic pattern and often biased towards the situation/condition. Making decisions concerning complex systems and often strains our cognitive capabilities. There is a substantial amount of empirical evidence that human intuitive judgment and decision making are far from optimal, and it deteriorates even further with complexity and stress. Even though individual interactions among a system's variables may be well understood, predicting how the system will react to any context especially policy decision is often difficult. Because in many situations the quality of decisions is important, aiding the deficiencies of human judgment and decision making has been a major focus of science throughout history. Recently, in information science, cognitive psychology, and artificial intelligence there has some techniques developed, mostly by using computer program, for complex decision making. Such system are often given the common name of decision support systems (DSSs). The concept of DSS is extremely broad, and its definitions vary, depending on the author's point of view. Here, we will explain some of them:

- DSS are a model-based set of procedures for processing data and judgments to assist a manager in his/her decision [Little, 1970]
- DSS couple the intellectual resources of individuals with the capabilities of the computer to improve the quality of decisions. It's a computer-based support for management decision makers who deal with semi-structured problems [Keen & Scott-Morton, 1978]
- DSS is a system that is extendable, capable of supporting ad hoc analysis and decision modelling, oriented towards future planning, and of being used at irregular, unplanned intervals [Moore & Chang, 1980]
- DSS enable mangers to use data and models related to an entity (object) of interest to solve semi-structured and unstructured problems with which they are faced [Beulens & Van Nunen, 1988]
- Main feature of DSS rely in the model component. Formal quantitative models such as statistical, simulation, logic and optimization models are used to represent the decision model, and their solutions are alternative solutions [Emery, 1987; Bell, 1992]
- DSS are systems for extracting, summarising and displaying data [McNurlin & Sprague, 1993]

Overall, DSS are a set of manual or computerized tools that assist in some decision making activity. In today's competitive environment, however, DSSs are commonly understood as:

- Specific class of computerized information system
- Interactive software based system
- Supports business and organizational decision making activities
- Compile useful information from raw data, documents, personal knowledge, business model to identify and solve problems and make decision.

ORIGIN OF DSS

The concept of decision support traced back to the late 1950s and early 1960s, when two main areas of research: the theoretical studies of organizational decision making done at the Carnegie Institute of Technology and the technical work on interactive computer systems carried out at the Massachusetts Institute of Technology. Fellow Harvard Ph.D. student Andrew McCosh asserts that the "concept of decision support systems was first articulated by Scott Morton in February 1964 in a basement office in Sherman Hall, Harvard Business School" (McCosh 2002) in a discussion they had about Scott Morton's dissertation. During these time J.C.R.Licklider also published paper titled "Man-Computer Symbiosis". Scott Morton studied about building, implementing and then testing an interactive, model-driven management decision system in 1964. It is considered that the concept of DSS became an area of research of its own in the middle of the 1970s, before gaining in intensity during the 1980s (Haettenschwiler 1999). In 1971 T.P.Gerrity studied came in the article titled "The Design of Man-Machine Decision System". The first use of the term decision support system was in Gorry and Scott-Morton's (1971) Sloan Management Review article. They argued that management information systems primarily focused on structured decisions and suggested that the supporting information systems for semi-structured and unstructured decisions should be termed "decision support systems". In the middle and late 1980s, Executive Information Systems (EIS), Group Decision Support Systems (GDSS), and Organizational Decision Support Systems (ODSS) evolved from the single user and modeloriented DSS. Beginning in about 1990, data warehousing and On-Line Analytical Processing (OLAP) began broadening the realm of DSS. As the millenium approached, new Web-based analytical applications were introduced.

CHARACTERISTICS OF DSS

Identifying characteristics, distinguishable features, attributes or aspects of all DSS helps distinguish such systems from other systems. Alter (1980) identified three major characteristics of DSS:

1. DSS are designed specifically to facilitate decision processes,
2. DSS should support rather than automate decision making, and
3. DSS should be able to respond quickly to the changing needs of decision makers.

Based on the study of Clyde Holsapple and Andrew Whinston (1996), Turban (1995) and Power (2002) following more characteristics can also be elaborated:

1. Facilitation : DSS facilitate and support specific decision-making activities and/or decision processes.

2. Interaction : DSS are computer-based systems designed for interactive use by decision makers or staff users who control the sequence of interaction and the operations performed.

3. Ancillary : DSS can support decision makers at any

level in an organization. They are NOT intended to replace decision makers.

4. Repeated Use : DSS are intended for repeated use. A specific DSS may be used routinely or used as needed for ad hoc decision support tasks.

5. Task-oriented : DSS provide specific capabilities that support one or more tasks related to decision-making, including: intelligence and data analysis; identification and design of alternatives; choice among alternatives; and decision implementation.

6. Identifiable : DSS may be independent systems that collect or replicate data from other information systems OR subsystems of a larger, more integrated information system.

7. Decision Impact : DSS are intended to improve the accuracy, timeliness, quality and overall effectiveness of a specific decision or a set of related decisions.

FUNDAMENTAL TYPES OF DSS

Model-driven DSS : Model-driven support systems incorporate the ability to manipulate data for statistical, financial, optimization, or simulation model. Model-based decision support systems can be extremely useful in forecasting the effects of changes in activity. Model-driven DSS use data and parameters provided by users to assist decision makers in analyzing a situation; they are not necessarily data-intensive. Decodess is an example of an open source model-driven DSS generator

Data-driven DSS : Data-driven DSS are a form of system that manipulate internal company data and, sometimes, external data to aid decision making. The database designed to store data in such a way as to allow for its querying and analysis by users. Geographical Information System is an example of data-driven DSS, which can be used to visually represent geographically dependant data using maps.

Document-driven DSS : Document-driven DSS is the newest field of study in Decision Support Systems. This types of system manages, retrieves, and manipulates unstructured information in a variety of electronic formats. While data-driven DSS rely on data that is already in a standardised format that lends itself to database storage and analysis, document-driven DSS makes use of data that cannot easily be standardised and stored. The three primary forms of data used in document driven DSS are: Oral (i.e. transcribed conversations); Written (i.e. reports, memos, e-mail and other correspondence); Video (i.e. TV commercials and news reports). Examples of document-driven tools can be found in Internet search engines, designed to sift through vast volumes of unsorted data through the use of keyword searches.

Knowledge-driven DSS : provides specialized problem-solving expertise stored as facts, rules, procedures, or in similar structures. Ideally, this type of systems are designed to sift through large volumes of data, identify hidden patterns in that data and present recommendations based on those patterns.

Communication Driven DSS : This is a type of DSS that enhances decision-making by enabling communication and sharing of information between groups of people. A simple example is Microsoft's NetMeeting, web-conferencing application, interactive videos.

Furthermore, Steven Alter published his MIT doctoral dissertation in 1980 describes seven types of DSS: They are:

File drawer systems that provide access to data items.

Data analysis systems that support the manipulation of data by computerized tools tailored to a specific task and setting or by more general tools and operators.

Analysis information systems that provide access to a series of decision-oriented databases and small models.

Accounting and financial models that calculate the consequences of possible actions.

Representational models that estimate the consequences of actions on the basis of simulation models.

Optimization models that provide guidelines for action by generating an optimal solution consistent with a series of constraints.

Suggestion models that perform the logical processing leading to a specific suggested decision for a fairly structured or well-understood task.

Another categorization has been made by Donovan and Madnick (1977) as *institutional* or *ad hoc*. Institutional DSS support decisions that are recurring. An ad hoc DSS supports querying data for one time requests. Hackathorn and Keen (1981) identified DSS in three distinct yet interrelated categories: Personal DSS, Group DSS and Organizational DSS.

COMPONENTS

Andrew (1991) explained three fundamental components of DSSs.

Database Management System (DBMS)

The role of DBMS in DSS is to supply data for operation. The data bank stores large quantities of data, collected from decision makers that are relevant to the class of problems for which the DSS has been designed. It provides logical data structures, as opposed to the physical data structures, with which the users interact. A DBMS separates the users from the physical aspects of the database structure and processing. It should also be capable of informing the user of the types of data that are available and how to gain access to them.

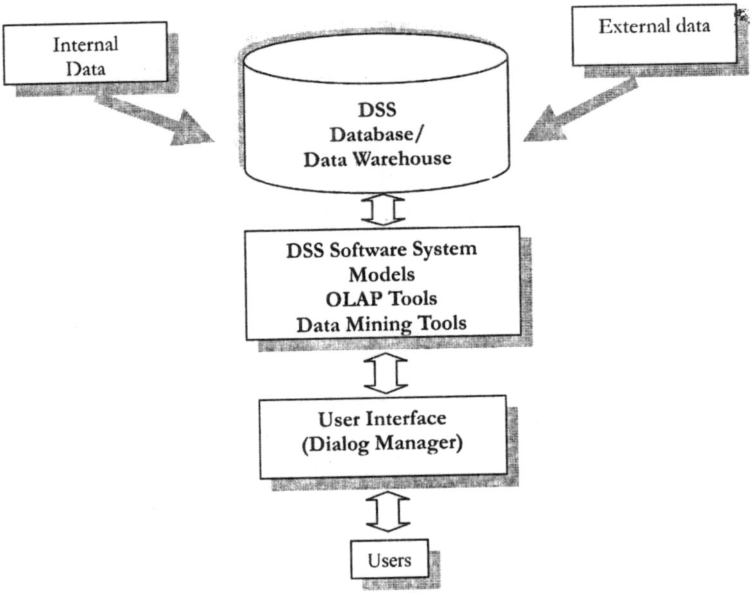

Fig. 1 : Main components of the DSS.

Model-Base Management System (MBMS)

The role of MBMS is analogous to that of a DBMS. Its primary function is providing independence between specific models that are used in a DSS from the applications that use them. The purpose of an MBMS is to transform data from the DBMS into information that is useful in decision making. Since many problems that the user of a DSS will cope with may be unstructured, the MBMS should also be capable of assisting the user in model building.

Dialog Generation and Management System (DGMS)

The main product of an interaction with a DSS is insight. The primary responsibility of a DGMS is to enhance the ability of the system user to utilize and benefit from the DSS. The dialog manager is also in charge for the information visualization.

User Interface

As the users of a DSS are often managers who are not computer-trained, DSSs need to be equipped with intuitive and easy-to-use interfaces. These interfaces aid in model building, but also in interaction with the model, such as gaining insight and recommendations from it. The DSS user interface permits easy interactions between users of the system and the DSS software tools. Many DSS today have Web interfaces to take advantages of graphics displays, interactivity, and ease of use. The DSS software system contains the software tools that are used for data analysis. It may contain various Online Analytical Processing (OALP) tools, data mining tools, or a collection of mathematical and analytical models that easily can be made accessible to the DSS users.

Marakas (1999) proposes a generalized architecture made of five distinct parts:

(a) the data management system,

(b) the model management system,

(c) the knowledge engine,

(d) the user interface, and

(e) the user(s).

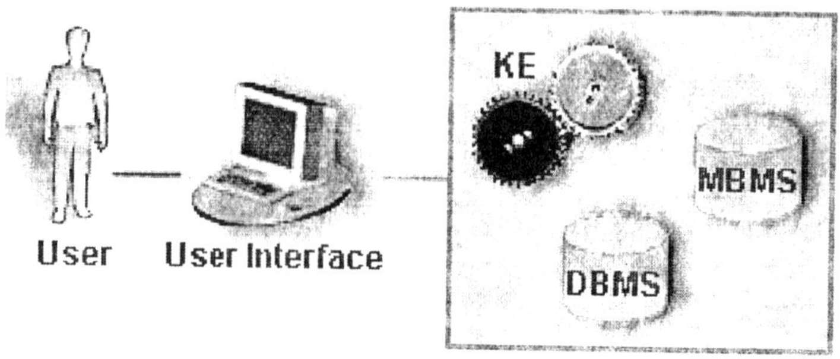

Similarly, Hättenschwiler (1999) identifies five components of DSS: *(a)* users with different roles or functions in the decision making process (decision maker, advisors, domain experts, system experts, data collectors), *(b)* a specific and definable decision context, *(c)* a target system describing the majority of the preferences, *(d)* a knowledge base made of external data sources, knowledge databases, working databases, data warehouses and meta-databases, mathematical models and methods, procedures, inference and search engines, administrative programs, and reporting systems, and *(e)* a working environment for the preparation, analysis and documentation of decision alternatives.

MODELS

There are three distinct models available in DSS

Passive DSS : Decision support systems that just collect data and organize it effectively are usually called passive models, they do not suggest a specific decision, and they only reveal the data.

Active DSS : An active decision support system actually processes data and explicitly shows solutions based upon that data.

Cooperative DSS : A cooperative decision support system is when data is collected, analyzed and then is provided to a human component which then can help the system revise or refine it. It means that both a human component and computer component work together to come up with the best solution.

ADVANTAGES & DISADVANTAGES

Power (2002) identify following as advantage in DSS

1. Time savings : For all categories of decision support systems, research has demonstrated and substantiated reduced decision cycle time, increased employee productivity and more timely information for decision making. The time savings that have been documented from using computerized decision support are often substantial. Researchers have not however always demonstrated that decision quality remained the same or actually improved.

2. Enhance effectiveness : A second category of advantage that has been widely discussed and examined is improved decision making effectiveness and better decisions. Decision quality and decision making effectiveness are however hard to document and measure. Most research has examined soft measures like perceived decision quality rather than objective measures.

3. Improve interpersonal communication : DSS can improve communication and collaboration among decision makers. In appropriate circumstances, communications-driven and group DSS have had this impact. Model-driven DSS provide a means for sharing facts and assumptions. Data-driven DSS make "one version of the truth" about company operations available to managers and hence can encourage fact-based decision making. Improved data accessibility is often a major motivation for building a data-driven DSS. This advantage has not been adequately demonstrated for most types of DSS.

4. Competitive advantage : Vendors frequently cite this advantage for business intelligence systems, performance management systems, and web-based DSS. Although it is possible to gain a competitive advantage from computerized decision support, this is not a likely outcome. Vendors routinely sell the same product to competitors and even help with the installation. Organizations are most likely to gain this advantage from novel, high risk, enterprise-wide, inward facing decision support systems. Measuring this is and will continue to be difficult.

5. Cost reduction : Some research and especially case studies have documented DSS cost saving from labor savings in making decisions and from lower infrastructure or technology costs. This is not always a goal of building DSS.

6. Increase decision maker satisfaction : The novelty of using computers has and may continue to confound analysis of this outcome. DSS may reduce frustrations of decision makers, create perceptions that better information is being used and/or create perceptions that the individual is a "better" decision maker. Satisfaction is a complex measure and often researchers measure satisfaction with the DSS rather than satisfaction with using a DSS in decision making. Some studies have compared satisfaction with and without computerized decision aids. Those studies suggest the complexity and "love/hate" tension of using computers for decision support.

7. Promote learning : Learning can occur as a by-product of initial and ongoing use of a DSS. Two types of learning seem to occur: learning of new concepts and the development of a better factual understanding of the business and decision making environment. Some DSS serve as "de facto" training tools for new employees. This potential advantage has not been adequately examined.

8. Increase organizational control : Data-driven DSS often make business transaction data available for performance monitoring and ad hoc querying. Such systems can enhance management understanding of business operations and managers perceive that this is useful. What is not always evident is the financial benefit from increasingly detailed data. Regulations like Sarbanes-Oxley often dictate reporting requirements and hence heavily influence the control information that is made available to managers. On a more ominous note, some DSS provide summary data about decisions made, usage of the systems, and recommendations of the system. Managers need to be very careful about how decision-related information is collected and then used for organizational control purposes. If employees feel threatened or spied upon when using a DSS, the benefits of the DSS can be reduced. More research is needed on these questions.

However, Klein and Methlie (1995) and Winograd and Flores (1986) identify following eight disadvantages of DSS.

1. Overemphasize decision making : Clearly the focus of those of us interested in computerized decision support is on decisions and decision making. Implementing DSS may reinforce the rational perspective and overemphasize decision processes and decision making. It is important to educate managers about the broader context of decision making and the social, political and emotional factors that impact organizational success. It is especially important to continue examining when and under what circumstances DSS should be built and used. We must continue to ask if the decision situation is appropriate for using any type of DSS and if a specific DSS is or remains appropriate to use for making or informing a specific decision.

2. Assumption of relevance : According to Winograd and Flores (1986), "Once a computer system has been installed it is difficult to avoid the assumption that the things it can deal with are the most relevant things for the manager's concern." The danger is that once DSS become common in organizations, that managers will use them inappropriately. There is limited evidence that this occurs. Again training is the only way to avoid this potential problem.

3. Transfer of power : Building DSS, especially knowledge-driven DSS, may be perceived as transferring decision authority to a software program. This is more a concern with decision automation systems (check DecisionAutomation.com) than with DSS. I advocate building computerized decision support systems because I want to improve decision making while keeping a human decision maker in the "decision loop". In general, I value the "need for human discretion and innovation" in the decision making process.

4. Unanticipated effects : Implementing decision support technologies may have unanticipated consequences. It is conceivable and it has been demonstrated that some DSS reduce the skill needed to perform a decision task. Some DSS overload decision makers with information and actually reduce decision making effectiveness. I'm sure other such unintended consequences have been documented. Nevertheless, most of the examples seem correctable, avoidable or subject to remedy if and when they occur.

5. Obscuring responsibility : The computer doesn't make a "bad" decision, people do. Unfortunately some people may deflect personal responsibility to a DSS. Managers need to be continually reminded that the computerized decision support system is an intermediary between the people who built the system and the people who use the system. The entire responsibility associated with making a decision using a DSS resides with people who built and use the system.

6. False belief in objectivity : Managers who use DSS may or may not be more objective in their decision making. Computer software can encourage more rational action, but managers can also use decision support technologies to rationalize their actions. It is an overstatement to suggest that people using a DSS are more objective and rational than managers who are not using computerized decision support.

7. Status reduction : Some managers argue using a DSS will diminish their status and force them to do clerical work. This perceptual problem can be a disadvantage of implementing a DSS. Managers and IS staff who advocate building and using computerized decision support need to deal with any status issues that may arise. This perception may or should be less common now that computer usage is common and accepted in organizations.

8. Information overload : Too much information is a major problem for people and many DSS increase the information load. Although this can be a problem, DSS can help managers organize and use information. DSS can actually reduce and manage the information load of a user. DSS developers need to try to measure the information load created by the system and DSS users need to monitor their perceptions of how much information they are receiving. The increasing ubiquity of handheld, wireless computing devices may exacerbate this problem and disadvantage.

DSS IN LIBRARIES

During the past few years, great progress has been made in research and commercial applications of decision support systems in various sectors like medical science, railway system etc. Library and information center is an organization in where there is need to take decision in many spares. Being of the service organization decision need to take for user service, manpower handling and overall management. In general, through Decision Support System, prediction of actions has been measured by studying model of the organization and its interaction with its environment. Data may be drawn from internal sources such as a data processing system or MIS, or from external sources like library user surveys. Decision support Systems (DSS) supports top librarians by allowing modeling of the organization. It also help librarians for strategic planning decisions to attain the objectives and policies governing acquisition, use and disposition of those resources. Acquisition of books, serials and other educational materials by libraries involves a complex decision process; especially when there are many books to choose from and the resources are meager. A DSS can held librarians to take decission for the combination of both structured and unstructured information in the library acquisitions decision process by considering.the past decisions concerning library acquisitions using structured information such as cost, availability of funds, and number of copies needed by the library, author and year of publication. Thie system can be used in solving the problem of decision-making in terms of selection of books from a long list of available books especially in areas where the resources are scarce.

Serials Solutions' 360 Counter, Thomson Reuters' Journal Use Reports, Swets' ScholarlyStats, and Serials Solutions', Ulrich's Serials, Analysis System, are considered as important DSS used by various commercial publisher in library & information sector.

A few examples of functional DSS have been found in library sectors. Akkamahadevi pointed followings as need for Decision Support Systems in Libraries.

1. To meet the challenges of providing users with increased access to information that is growing at an alarming rate, it is vital that libraries' resources - human, material and financial be used in the most effective and efficient manner.
2. Improved decision making and planning is required to use the library's resources most effectively.
3. The library manager much be able to identify problems, needs and trends, areas in to library activities which require some change to be implemented.
4. Library manager can make decisions and programs that direct resources in such a manner as to best support the overall objectives of the institution.
5. Sound decision making and planning, requires appropriate management information and models. Most of this information is available from the existing databases (as a by product of) automated or computerized operating systems or can also be captured from various sources.

Similarly, Michael E. Gleeson, John R. Ottensmann had

developed a Decision Support System for Acquisitions Budgeting in Public Libraries. The DSS has four modules: a database module that allows comparison across budget categories and inspection of trends in costs, circulation, acquisitions, stocks, turnover rates, and discards; a forecasting module that uses time series techniques to make cost and circulation forecasts; a budget-allocation module that produces a satisfactory allocation by iteratively solving a continuous knapsack problem; and a scenario-testing module that calculates future stock.

CONCLUSION

Decision support systems is now become one of the popular information processing system in various domains, including business, engineering, the military, and medicine. This type of system is extremely valuable in situations where the amount of available information is prohibitive for the intuition of an unaided human decision maker and in where precision and optimality are of importance. It supports in gaining high level cognition by integrating various sources of information, providing intelligent access to relevant knowledge, and aiding the process of structuring decisions. They are using as an useful tool in engineering economics, operations research, statistics, and decision theory. Applying artificial intelligence methods DSSs address heuristically problems that are intractable by formal techniques. Proper implication of decision-making tools increases productivity, efficiency, and effectiveness and gives many businesses a comparative advantage over their competitors, allowing them to make optimal choices for technological processes and their parameters, planning business operations, logistics, or investments.

REFERENCES

Alter, S.L. (1980). Decision Support Systems: Current Practice and Continuing Challenge. Reading, MA: Addison-Wesley.

Sage, Andrew P. (1991). Decision Support Systems Engineering. John Wiley & Sons, Inc., New York, 1991.

Bell, P. C. (1992). Decision Support Systems: Past, Present and Prospects", *Revue des systèmes de decision,* 1(2-3), 126-137.

Beulens, A. J. and J. A. van Nunen (1988). The Use of Expert System Technology in DSS, *Decision Support Systems,* 4(4), 421-431.

Donovan, J.J. and S.E. Madnick (1977). Institutional and Ad Hoc DSS and Their Effective Use, Data Base, 8,3.

Emery, J. C. (1987). *Management Information Systems. The Critical Strategic Resource.* New York: Oxford Univ. Press.

Gorry, A. and M.S. Scott Morton (1971). A Framework for Information Systems, *Sloan Manage Rev,* 13(1), 56–79.

Hackathorn, R.D. and P.G.W. Keen (1981). Organizational Strategies for Personal Computing in Decision Support Systems, *MIS Quarterly,* 5(3), 21-26.

Haettenschwiler, P. (1999). Neues anwenderfreundliches Konzept der Entscheidungsunterstützung. Gutes Entscheiden in Wirtschaft, Politik und Gesellschaft. Zurich, vdf Hochschulverlag AG: 189-208.

Holsapple, C. and A. Whinston (1996). Decision Support Systems: A Knowledge-Based Approach, Minneapolis/St. Paul, MN: West Publishing,

Keen, P. G. W. and M. S. Scott Morton (1978). Decision Support Systems: An Organizational Perspective. Reading, MA: Addison-Wesley.

Klein, M. and L. B. Methlie (1995). Knowledge-based Decision Support Systems with Applications in Business. Chichester, UK: John Wiley & Sons.

Little, J. D. C. (1970). Models and Managers: The Concept of a Decision Calculus. *Management Science,* 16(8), B466-485.

Marakas, G. M. (1999). Decision support systems in the twenty-first century. Upper Saddle River, N.J., Prentice Hall.

McCosh, A.M and Scott Morton, M.S. (1978). *Management Decision Support Systems*. London: Macmillan.

McNurlin, B. C. and Sprague, R. H., Jr. (1993). *Information Systems Management in Practice,* Engelwood Cliffs, NJ: Prentice Hall.

Michael E. Gleeson, John R. Ottensmann (1999). A Decision Support System for Acquisitions Budgeting in Public Libraries INTERFACES, 24(5), September-October 1994, pp. 107-117

Moore, J.H.,and M.G.Chang (1980). Design of Decision Support Systems. *Data Base,* 12(1 and 2).

Power, D. J. (2002). Decision support systems : concepts and resources for managers. Westport, Conn., Quorum Books.

Power, D. (2003) What are the characteristics of a Decision Support System? *DSS News,* 4(7).

Turban, E. (1995). Decision support and expert systems : management support systems. Englewood Cliffs, N.J., Prentice Hall.

Turban, E. and Aronson , J. E. (1995). Decision Support and Intelligent Systems. (5th edition) Upper Saddle River, N.J.: Prentice-Hall, Inc.

Winograd, T. and Flores, F. (1986). Understanding Computers and Cognition, Reading, MA: Addison-Wesley.

8
Information Profession

"Every person who has mastered a profession is a skeptic concerning it." - **George Bernard Shaw**

CONCEPT

It has doubts as when exactly the phrase information profession was first introduced. However, the concept informal professional was popularized during 1970s.

Although, profession and vocation seems similar to some extent but have some basic difference.

In this chapter we have attempted to understand the concept profession and how it differs from vocation and after that we have discussed various facets of information profession in detail. The increasing influences of the field of Information Technology and the advent of networked information services have prompted to review the Library and Information Science profession in present context. This chapter is an attempt to know the recent structure of LIS profession. Later part of this chapter particularly discusses how library profession has convergence with technology.

The dictionary meaning of Profession (noun) is -

1. An occupation, especially one that requires specialist academic and practical training, eg medicine, law,

teaching, engineering, etc.

2. The body of people engaged in a particular one of these.
3. An act of professing; a declaration. Example: a profession of loyalty. Thesaurus: declaration, confession, affirmation, acknowledgment, claim, assertion, statement, testimony, manifesto, attestation, vow, avowal.
4. A declaration of religious belief made upon entering a religious order.

Thesaurus meaning of profession is: occupation, job, line of work, career, vocation, employment, calling, position, business, office, sphere, metier, walk of life.

Whereas, the term Vocation (noun) reveals

1. A particular occupation or profession, especially one regarded as needing dedication and skill.
2. A feeling of being especially suited for a particular type of work.
3. A divine calling to adopt a religious life or perform good works.

Thesaurus meaning of vocation is: career, employment, profession, job, work, calling, position, business, niche, office, post, role.

In gist, a profession is an occupation that requires extensive training and the study and mastery of specialized knowledge, and usually has a professional association, ethical code and process of certification or licensing. Examples are accounting, law, teaching, architecture, nursing, pharmacy, medicine, finance, the military, the clergy and engineering.

On the other hand, a vocation is an occupation, either professional or voluntary, that is carried out more for its altruistic benefit than for income, which might be regarded as a secondary aspect of the vocation, however beneficial.

Vocations can be seen as fulfilling a psychological or spiritual need for the worker, and the term can also be used to describe any occupation for which a person is specifically gifted, and usually implies that the worker has a form of "calling" for the task. The word "vocation" comes from the Latin vocare, meaning "to call."

In fact, post-industrial society is characterized by increasing demand of theoretical knowledge, the professionalization of everyone, and a economy which gives better value to services than goods itself. As a result, the concept of profession and professional knowledge becomes the central idea of post-industrial economy. While there is no agreed definition of a profession, the Australian Council of Professions defines a profession as:

> *'A disciplined group of individuals who adhere to high ethical standards and uphold themselves to, and are accepted by, the public as possessing special knowledge and skills in a widely recognised, organised body of learning derived from education and training at a high level, and who are prepared to exercise this knowledge and these skills in the interest of others.*
>
> *Inherent in this definition is the concept that the responsibility for the welfare, health and safety of the community shall take precedence over other considerations.'*

Ever since the concept conceived by Flexner (1915) to determine whether or not social work could qualify as a profession, various people have defined it in various ways. Elias (1964) defines 'profession' as an occupation which demands highly specialized knowledge and skill, acquired at least in part by courses of a more or less theoretical nature and not by practice alone, tested by some form of examination either at a university or some other authorized institution and conveying to the persons who possess them considerable authority in relation to 'clients'. According to him, a profession is intellectual in that it carries with it personal responsibility for the exercise of choice and judgment. It is learned because its exercise is based on a substantial body of knowledge which could be passed on from generation to generation. It is also practical in that its corpus of knowledge is put to practical benefit of society. Finally, Flexner stated that a profession is characterized by idealism, which in theory puts the aims and practice of the profession above mere monetary rewards.

On the other hand, Logan (1953) describes a profession as a vocation whose practice is founded upon an understanding of the theoretical structure of some department of learning or science, and upon the abilities accompanying such understanding. Similarly, Chadwick (1998), who defined a profession as a vocation founded upon specialized educational training, the purpose of which is to supply disinterested counsel and service to others, for a direct and definite compensation, wholly apart from expectation of other business gain (emphasis added).

Although the discipline 'library science' have been established in 1887, the occupation from which it is derived, that is librarianship, is one of the oldest discipline. However, as Benge (1979) pointed that the irony in the situation of the librarian is that, unlike the doctor or the lawyer or even the priest, he is not suddenly required in time of crisis or dismay; he is just there all the time like the weather. He argued that the librarian is part of the foundation of a civilized life whereas neither doctor nor lawyer is needed all the time. He further contended that librarians, like teachers, are embedded in the foundation of the cultural process. However, the tragedy is that their absence ought to be most noticeable, but in many countries this does not happen. This may have to do with the mute nature of the profession. Asheim (1979), in this regard, also argues that of all the characteristics identified or associated with profession, which library and information science has been striving to attain, the one in which LIS practitioners have been least successful is what he calls "sanction of the community" which means societal or social recognition. Societal recognition is indeed very critical and has been the bane of LIS growth, especially in less literate societies.

CHARACTERISTICS OF PROFESSION

Information profession is characterized by parochialism, particularly at national level. As pointed Flexner (1915), and Millerson (1964) certain characteristics of a profession are:

1. A Common Body of Knowledge and Skills

A profession must have a body of knowledge and skills based on that knowledge and extended by united effort. This attribute cuts across national and cultural boundaries. The body of knowledge and skills must be unique to the profession and must not easily be assimilated by a non-professional.

2. Formal System of Education and Training

Closely related to the common body of knowledge and skills is the possession of a formal system of education and training. The importance of this attribute lies in the fact that a professional body without a formal system of education and training cannot regenerate itself and cannot extend or expand its accumulated body of knowledge.

3. Professional Ethics

Ethics is designed to educate people, to help them to behave properly with others, to communicate at the workplace, etc. The tasks of professional ethics are to identify moral standards and assessments, judgments and concepts, characterizing people as representatives of a particular profession. Professional ethics develops norms, standards, requirements, typical to certain activities.

Most professions are regulated by their code of ethics, which concerns one's conduct or behaviour and practice when carrying out professional duties. A professional code of conduct sets out in general terms the standards and duties which it is reasonable to expect a professional to observe. This is not only to the benefit of the client but also to the benefit of those belonging to the profession. A professional code of ethics engenders public trust and confidence in the profession. Professionals are also expected to uphold professional ethics by not getting involved in any type of conflict of interest. A conflict of interest situation may occur when an individual tries to accomplish personal goals as a result of being in a certain profession. Generally, ethical rules are agreed and subscribed to by all the practitioners in each profession (Stevenson, 1968). Salisu (2001) notes that, in some particular cases, new entrants into some professions are expected to swear an oath binding them to certain ethics in the day-to-day performance of their duties. However, no two codes of ethics are identical. While the principles may be the same, the emphasis and priorities may differ from country to country.

4. Professional Association

A profession must be organized into a professional association of practitioners. Membership of such a body is an indication that a person is a member of the profession. It is the statutory responsibility of a professional association to ensure that institutions providing professional education maintain the standards set by the association (Oderinde, 1969). For LIS education, this system of accreditation ensures that LIS schools are not established without full consultation with, or approval of, the professional association. A professional association is a byproduct of the legal recognition of a profession.

5. Legal Recognition

Perhaps the most important characteristic of a profession is the possession of legal recognition. It is through legal recognition that society expresses the importance of the services a professional body renders to it. This recognition enhances the social image of the profession. Without legal empowerment, no profession can regulate the practice of the profession in any given society and the other attributes may not be attained or strengthened. Legal recognition presupposes that the body seeking recognition has a common body of knowledge and skills as well as a formal system of education and training. Therefore, legal recognition will be pivotal to the attainment of the other traits.

6. Service Orientation

A profession must be characterized by an idealism which in theory, if not in practice, puts the aims and practice of the profession above mere money making. This implies that a profession provides a service for public good. It requires that members of the profession should adhere strictly to a sense of social responsibility. This means that a profession must possess a service principle that places the welfare of society above personal gains.

In addition to all these, we believe that there are three more important characteristics of a profession. They are:

7. Professional Responsibility

The professional carries additional moral responsibilities to those held by the population in general. This is because professionals are capable of making and acting on an informed decision in situations that the general public cannot, because they have not received the relevant training and the relevant knowledge. In contrast, a fully trained professional, like a doctor (with the correct equipment) would be capable of making the correct diagnosis and carrying out the procedure and we would think it wrong if they stood by and failed to help in this situation.

8. Code of Practice

Questions arise as to the ethical limits of the professional's responsibility and how power and authority should be used in service to the client and society. Most professions have internally enforced codes of practice that members of the profession must follow, to prevent exploitation of the client and preserve the integrity of the profession. This is not only to the benefit of the client but to the benefit of those belonging to the profession.

9. Separatism

Separatists argue that professions should be allowed to go beyond such confines when they judge it necessary. This is because they are trained to produce certain outcomes which may take moral precedence over other functions of society.

On the basis of above characteristics if we try to compensate our own discipline, we can fairly claim that librarianship is a truly a profession. William J. Goode in his article *The Librarian: From Occupation to Profession?* mentioned six reasons to claim librarianship as profession.

First, they are thought to be, and in fact are, attached to learning. Identified as they are with knowledge, a prime source of occupational prestige in our society, their claims can not be dismissed lightly.

Second, they are service-oriented, rather than self-interested, at least in certain senses. As one researcher put it, "the discontent of librarians with their salaries tends to be tame and genteel. Librarians administer large budgets, but none of the relevant publics even conceives of graft as a possibility. Librarians view as unworthy an intense concern with money. Almost no peripheral work is available to them, as it is to the university scholar, which would bring in additional income but which would carry the stigma of popularization or commercialization. The public believes that the librarians' main task is service to the reader, and librarians agree, at least with certain qualifications to be noted later.

Third, an increasing number of librarians are trained in professional schools, some of which offer a doctorate and are associated with universities. Much energy is devoted to curriculum development, and a serious attempt has been made to evaluate these schools.

Fourth, librarians belong to professional associations, both state and national, and have formulated a code of ethics.

Fifth, unlike several other occupations striving for recognition as professions, such as nursing or pharmacy, librarians are not subordinate to any other group in the same situs or organization.

Finally, the librarian has no competitors, and indeed librarians themselves have a sense that their occupation is unique.

INFORMATION PROFESSIONAL

Before discussing the concept information professionals firstly we should consider the pioneer work by Fritz Machlup and his colleague Stephen Kagan. According to them "Information science, at present stage of its development, is a not fully integrated assemblage of systematic studies of the processes regarded as information, particularly of the system, operations and devices, technology, and organization by which men - which of course stands for men and women, transmit and receive, and therefore transfer, knowledge among one another". They stress community of information professional as communicators and describing their job as transporting of *package of knowledge* (commodities). These author attempted to explain these knowledge producing labour force into eight categories:

1. A transporter of knowledge is one who delivers what he receives without changing it in the least.
2. A transporter of knowledge changes the form of a message but not its content.
3. A routine processor of knowledge who changes both the form and the content of the message received.
4. A discretionary processor of knowledge is very like a routine processor, except that the person must make judgment in choosing what rules or procedures to follow to modify a given message. Decision involved in inventory evaluation are example of this type of knowledge.
5. A managerial processor of knowledge receives a variety of message and generate extracts, summaries and so forth based on them. This individual also receives message in the form of instructions from others higher up in the processor will change the form and contents of message to whatever extent is deemed necessary.
6. A interpreter of knowledge changes both form and contents of message received but must do so in a way that preservers as accurately as possible their essential meaning. Language translator are an obvious example.
7. An analyzer of message received, in contrast to the interpreter, may use judgment, craft and skill to such an extent that the message communicated may bear little or no resemblance to the message received.
8. An original creator of knowledge gathers a variety of input from numerous sources and, based on personal creativity and other attributes, communicates a synthesis of collective message that is wholly different

from any one message. Poets,. Novelists, and such fall into this category.

According to Special Library Association, USA, an Information Professional ("IP") strategically uses information in his/her job to advance the mission of the organization. This is accomplished through the development, deployment, and management of information resources and services. The IP harnesses technology as a critical tool to accomplish goals. IPs include, but are not limited to, librarians, knowledge managers, chief information officers, web developers, information brokers, and consultants.

According to a study of Shiery, Gupta and Debons (1974), there are four categories of people who are associated with information profession. They are:

1. Information theorists/scientists who are concerned with the laws, theories, philosophy, sociology etc. of information science.
2. Information systems specialists who analyze information problems and design systems or network to solve.
3. Information intermediaries who work between the decision maker and the body of knowledge.
4. Information technologists who operate, maintain, and control information system, consisting of individuals, acquisition, transmission and processing technologies and related working procedures.

   In later, Debons (1981) added two more categories:

5. Manager of information, who plan, develop, coordinate and control information programs and the human and materials resources needed for their implementations.
6. Educators and trainers of information, workers, who provide education and/or training for all categories

of information professional and nonprofessionals workers.

DUTIES OF INFORMATION PROFESSIONALS

In fact, information professionals is concerned primarily with users of information, and secondly with logistics of handling (acquiring, storing, retrieving) materials that has the potential for informing individuals. In context of activities of information workers Becker explained duties as:

a) coordinating relevant information activities;
b) providing policy oversight and guidance;
c) planning, progarmme and budgets;
d) managing personnel;
e) planning, developing and operating automated and non-automated information system; and
f) providing information technology support service.

Similarly, Special Library Association of USA identifies diverse responsibilities that Information Professionals may have include:

- Developing and maintaining a portfolio of cost-effective, client-valued information services that are aligned with the strategic directions of the organization and client groups
- Building a dynamic collection of information resources based on a deep understanding of clients' information needs
- Gathering evidence to support decisions about the development of new services and products
- Maintaining current awareness of emerging technologies
- Assessing and communicating the value of the information organization, including information

services, products and policies to senior management, key stakeholders and client groups

- Contributing effectively to senior management strategies and decisions regarding information applications, tools and technologies, and policies for the organization

Competencies of Information Professionals

There is growing need to understand the competencies for the library & information profession. Flynn and Shirey (1983) have identified following as competencies:

Understanding of principles, facts, concepts, and procedures, problem solving by the principles of information transfer; appreciation of the social role of the profession, knowledge of client's capacity to establish systemic relationships; self-understanding and self-reliance; critical attributes towards the profession's rationale and tools/ technologies; continued professional growth; and identification and use of ethical principles.

Whereas, Graffiths and King (1984) in their study pointed several types of knowledge considered critical to information work:

1. Basic knowledge in such areas as language, communication, arithmetic operations.
2. Subject knowledge of primary subject field of user served, such as medicine, chemistry, law.
3. Library & information science knowledge, such as the definition, structure and format of information.
4. Knowledge about information work environments, such as the information community, its participants, and their social, economic and technical interrelationship.
5. Knowledge of what work is done, such as that required to provide services and produce products.

6. Knowledge of how to do work, such as how to perform various activities, apply techniques, use materials and technology.
7. Knowledge of the organization or user community served, such as mission, goals, and objectives, user's information needs and requirements.

Competencies also explained into three fold: Professional Competencies, Personal Competencies and Core Competencies.

Professional Competencies : This competency relate to the practitioner's knowledge of information resources, access, technology and management, and the ability to use this knowledge as a basis for providing the highest quality information services. There are four major competencies, each augmented with specific skills:

A. Managing Information Organizations
B. Managing Information Resources
C. Managing Information Services
D. Applying Information Tools and Technologies

Personal Competencies : This competency represent a set of attitudes, skills and values that enable practitioners to work effectively and contribute positively to their organizations, clients and profession. These competencies range from being strong communicators, to demonstrating the value-add of their contributions, to remaining flexible and positive in an ever-changing environment.

Core Competencies

I. Information professionals contribute to the knowledge base of the profession by sharing best practices and experiences, and continue to learn about information products, services, and management practices throughout the life of his/her career.
II. Information professionals commit to professional

excellence and ethics, and to the values and principles of the profession.

Library Profession & Technologies - Convergence

There has wide discussion everywhere that computers especially technologies will completely take the job of library professionals within few years and there will be no library at all. Everybody will access data in their terminals and no body will use library. Times will only say what the situation will be after 15 years or so on, here, however, we will try to discuss the roles of librarian and information technologist, how they relate, and sets of factors which affect the success of any effort to join the two together in partnership.

At present we are witness with the fact that Digital libraries and networked information provide a great area of shared interest for librarians and technologists. And these same innovations have also led to increasing specialisation in both professions. Librarians should encouraged to reinterpret "traditional" library skills, to explore new ways of putting those skills to work, and to promote themselves to administration. Models for "electronic libraries" show librarians taking responsibility for the provision and management of information that comes not from traditional collections, but from databases.

As pointed Bernbom Librarians and technologists, especially those technologists who design and deploy information systems, have similar interests with respect to the three primary components - *information, users, services* - that are common to libraries, digital libraries and, more generally, information systems.

Information : in all cases, can be analysed according to its lifecycle. It is created, acquired, organised, accessed, and preserved. It can be arranged according to systems of classification, and can be described using a standard reference language.

Users : in all cases, have some specific need for information. They can express their requirements for information, and can be understood to use information in some intellectual, social or organisational context.

Services : in all cases, represent the bridge between information and user. These may be distinctly *human services* such as reference services ("analysing unclear communication in order to locate knowledge for patrons"). They may be *automated* services, ranging from highly structured and specialised information systems to general-purpose search engines and retrieval tools. Often they are combining some human activity (e.g.. cataloguing and classification) with automation (e.g. an OPAC).

John Henderson identify certain factors which act to create and sustain purposeful partnership between librarian and information technologist. They are:

Mutual Benefit

This is the essential reason for the partnership. A partnership can achieve things which its partners cannot do alone. This can lead to innovation, as the expertise of the two professions is combined, and financial savings based on efficiencies. The benefits to each partner must be articulated explicitly.

Commitment

Commitment relies on the seeking of shared goals which are common to both partners. There is a place for incentive systems which are designed to reinforce the common goals. It can also be a good idea to develop jointly a contract, intended to state formally how the partners will work together. A contract often serves as much as a symbol of co-operation as a reference document.

Predisposition

It is a fact that good partnerships are often built by

people who are predisposed to build good partnerships. A successful partnership is based on a willingness to trust each other. Trust in turn is based on an explicit track record of performance and personal contacts with partners. Consequently, the way in which you interact today creates the predisposition for partnership tomorrow.

Shared Knowledge

Partners can work together better if they each know what the other does. Additionally, the act of building shared knowledge can improve predisposition.

Mutual Dependency on Distinctive Competency

Good partnerships bring together people who make unique and distinctive contributions, and who are willing to rely on someone else's skill or knowledge for mutual success.

Organisational Linkage

Organisation is often a "hot spot" in library/IT relations. The focus need not be on a formal hierarchy, instead it is on:

- process integration: linking activities;
- information sharing: especially informally, outside of "channels";
- social networks: communication across boundaries at all levels.

LIBRARY PROFESSION IN DIGITAL AGE

In the last few years, librarianship and libraries, the pervasive influence of digital computing is transforming the expression and communication of shared ideas and knowledge. The power of technology has not only allowed libraries to share resources more easily and less expensively, it has also allowed the library to bring more information and more up-to-date information to its users. The enormous developments in the field of Information Technology and the advent of networked information in the last twenty five year, the technological development such as electronic databases, on-line services, CD ROMs, and the introduction of the Internet, have radically transformed access to information, making information readily available, especially for the end user. However, the information overload is such that greater expertise is demanded in retrieving and analyzing relevant information. In this period of constant change, the library's traditional roles of preserving, cataloging, classifying, and readers' services are undergoing a transformation. Many academic research studies discuss expected changes that the LIS profession is undergoing.

At the same time a very common question arises to us will the easy access to information completely eliminate the need for the librarian as? Or, whether the traditional library will be transformed into a virtual entity with the majority of the information in electronic format? Let us take some discussion as mentioned by Baruchson-Arbib and Bronstein (2002):

With the advent of the World Wide Web an enormous amount of information is now available on the web, which may appear easy to use at first glance but can also be confusing. The information retrieved by a researcher from the Internet depends on the adequacy of the search engines and data bases used, and on the user's skills in using them (Griffiths, 1999). Today there is a need for skilled librarians that are specialists in managing, retrieving, filtering, and evaluating information. Just as a person walking into a library for the first time must learn to translate the organizational design into the ability to find a book on a shelf, anyone using database must be trained to appreciate the value and benefits of a similar investigative process (Adams, 1997). Today, many users start out searching on their own and then come back to the LIS professional for help and advice when they are tangled in an irrelevant flood of information (Schulman, 1998).

The very popular concept hybrid library is a concept rather than an actual physical entity. The hybrid library is found on the continuum between the conventional and the digital library, where electronic and paper-based information sources are used jointly. The hybrid library should be viewed as more than a transition between the conventional and the digital library; the hybrid library is a worthwhile model in its own right, which can be developed and improved (Garrod, 1999). As mentioned Baruchson-Arbib and Bronstein (2002) Libraries and information centers will survive the Information Revolution because of the added value their services will continue to provide to users. Although those centers will be radically transformed in the next decades, their essence will be preserved. Both the traditional and virtual library models will coexist in a symbiotic relationship, each one bringing its most valued qualities into the new library model. Libraries should not be afraid to be identified as "museums of information," because in an era of information uncertainty, in which information seems ephemeral, great value will be placed on the preservation of human knowledge.

History says that LIS professionals have always been willing to explore a new outlook and adapt to new challenges. We are the first to adopt virtually every major technological innovation of the past hundred years than others – we adopt microfilm before spies, online databases before Dow Jones, CDs before Bruce Springsteen, and the Internet before it captured the imagination of the mass media and the average consumer (Dysart and Abram, 1997). However, to survive the challenges presented by the Information Age, the LIS profession must undergo a major transformation. The basic need to cope-up with transformation is skills and competencies, such as social and communication skills; technological and information skills both in the library and other settings that manage information. Librarians must build on their skills and be able to confidently instruct, inform, inspire, and guide others. Although the information environment may have changed, the methods and competencies remain essentially the same. LIS professional should acquire new roles and also to pursue new jobs beyond the library walls. In addition, management skills (Crosby, 2000) are viewed as an important set of competencies required at almost every level, every set-up libraries-small, medium, big. In this regard, Kinnell, (1996) mentioned that "Resourcing, staffing, procurement, materials organization, inventory, delivery, marketing and, above all, satisfying clients' needs, are at least as relevant to the information manager as to a McDonalds restaurant manager".

Librarian can also perform as information architect of a web site by ensuring the logic of the navigational schemes, deciding the content and location of information defining the parameters for searching the site, defining classification schemes, and generally ensuring an overall level of consistency and accuracy (Rowbotham, 1999). They can expand their experience to organize digital material—such as scanned photos and documents and digitized videotapes—and then decide how people will move from one piece of material to another, they might link videotape news with a map that shows the location of the story (Crosby, 2000).

In an environment where the available information content is expanding so rapidly, users need help retrieving relevant information and interpreting it. Librarians can serve themselves as analyst/knowledge interpreter. With their excellent research skills, can target the specific needs of each departments, and help prevent employees from wasting time surfing the Internet (Dolan & Schumacher, 1997).

Baruchson-Arbib and Bronstein (2002) in their study mentioned that the library's traditional roles of preserving, cataloging, classifying, and readers' services are undergoing a transformation. Library schools worldwide have confronted technological challenges and adapted their curriculum according to the new developments. The authors of that study, however, assume that the Web is not a library substitute, and that there will always be a need for libraries and librarians to help users cope with the ever changing information environment. The overall findings of their study were:

- The traditional library system will continue, intertwined with the new information technologies. The virtual library model will not, in our lifetime, replace the traditional library model.
- Libraries will continue to serve as an archive/ museum for special materials, such as rare or antique books, or maps.
- As a result of technological and financial changes, libraries will move from a holdings/ownership strategy to an access strategy.
- For budgetary as well as for efficiency reasons many traditional operations such as cataloging and acquisitions, will be handled by external contractors, greatly reducing, if not completely eliminating, the need for these library departments.
- Libraries/information centers will have to promote themselves and market their services within their organizations to justify their existence.
- Libraries/information centers will have to concentrate their efforts on delivering services such as Internet publishing, and integration of electronic and printed sources.

- In the future, libraries will be judged not by the size of its collection, but by its success in providing information quickly and accurately.
- Within 10 years, over half of the services provided to library users will be to individuals who never come into the library.
- For those users who do come to the library, it will be for assistance with special problems, recreational reading of books not in electronic format or access to special equipment.
- Libraries will be forced to find additional income by introducing a wider range of fee-based services and by seeking sponsors among the private sectors, to cover increasing costs.
- Academic libraries, computing centers, and networking and telecommunication units will come together to create a logical and effective system of information provision for teaching, research, and service support.
- The library/information center will assert a leadership role in the organization's overall information structure.
- As an enterprise the library represents the societal values of amassing and preserving information of value to the community. The task of library leaders will be to carry forward the "idea" of the library in an age when information is not hostage to format, time or space.
- Corporate libraries will be in demand because companies increasingly recognize that librarians have excellent research skills, and can target the specific needs of each employee and each department.
- Public Libraries will provide free Internet and other networked information access to ensure that every member of society has one free access point to

electronic information.

- To survive, libraries/information center will have to become the public's main access link to a network of knowledge containing all types of information in all sort of formats.
- Front-end systems for accessing databases will be much more intuitive, while users will become more information knowledgeable, greatly reducing the need for library and Information Science professionals.
- Automated reference will go farther than just adding a few terminals at the delivery site. In the near
- future change in this area will mean having librarians work at home, communicating with patrons via e-mail or phone, or being able to electronically help a patron who is having trouble with an on-line search in the catalog.
- Libraries/information centers will focus more on disadvantage socio-economic groups, giving them equal access to information resources, technology, and skills.
- Libraries/information centers will deliver any and all information where patrons need it from decentralized, ubiquitous locations such as kiosks, booths, mobile vans, Web sites and so on, while becoming financially self-sufficient.
- Libraries/information centers will become training centers in PC and basic office software use. These new functions will force the libraries to increase the number of staff in the training department while decreasing the number of staff in more traditional library departments.
- As a result of the Information Revolution libraries, as we know them today, will eventually disappear.

In their study the role of *The Library/Information Professional (LIP)* also viewed as:

- The library/information professional (hereafter LIP) will present a more assertive behavior in order to confront the challenges presented by the Information Age.
- The Internet presents the LIP with a unique opportunity for reinventing itself.
- The profession will devote itself to how people seek, organize. and consume information.
- The ability to seek, find, and process information will be a fundamental skill of the information society. As a result, LIP will have a central place in this society.
- In the academic setting LIP will work as partners in the research process with the discipline-based scholars.
- In the corporate setting LIP roles will become more analytical coordinating and advisory in nature.
- The traditional skills of the LIP such as devising search strategies, database design, system analysis, and user guidance will still be very important in the Information Age.
- The absence of any intermediary agency that monitors, selects, or edits Internet contents will emphasize the need for LIP to mediate the use of the Internet.
- The user-centered approach calls for a new breed of LIP with advance social and communication skills. As a result, Library Schools will need to integrate social and communication skills in their curriculum.
- One of the more important issues that LIP will be facing is their ability to predict their future clients' needs.
- Future LIP will have to have a very strong sense of leadership. Leadership in the use of new media, knowledge of information sources, and their

characteristics.

- One of the fundamental shifts in the profession will come from serving the public not in the library but in the community itself.
- Catalogers will merge the systems maintenance skills currently held by the computing professional in addition to their information skills.
- LIP will lead in designing training programs that help end users maximize the tools available to them at the desktop.
- Library/information center managers will be graduates from economic and business schools rather than LIS professionals.
- LIP will have to combine specialized expertise of library training, wedded with interpersonal/ communication skills, and subject knowledge with technical capabilities such as HTML literacy, demands of coping with basic hardware problems, knowledge of networking concepts and operating systems skills.
- New roles of advisor, trainer, and facilitator will necessitate instructional/teaching abilities and strong oral/written communication skills.
- School librarians will become more involve in planning course content and in devising methods of integrating information skills into curricula.
- The future LIP will be a promoter. He/she will promote products and services, making his public aware of new IT developments and carrying this promotion to the highest reaches of the corporation or institution.
- To reaffirm their place in the new Information Age, LIP will have to rely on innovative ideas such as the concept of "knowledge management," by which IS take an active role with users at the beginning of the

information process rather than at its end, assisting in the development and structuring of databases even as research is ongoing.

- Future LIP will have to have a deep professional understanding of both information applications and the human information interface. Not so much how technology works but rather what to do with it and how easily information can be turned into knowledge.
- LIP will be a market analyst, he/she will be surveying users to determine their needs and how well they meet those needs.
- LIP will be technology transfer agents, as the catalysts of the Information Age.
- Although the skills and competences of the LIS professional will be central in the Information Age, the Library and Information Science will be transformed to such an extent that it will eventually disappear as a profession.

SWOT ANALYSIS OF INFORMATION PROFESSION

Present day information professionals need characteristics of creativity and innovation to remain relevant. SWOT analysis is a tool to know the strengths and weaknesses of an organization versus its competitors and identifies the associated opportunities and threats in the larger business environment. It offers *professional* managers like librarians an effective evaluative technique to aid the decision making process.

Strengths

Elaborative knowledge and skills to order and organize information Rich experience in reference and information service and searching various database. A bird's-eye view to the present disciplines and subjects

Weaknesses

Not deep knowledge and judgment in an individual discipline or on a subject Difficulties to understand end-users' information needs completely

Opportunities

- Explosion of information
- Problem-oriented access to information
- Multidisciplinary approach
- Higher cost to search commercial databases
- New rights on databases

Threats

- End-user searching
- Decrease of bibliographic databases well-indexed
- The development of search engine services on the Internet

REFERENCES

Adams, V. (1997). Concept in end-user training: How to convert end users into effective searchers. *Searcher*, 5(9), 8–20.

Asheim, L.E. (1979). Librarians as professionals. *Library Trends*, 27(3), 225–257.

Baruchson-Arbib, Shifra and Bronstein, Jenny (2002). A View to the Future of the Library and Information Science Profession: A Delphi Study. *Journal of the American Society for Information Science and Technology*, 53(5),397–408.

Becker, Louise Giovane (1980). Information resource management (IRM): a revolution in progress. *Bulletin of the American Society for Information Science*. 6(6), 26-27.

Benge, Ronald C. (1979). Cultural crisis and libraries in the third world. London: Bingley.

Bernbom, Gerry (1998). The Information Professions and the Information Professional. Coalition for Networked Information, United States of America. Available at: http:/

/www.cni.org/regconfs/1997/ukoln-content/repor~11.html

Chadwick, Ruth. (1998). Professional ethics. In E. Craig (Ed.). Routledge encyclopedia of philosophy. London: Routledge.

Crosby, O. (2000). Librarians: Information experts in the information age. *Occupational Outlook Quarterly*, 44(4), 3–15.

Debons, A.; King, Donald W. Mansfield, Una and Shirey, Donald (1981). The information professional: a survey of an engineering field. New York, Marcel Dekker.

Dolan, D.R., & Schumacher, J. (1997). New jobs emerging in and around libraries and librarianship. *Online*, November, 70–76.

Dysart, J.I., & Abram, S.K. (1997). What is your information outlook? *Information Outlook*, January, 34–36.

Elias, N. (1964) Professions. In Gould, J. and Koll, W.L. (eds.) Dictionary of the social sciences. New York: Free Press.

Flexner, A. (1915). Is social work a profession? *Social and Society*, 1 (26), 901–906.

Flynn Roger and Donald L. Shirey (1983). Towards a paradigm for education in information science. *In: Information science in action: system design*, edited by A. Debons and Arvid Larson, Boston: Martinus Nijhoff Publishers.

Garrod, P. (1999). Survival strategies in the learning age – Hybrid Staff and Hybrid Libraries. *Aslib Proceedings*, 51(6), 187–194.

Goode, William J. (1961). The Librarian: From Occupation to Profession? *The Library Quarterly*, 31(4), 306-320

Griffiths, J.-M. (1999). Why the Web is not a library. *FID Review*, 1(1), 13–20.

Griffiths, Jose-Marie and King, Donald W. (1984). Educating the information professional of the future. *Challenges to an information society*, Proceedings of the 47th ASIS Annual Meeting, Vol. 22 White Plains, N.Y. Knowledge Industry Publication, 68-74.

Henderson, John (1990). Plugging into Strategic Partnership: The Critical IS Connection, *Sloan Management Review*, Spring, 7-18

Kinnell, M. (1996). Management development for the information professional. *Aslib Proceedings*, 48(9), 209–214.

Logan, Morris L. (1953). Towards a definition of profession. *Harvard Education Review*, 23(1), 33–50.

Machlup, Fritz and Stephen Kagan (1978). The changing structure of the knowledge-producing labour force. Discussion paper series, New York University, Centre for Applied Economics. Paper no. 78-01, January.

Millerson, G. (1964). The qualifying association: a study in professionalization. London: Routledge and Kegan Paul.

Rowbotham, J. (1999). Librarians—Architects of the future? *Aslib Proceedings*, 51(2), 59–63.

Salisu, Taofiq, M. (2001) Ethical issues in library management: a critical perspective. *Nigerian Libraries*, 35(1), 56–62.

Schulman, S. (1998). Applying a proactive ounce of prevention: Librarians helping their users in different ways. *Information Today*, 15(7), 46–51.

Shirey, Donald L., Armand B. Gupta and Anthony Debons (1974). The future market for professional in information. In: *Information science: search for identity*, edited by Anthony Debons. Proceedings of the 1972 NATO Advanced Study Institute in Information Science, New York, Marcel Dekker, 1974.

Stevenson, G.T. (1968). American Library Association. In Kent, Allen and Lancour, Harold (eds.) Encyclopedia of library and information science. New York: Marcel Dekker. p. 284.

9
Methods in Information Science

"Research is to see what everybody else has seen, and to think what nobody else has thought" - **Albert Szent-Gyorgyi**

The term methods simply refers to matters of practical research technique. This chapter provides a general framework regarding research methods that are useful in information science perspective. Information science had its origins in a variety of disciplines with distinct theoretical research perspectives on the important issues to study and the methods to study them. Research methods in any discipline, including information science, can be classified in various ways, however one of the most common distinctions is between qualitative and quantitative research methods. **Quantitative research methods** are originally developed in the natural sciences to study natural phenomena. Examples of quantitative methods now well accepted in the social sciences include survey methods, laboratory experiments, formal methods (e.g. econometrics) and numerical methods such as mathematical modeling. While, Mayer mentioned that **qualitative research methods** are developed in the social sciences to enable researchers to study social and cultural phenomena. Examples of qualitative methods are action research, case study research and ethnography. Qualitative data sources include observation and participant observation (fieldwork), interviews and questionnaires, documents and texts, and the researcher's impressions and reactions. Although most researchers do either quantitative or qualitative research work, some researchers have suggested combining one or more research methods in the one study (called triangulation). Research methods have also been classified as objective versus subjective methods (Burrell and Morgan, 1979). As being concerned with the discovery of general laws (nomothetic), verses being concerned with the uniqueness of each particular situation (idiographic), as aimed at prediction and control versus aimed at explanation and understanding; as taking an outsider (etic) versus taking an insider (emic) perspective etc.

As pointed out by Orlikowsky and Baroudi (1991), a quantitative research methodology is appropriate where quantifiable measures of variables of interest are possible, where hypotheses can be formulated and tested, and inferences drawn from samples to populations. Qualitative methods, on the other hand, are appropriate when the phenomena under study are complex, are social in nature, and do not lend themselves to quantification. Typically, qualitative methods are used when understanding the cultural context from which people derive meaning is an important element of a study. Such cultural context is usually not susceptible to quantification and aggregation and is, therefore, usually ignored in quantitative studies.

In LIS, both qualitative and quantitative are implacable because researchers in information science beginning to recognize that resorting to a single methodological paradigm in LIS research does not provide the understanding needed to design and maintain effective services.

PHILOSOPHICAL PERSPECTIVE OF RESEARCH METHODS

All research (either quantitative or qualitative) is based on some philosophical assumptions about what constitutes 'valid' research and which research methods are appropriate. While Guba and Lincoln (1994) suggest four underlying "paradigms" for research: positivism, post-positivism, critical theory, and constructivism, Orlikowski and Baroudi (1991) suggest three categories, based on the underlying research epistemology: positivist, interpretive and critical. This three-fold classification is discussed here.

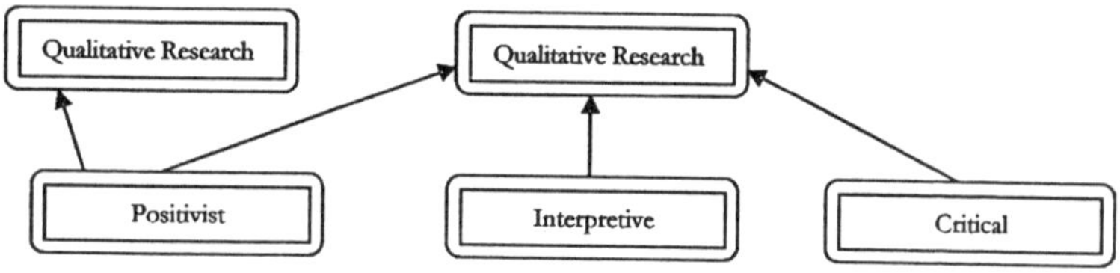

Positivist Research

Positivists generally assume that reality is objectively given and can be described by measurable properties which are independent of the observer (researcher) and his or her instruments. Positivist studies generally attempt to test theory, in an attempt to increase the predictive understanding of phenomena. In information science perspective, a research can be positivist, if there is evidence of formal propositions, quantifiable measures of variables, hypothesis testing, and the drawing of inferences about a phenomenon from the sample to a stated population.

Interpretive Research

Interpretive studies generally attempt to understand phenomena through the meanings that people assign to them and interpretive methods of research in IS are "aimed at producing an understanding of the context of the information system, and the process whereby the information system influences and is influenced by the context" (Walsham 1993, p. 4-5). Interpretive research does not predefine dependent and independent variables, but focuses on the full complexity of human sense making as the situation emerges (Kaplan and Maxwell, 1994).

Critical Research

Critical researchers assume that social reality is historically constituted and that it is produced and reproduced by people. Although people can consciously act to change their social and economic circumstances, critical researchers recognize that their ability to do so is constrained by various forms of social, cultural and political domination.

A research method is a strategy of inquiry which moves from the underlying philosophical assumptions to research design and data collection. Above mentioned are various philosophical perspectives of research. In the next we will be proceed with various research methods that are applied during various stages of research, irrespective qualitative and quantitative. Let's start with by methods in research design.

A. RESEARCH DESIGN METHODS

Action Research

Action research, sometimes called "practitioner research, is a systematic form of inquiry that is collective, collaborative, self-reflective, critical, and undertaken by the participants of the inquiry [McCutcheon, G. & Jung, B. (1990). Rapoport, (1970) explained that Action research aims to contribute both to the practical concerns of people in an immediate problematic situation and to the goals of social science by joint collaboration within a mutually acceptable ethical framework. The process begins with the development of questions, which may be answered by the collection of data. Action implies that the practitioner will be acting as the collector of data, the analyst, and the interpreter of results.

It has been accepted research method in applied fields such as organization development and education (e.g. study of Kemmis and McTaggart, 1988), in information science, however, a few exceptions have been noted (e.g. Baskerville and Wood-Harper (1996) in spite of the fact this research was for a long time largely ignored.

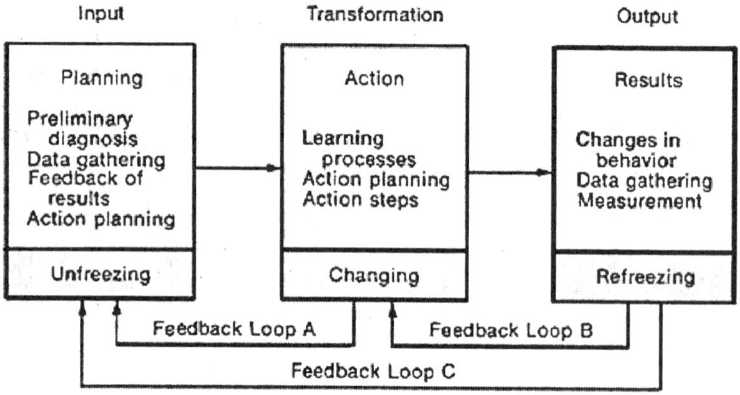

Source: Kurt Lewin, 1948, p. 202-3.

Case Study Research

This type of research is used to describe a unit of analysis (e.g. a case study of a particular organisation or to describe a research method. According to Yin (2002) case study investigates a contemporary phenomenon within its real-life context, especially when the boundaries between phenomenon and context are not clearly evident. the case study research method is particularly well-suited to IS research, since the object of our discipline is the study of information systems in organizations, and "interest has shifted to organizational rather than technical issues" (Benbasat et al. 1987). Case study research can be positivist, interpretive, or critical, depending upon the underlying philosophical assumptions of the researcher.

Ethnography

Ethnographic research comes from the discipline of social and cultural anthropology where an ethnographer is required to spend a significant amount of time in the field. Ethnographers immerse themselves in the lives of the people they study (Lewis 1985) and seek to place the phenomena studied in their social and cultural context. Ethnographic studies are ideal for exploratory projects where the objectives are initially undefined but become clearer as fieldwork progresses. Through ethnographic research, one can learn behavious, values and culture influence of product/service and how they make use of products and services. Ethnographers spend time in their customers' natural environments to study interactive behaviors and both spoken and unspoken needs.

In the area of the design and evaluation of information systems, some very interesting work is taking place in a collaborative fashion between ethnographers on the one hand, and designers, IS professionals, computer scientists and engineers on the other.

Grounded Theory

According to Martin and Turner (1986), grounded theory is "an inductive, theory discovery methodology that allows the researcher to develop a theoretical account of the general features of a topic while simultaneously grounding the account in empirical observations or data." The major difference between grounded theory and other methods is its specific approach to theory development - grounded theory suggests that there should be a continuous interplay between data collection and analysis. The phrase "grounded theory" refers to theory that is developed inductively from a corpus of data, and the resulting theory at least fits one dataset perfectly. The basic idea of the grounded theory approach is to read (and re-read) a textual database (the data do not have to be literally textual – they could be observations of behavior) and "discover" or label variables (called categories, concepts and properties) and their interrelationships. The ability to perceive variables and relationships is termed "theoretical sensitivity" and is affécted by a number of things including one's reading of the literature and one's use of techniques designed to enhance sensitivity.

Grounded theory approaches are becoming increasingly common in the IS research literature because the method is extremely useful in developing context-based, process-oriented descriptions and explanations of the phenomenon (see, for example, Orlikowski, 1993).

B. DATA COLLECTION METHODS

Over the years there has been a large amount of complex discussion and argument surrounding the qualitative versus quantitative inquiry. Different methodologies become popular at different social, political, historical and cultural times in our development, and, due to that it is fair to deal with various techniques, without particularly mentioning whether it is qualitative and quantitative. In information science perspective, there are many techniques used for collecting empirical data. The remaining parts are discussing some of them. Written data sources can include published and unpublished documents, company reports, memos, letters, reports, email messages, faxes, newspaper articles and so forth.

Questionnaires, Opinion Poll

The questionnaire is the most commonly used method of gathering information about use and users. A questionnaire consist a list of written questions that can be completed in one of two basic ways

Firstly, respondents could be asked to complete the

questionnaire with the researcher either by sending question to post-mail, email or by verbally responding to questions in the presence of the researcher. This variation is called a structured interview. In the present days there are one popular website, namely sourveymonkey.com which allow respondents to ask question by online to anyone who wants to response. This becomes one of the most popular methods of asking question in western countries, yet to successful in India. Although the two variations are similar, the difference between them is when we are concerned with protecting the respondent's anonymity then it might be more appropriate to use a postal questionnaire than a structured interview.

Questionnaires are restricted to two basic types of question:

Closed-ended (or "closed question") is a question for which a researcher provides a suitable list of responses (e.g. Yes / No). This produces mainly quantitative data.

Open-ended (or "open question") is a question where the researcher doesn't provide the respondent with a set answer from which to choose. Rather, the respondent is asked to answer "in their own words". This produces mainly **qualitative** data.

One of advantages of using questionnaires is questionnaires are a less expensive way to reach more people, including people at some distance. Depending upon the mode of distribution, this can be quickly done and data analysis can begin right away. Additionally, the questionnaire avoids interviewer bias, guiding, and cues that can impact the validity and reliability of the data collection. However, disadvantages includes the use of questionnaires for a variety of commercial purposes as well as for "real" research have created a situation in which response rates have fallen over time. A response rate between 20 and 30 percent is now considered to be a good one. Even after follow-ups, the response rate may still be low.

An opinion poll is a process to receive opinion from a particular sample. These are usually designed to explain the opinions of a population for a particular event by conducting a series of questions and then extrapolating generalities in ratio or within confidence intervals. Mass media like newspapers, television try to infer findings by gathering opinion in respect of various issues from their readers/ viewers. These are very popular method in present days.

Observation

Observation is one of the most common methods for qualitative data collection. Being a researcher one have to observe the characteristics of the population. There are two way to observe, either being a participant of the event or may involved indirectly. Participant observation requires that the researcher become a participant in the culture or context being observed. For example being a teacher/tutor to get real access to the pupils'/students' perspectives is a participatory observation techniques to evaluate students. On the other hand, without participate in examination, knowing psychological condition of examinee in examination process is non-participatory observation.

Interview

This method seeks to describe the meanings of central themes of the subjects. The main task in interviewing is to understand the meaning of what the interviewees say. It covers both a factual and a meaning level, though it is usually more difficult to interview on a meaning level. There are two types of interview: informal, conversational interview and closed, fixed-response interview. In former case no predetermined questions are asked, during the interview, while in close ended interviewees are asked the same questions and asked to choose answers from among the same set of alternatives. Interview can be conducted through written (including email) or through telephone.

Focus Group

According to Powell et al a focus group is a group of individuals selected and assembled by researchers to discuss and comment on, from personal experience, the topic that is the subject of the research. (1996: 499). The main purpose of focus group research is to draw upon respondents' attitudes, feelings, beliefs, experiences and reactions in a way in which would not be feasible using observation, one-to-one interviewing, or questionnaire surveys. The benefits of focus group research include gaining insights into people's shared understandings of everyday life and the ways in which individuals are influenced by others in a group situation. However, the problems arise when attempting to identify the individual view from the group view, as well as in the practical arrangements for conducting focus groups. The role of the moderator is very significant. Good levels of group leadership and interpersonal skill are required to moderate a group successfully. This types of research is very useful for new product development studies, positioning studies, habit and usage studies, packaging assessment, attitude studies, copy evaluation, promotional evaluation, employee attitude and motivation studies.

Survey method

Survey method is a non-experimental, descriptive research method and can be useful when a researcher wants to collect data on phenomena that cannot be directly observed (such as opinions on library services). Data are usually collected through the use of questionnaires, although sometimes researchers directly interview subjects. Surveys can use qualitative (e.g. ask open-ended questions) or quantitative (e.g. use forced-choice questions) measures. There are two basic types of surveys: cross-sectional surveys and longitudinal surveys. Cross-sectional surveys are used to gather information on a population at a single point in time, while longitudinal surveys gather data over a period of time. An example of a cross sectional survey would be a questionaire that collects data on how parents feel about use of social networking site by their child.

Surveys are used extensively in library and information science to assess attitudes and characteristics of a wide range of subjects, from the quality of user-system interfaces to library user reading habits. One criticism of library surveys is that they are often poorly designed and administered (Busha and Harter 1980), resulting in data that is that is not very accurate, but that is energetically quoted and used to make important decisions.

Discourse Analysis

Discourse Analysis is neither a qualitative nor a quantitative research methods, it is a manner of questioning the basic assumptions of quantitative and qualitative research methods. In fact, discourse analysis enable us to reveal the hidden motivations behind a text or behind the choice of a particular method of research to interpret that text. It enables researcher to access the ontological and epistemological assumptions behind a project. When we apply discourse analysis to the theory of Library Science, it would not argue for or against the validity and "truth" of a certain research method (qualitative or quantitative), statement, or value (i.e. the Library Bill of Rights, or policies concerning free speech). Rather, discourse analysis would focus on the existence and message of these texts and locate them within a historical and social context. Although, no technology or funds are necessary and authoritative discourse analysis, it does not provide definite answers; it is not a "hard" science, but an insight/knowledge based on continuous debate and argumentation.

Content Analysis

Bernard Berelson defined Content Analysis as "a

research technique for the objective, systematic, and quantitative description of manifest content of communications" (Berelson, 74). Content analysis is used to determine the presence of particular words, ideas, concepts, themes, phrases, characters, or sentences within texts or sets of texts and to quantify this presence in an objective manner. Present day content analysis is one of the most useful techniques in library science to develop semantic web, federated search and relevancy ranking of search results.

There are two general categories of content analysis: conceptual analysis and relational analysis. Conceptual analysis can be thought of as establishing the existence and frequency of concepts in a text. Relational analysis builds on conceptual analysis by examining the relationships among concepts in a text.

Historical Research

The process by which a researcher try to identify the background and growth of a chosen field of study or profession its organizational culture, current trends, and future possibilities, historical method is best suitable techniques to collect data. Both quantitative and qualitative variables can be used in the collection of historical data. In the field of library and information science, there are vast areas that may be considered for conducting historical research. For instances, a researcher may chose to answer questions about the development of various types of libraries in a country, the invasion and use of technology and the benefits/ problems it brings, the development of preservation methods, famous personalities in the field, library statistics, or geographical demographics and how they effect library distribution.

C. DATA ANALYSIS METHODS

Content Analysis

Content Analysis is used by social scientists (and other social scientists) to explore the content of various media (books, journals, web resources etc.) in order to discover how particular issues are presented. At its most basic, content analysis is a statistical exercise that involves categorising some aspect or quality of people's behaviour and counting the number of times such behaviour appears (a simple content analysis might involve counting the number of minutes men and women appear on library in a Particular span of time). In this way, content analysis helps us to build-up a picture of the patterns of behaviour that underlie (and are usually hidden from view) the social interaction portrayed in the media. It produces highly reliable (usually quantitative) data. Content Analyses are usually easy to repeat ("replicate"). Complex forms of social interaction can be quantified using a standardised framework (the content analysis grid) that can be applied across a wide range of media. It can present an objective account of events, themes, issues and so forth that may not be immediately apparent to a reader, viewer or general consumer.

Overall, it is an unobtrusive method - it doesn't involve the researcher interacting with the people / things being studied. The researcher cannot, therefore, influence the behaviour of the people being studied. However the major drawbacks of this method can be explained as this method may not be as objective as it claims since the researcher must select and record data accurately. In some instances (such as a television programme) the researcher must make choices about how to interpret particular forms of behaviour (for example, when a character is acting aggressively). For example, the researcher decides things like: what categories will be used and whether or not everyone be put neatly into a particular category). By attempting to quantify behaviour (such as the relationship between people), this method may not tell us very much about the quality of people's relationships.

Statistical Analysis

In order to evaluate collected data, the information science professional applied numerous statistical techniques. Before the world wide web, there are few number of techniques available. With the presence of web, this is one of the most prolific areas in information science where wide number of new research method has developed. Followings are some of the important techniques.

a. Before the World Wide Web : Historically, various quantitative techniques or statistical studies are widely used for measuring impact of scientific work. Dr. S.R. Ranganathan first coined the term 'Librametry' (Gopinath, 1992) [some times 'Librarmetrics'] at the Aslib conference in Leamington Spa in 1948. After Ranganathan's achievement, there were hardly any researches in this area for the next twenty years. A. Prichard in 1969 used the term 'Bibliometrics' as a redevelopment of the term 'Statistical Bibliography' (this term was coined by Hulme in 1923). Bibliometrics is defined as "the study of quantitative aspects of the production, dissemination and use of recorded information". Borgman and Funer (2002) contend, "bibliometrics is now an accepted method in sociology of science" which "can be applied to a border array of behaviour and to a border array of content than in the past". Overall, bibliometrics is a tool by which the state of science and technology can be observed through the trace of communication in science-technology system, most notably the published papers in refereed journals. Originally, it is means for situating a country in relation to world, and institution in relation to country (Heimeriks and Besselaav, 2002).

In late 1960s, Vassily V. Nalimov of Russia had coined the term 'Scientometrics' (Hood, *2001)* as all quantitative aspects of studies in the field of science of science, communication in science and science policy. Tague-Sutcliffe (1992) pointed "Scientometrics" as "the study of quantitative aspect of science as a discipline or economic activity".

In 1989, Jean Tague being organizer of the conference "*Second International Conference on Bibliometrics, Scientometrics and Informetrics*" first introduce a extended term of bibliometrics. Interestingly, during the same conference editor Leo Egghe and Ronald Rosseau strongly endorse the use of term 'Informetrics' (Informetrics 89/90). According to Tague-Sutcliffe (1992), informatics is "the study of the quantitative aspects of information in any form, not just records or bibliographies and in any social group, not just scientists".

The route from Librametry/Librametrics via bibliometrics to Scientometrics and Informetrics has revealed that the emergence and the disappearance of these terms is only partly related to their scientific content and common aspects (overlapping) to other contents, social process in scientific communities are also reflected (Kretschmer and Thelwall, 2004).

b. After the World Wide Web : With the advent of Web and to perform Web based statistics, the term 'Webometrics' (Abraham, 1996) came into existence. According to Bjornebron and Ingwersen, Webometrics is "the study of the quantitative aspects of the construction and use of information resources, structure and technologies on the WWW drawing on bibliometrics and informetric approaches" (Bjornebron & Ingwersen, 2001). The main four areas of webometric research are: (a) Web page content analysis; (b) Web link structure analysis; (c) Web usage analysis (by exploiting log file of users' searching and browsing behaviour); and (d) Web technology analysis (including search engine performance) (Bjorneborn, 2004; Thelwall, 2005).

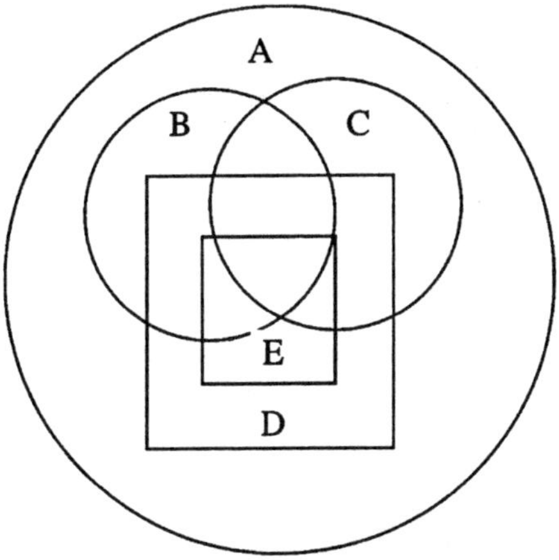

A – Informetrics,

B – Bibliometrics,

C – Scientometrics,

D – Cybermetrics,

E - Webometrics

Fig. 1 : Relation between the Infor- / biblio- / sciento- / cyber - / webo-metrics.

The term Cybermetrics is also used in parallel with Webometrics these days to perform statistical analyse of electronic communications. Bjorneborn and Ingwersen pointed cybermetrics as "the study of the quantitative aspects of construction and use of information resources, structures and technologies on the whole Internet, drawing on bibliometrics and informetrics approaches".

During mid 1990s a range of new terms has emerged in this field as coined by various scientists. They are 'netometrics' (Bossy, 1995), 'Webometry' (Abraham, 1996), 'internetometrics' (Almid & Ingwersen, 1996) 'Webomterics' (Almid & Ingwersen, 1997) 'Web bibliometry' (Chakravarti *et al.* 2002). Webomterics and cybermetrics often used synonyms are two most widely adopted term among research communities.

Traditional Techniques in Bibliometric Researches

One of the main areas in bibliometric research concerns

Table 1 : Comparison of the applications of the distinct quantitative methods:

Typology	Bibliometrics	Scientometrics	Informetrics	Webometrics
Objects of study	Books, documents, magazines, articles, authors, users	Any discipline, subjects, areas, fields	Words, documents, databases	Citation, WWW, link, Search engines
Variable	Number of loans (circulation) and of citations, frequency of citation of words, extension of phrases etc.	Factors that differentiate one discipline withsub-disciplines. Journals, authors documents. As scientists if communicate.	It differs from the Scientometrics in the intention of variable; for example, to measure the recovery, relevance, the revocation etc.	Number of Web pages and number of Web citations, number of downloads.
Methods	Ranking, frequency, distribution.	Analysis of set of correspondence.	Model vector-space, Boolean models of recovery, probabilistic models; language of processing etc.	WIF, density of link, sitations (citation to web), strategy of search, Web citation analysis
Objectives	To place resources: time, money etc.	To identify domain of interest, where subjects are concentrated. To underst and leading scientists and their area of interests.	To improve the efficiency of the recovery.	To evaluate the success of a sites, to detect presence of individuals, institutions and researchers in the net and to improve efficiency of the search engines use in research
Tools	Tradition quantitative Techniques	Tradition quantitative Techniques	Tradition quantitative Techniques	Tradition quantitative Techniques as well as Search Engines

the application of bibliometrics laws. The three most commonly used laws in bibliomterics are: Lotka's Law of Scientific Productivity (Lotka, 1926), Bradford's Law of Scattering of literature on a particular topic over different journals or to identify core journal of a subject (Bradford, 1934); and Zipf's Law of word occurrence in text (Zipf, 1949).

Lotka's Law

Lotka's Law describes the frequency of publication by authors in a given field. Lotka's Law describes the frequency of publication by author in a given field. It states "if x authors contribute one paper each to a field, the number of contributing two papers should be approximately $x/2^2$ and the number producing three papers should be $x/3^2$ and so on This means that out of all the authors in a given field, 60 percent will have just one publication, and 15 percent will have two publications ($1/2^2$ times .60). 7 percent of authors will have three publications ($1/3^2$ times .60), and so on. According to Lotka's Law of scientific productivity, only six percent of the authors in a field will produce more than 10 articles. Lotka's Law, when applied to large bodies of literature over a fairly long period of time, can be accurate in general, but not statistically exact. It is often used to estimate the frequency with which authors will appear in an online catalog (Potter 1988).

Bradford's Law

Bradford proposed the Law of Scattering, which states "if scientific journals are arranged in order of decreasing productivity of articles in a given subject, they may be divided in a nucleus of periodicals more particularly devoted to the subject and several other groups of zones containing the same number of articles as the nucleus" Bradford's Law serves as a general guideline to librarians in determining the number of core journals in any given field. It states that journals in a single field can be divided into three parts, each containing the same number of articles: 1) a core of journals on the subject, relatively few in number, that produces approximately one-third of all the articles, 2) a second zone, containing the same number of articles as the first, but a greater number of journals, and 3) a third zone, containing the same number of articles as the second, but a still greater number of journals. The mathematical relationship of the number of journals in the core to the first zone is a constant n and to the second zone the relationship is n^2. Bradford expressed this relationship as $1:n:n^2$. Bradford formulated his law after studying a bibliography of geophysics, covering 326 journals in the field. He discovered that 9 journals contained 429 articles, 59 contained 499 articles, and 258 contained 404 articles. So it took 9 journals to contribute one-third of the articles, 5 times 9, or 45, to produce the next third, and 5 times 5 times 9, or 225, to produce the last third. As may be seen, Bradford's Law is not statistically accurate, strictly speaking. But it is still commonly used as a general rule of thumb (Potter 1988).

Zipf's Law

Zipf's Law is often used to predict the frequency of words within a text. Zipf's Laws of word occurrence states "if words are ranked according to their frequency of occurrence (f), the nth ranking word will appear approximately k/n times where k is a constant, or f(n)=k/n Zipf illustrated his law with an analysis of James Joyce's *Ulysses*. "He showed that the tenth most frequent word occurred 2,653 times, the hundredth most frequent word occurred 265 times, the two hundredth word occurred 133 times, and so on. Zipf found, then that the rank of the word multiplied by the frequency of the word equals a constant that is approximately 26,500" (Potter 1988). Zipf's Law, again, is not statistically perfect, but it is very useful for indexers.

Another major area of bibliometric research uses

various methods of citation analysis in order to establish relationships between authors or their work. Here is a definition of citation analysis, and definitions of co-citation coupling and bibliographic coupling, which are specific kinds of citation analysis.

Citation Analysis

When one author cites another author, a relationship is established. Citation analysis uses citations in scholarly works to establish links. Many different links can be ascertained, such as links between authors, between scholarly works, between journals, between fields, or even between countries. Citations both from and to a certain document may be studied. One very common use of citation analysis is to determine the impact of a single author on a given field by counting the number of times the author has been cited by others. One possible drawback of this approach is that authors may be citing the single author in a negative context (saying that the author doesn't know what s/he's talking about, for instance) (Osareh 1996).

Co-citation Coupling

Co-citation coupling is a method used to establish a subject similarity between two documents. If papers A and B are both cited by paper C, they may be said to be related to one another, even though they don't directly cite each other. If papers A and B are both cited by many other papers, they have a stronger relationship. The more papers they are cited by, the stronger their relationship is.

Bibliographic Coupling

Bibliographic coupling operates on a similar principle, but in a way it is the mirror image of co-citation coupling. Bibliographic coupling links two papers that cite the same articles, so that if papers A and B both cite paper C, they may be said to be related, even though they don't directly cite each other. The more papers they both cite, the stronger their relationship is.

Similarly, for Web, a number of power laws have also been developed, for example, distribution of TLD (top level domain) on a given topic (Rousseau, 1997) or links per Web site (Albert, Jeong & Baranasi, 1999; Adamic & Huberman, 2000).

Another important area on bibliometric research uses various methods of citation analysis in order to establish relationship between authors and works. Citation analysis uses citation in scholarly works to establish links (Garfield, 1972). Many different links can be ascertained, such as between authors, between scholarly works, between journals, between fields, or even between countries. One very common use of citation analysis is to determine the impact of a single author on a given field by counting the number of times the author has been cited by others. Impact factor, i.e. mean citedness, can be calculated using either a synchronous or a diachronous approach, and with different time windows for publication and citation data. The term "synchronous" refers to the fact that citations used for the calculation were all received in the same year. Whereas, the term "diachronous" refers to the fact that the data used to calculate it derive from a number of different years with a starting point somewhere in the past and encompassing subsequent years. Thus the diachronous impact factor can be said to reflect the development over time (Ingrwersen *et al.*, 2001).

Thomson ISI's Journal Citation Report (JCR) applies synchronous technique to measure impact of journals as well as work of any author. Generally speaking, the JCR is a statistical data set providing information on how often journals are cited, how many items are published, and how often, on average, each item is cited. It also reports those source journals responsible for the references of each journal, the number of references each journal has published and the distribution of these references in time.

Relationship between Bibliometrics and Webometrics

Webometrics is a concept which deals with Web based phenomena, using methods originally designed for bibliometric analysis of scientific journal article citation pattern. The hope that Web links could be used to provide information similar to that extracted from journal citations has been a key factor in stimulating much Webometrics research (Borgman & Furner, 2002; Cronin, 2001; Davenport & Cronin, 2000, Thelwall, 2002). The co-citation coupling as used to establish subject similarities between two documents in print documents are also visualized in two Web documents. These similarities of citation and links can be visualized in following diagram.

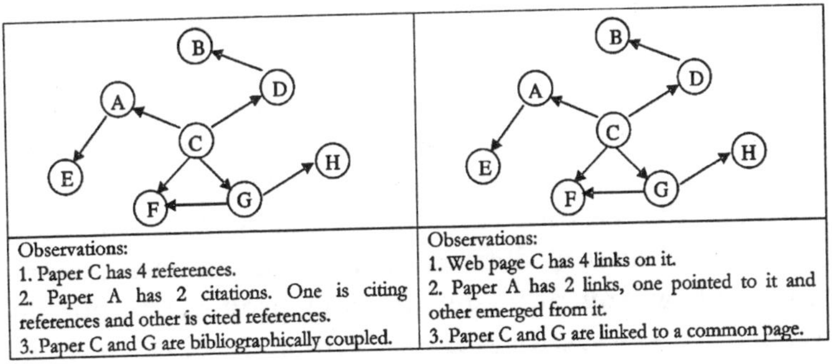

Fig. 2 : Diagram Represents Functional Relation between Citation and Link

Terminology being followed by bibliometrics and webometrics is to a large extent similar. The term 'citation index' used in print based journals is similar to 'Web Citation Index' in Web. The print based scientometrics indicators 'Journal Impact Factor' has also applied to the e-journals and Prof. Ingwersen termed it as Web Impact Factor (WIF)[1]. There are some structural similarities between journal citations with Web links. In print based journals citation analysis is measured by counting number of citations of a journals has received in a given time. In Web, citations can be calculated by counting hyperlinks[2] or specifically by counting inlinks[3]. Additionally, in Web authors also use outlinks[4] selflinks[5] in their scholarly articles. It is easy to calculate outlinks and selflinks of a scholarly article but it is quite difficult to measure the inlinks of the same. In this regard search engines serve as a unique tool to excavate the linking pattern of any page or site or, say, any scholarly article.

Tools for Webometric Researches – Search Engine

The term 'Web Search Engine' has different meanings in different contexts. *Oxford English Dictionary* (2002, online) defines 'search engine' as "a piece of hardware or software designed for searching, *esp.* a program that searches for and identifies items in a database that correspond to one or more keywords specified by the user; *spec.* such a program used to search for information available over the Internet, using its own previously compiled database of Internet files and documents". The search engines may be deployed for textual search of the Web or for non-textual search. Harrod's *Librarians' Glossary* defines search engine as software produced by any publisher or data provider to enable detailed access – via, for example, author, title, keyword – to their information (e.g. Google Scholar). On the World Wide Web, third party search engines are available for searching the whole Web, and these rely on robots (robot is a tool which identifies and fetches Web pages, usually for indexing, by traversing the Web link graph from a set of starting point) that traverses the Web following links between pages and copying relevant information to create a database which is then indexed to form searchable keywords" (Prytherch, 2000). Oppenheim, *et al.* (2000) classified search engines into four categories: robot (tool that automatically collects and indexes documents, e.g. Google, Altavista), directories (that rely mainly on human to identify and categories resources, e.g. Yahoo), meta-search engines (that does not crawl individual site rather collect results of various search engines and display them, e.g. Metacrawler, Vivisimo) and software tools (software for searching the Web that is installed in the user's computer, e.g. Copernic). And they noted that others also include geography-specified and subject-specified search tools (e.g. SOSIG, BUBUL, Infolibrarian etc. in our field).

Working of Crawler Based Search Engine

A crawler based search engine is made up of three major parts: the crawler, the indexer and the query engine (Brin & Page, 1998). The job of crawler is to collect data by visiting URLs of the Web. The crawling policy i.e. which page to visit, in which order and how often, is different in different search engines. These differing policies make search engines different from one other in terms of size, coverage and freshness. Revisiting Web pages are necessary for search engines as Web undergoes changes from time to time. The job of an indexer is to extract words from the pages forwarded to it by crawlers, and to turn each document into a list of words. This list of words is then inverted into 'inverted index' or 'inverted file', and it facilitates the work of the query engines. The search engines may also decide to save other information about documents such as metadata describing their contents, URLs of page linking to this page. The query engine is responsible for receiving request and providing answers to the users. The query engines consult the inverted file and the database of additional information to match the query. The capability to handle various advanced techniques such as phrase search, Boolean expression, domain specific search, time specific search etc. of various search engines allow it to display more specified results. But before display search engines rank the list of results, with most relevant results (as their policy determines) displayed at the top of the list. Here various ranking algorithms, including the classical one based on similarity between the documents and the query (a function of the frequency of the search terms in the document, and the rarity of the search terms in the database), the location of search terms in the documents (terms in title or headers receive more weight) and algorithms that are applicable to hypertext system (e.g. link analysis, most frequency clicked Web pages, most downloaded Web pages etc.) are used for ranking pages. Each search engine uses different secret techniques to compute the ranks. In addition to this some search engines provide refined search, suggested search terms, groups, similar pages, cache etc. which make them different from the others.

Application of Search Engine in Webometric Research

Commonly search engines are widely used to locate relevant information from the sea of information World Wide Web. The efficiency and popularity of search engines basically depend upon how much information it can excavate from the Web against a query of user. The quantity as well as quality issues are very important for measuring efficiency of search engines. The notion of quality is based on the number of links pointing to a page and it is measured by applying various mathematical theories of random rinks. At present search engines are used widely in various webometric research. The main areas are: (a). Link Analysis; (b) Web/URL Analysis; and (c) Web Citation analysis

Link Analysis

Web consists of number of pages interconnected with hyperlinks. These hyperlinks are inserted not for navigational purposes, but to point to pages with similar and relevant contents. These hyperlinks are generally termed as 'outlink' of the page. Total number of such pages can be measured by using some inbuilt command [site:page address] of search engines. Using this command along with some advanced command one can extract the total page, file format etc. of the whole site. They add structure to the collection and it is important to explore the ways these links are employed for characterization of the Web. These interconnected structures probably help the search engines rank the pages.

Web/URL Analysis

Web/URL analysis is different from link analysis because, by this analysis it is possible to know how many pages are inlinked towards the particular Web page. These links are termed as 'inlink' to a page. At present, most of the search engines [e.g. Altavista, Google, AlltheWeb etc.] provide some in-built command [link:page address] to extract inlink towards a particular Web page but not the whole Web site. Some of the search engines [Microsoft based MSN], however, claim that they have a different string command to excavate total inlinked page of whole Web site [linkdomain:web address]. But it is always recommended to use these results with caution because no search engines is able to fetch all pages of the Web and most of the search engines display duplicate results to attract user towards their coverage.

Web Citation Analysis

Previously, Web link analysis was assumed as successor of citation analysis. But later it was observed that a Web page can be linked (inlinks) from different Web sites or different Web contents. Inlinks may come from journal articles, conference papers, research reports etc., as also from author's personal Web sites, Web CVs, or simply from a Web page. In terms of citation analysis it is not fair to consider all such inlinks for scholarly impact measurement. So, there is need to compare inlinks for formal reasons from inlinks for informal reasons. Google and AltaVista are two widely used tools for measuring Web links. However, the newly emerged Google Scholar mostly extracts Web citations from scholarly sources than less-scholarly sources. As mentioned on the Web site of Google "Google Scholar has boosted the worldwide visibility and accessibility of [the] content. [They] work with publishers of scholarly information to index peer-reviewed papers, theses, preprints, abstracts, and technical reports from all disciplines of research and make them searchable on Google and Google Scholar". In addition, Google scholar's "Cited by", "Group of" or "Related sites" are widely used presently for statistical analysis of the Web results.

CONCLUSION

The field off webometrics, a new research area that has grown out of bibliometrics, has established an important independent domain in quantitative research. In the last few years there has been wide applicability of webometric research for Web Impact Assessment, Link Analysis, Blog Searching, Tracking User Actions Online etc. However, one of the major breakthrough is the application of search engines for measuring impact of web content. In order to measure the Impact factor, h-index, researchers are using Google Scholars, Yahoo Beta etc. as a supplement tool for impact measurement.

REFERENCES

Abraham, R.H. (1996). *Webometry: Measuring the complexity of the World Wide Web*, Santa Cruz, CA. Visual Math Institute. University of California at Santa Cruz. Available at: http://www.ralph-abrahamorg/vita/red.wood/vienna.html

Adamic, L.A. & Huberman, B.A (2000). Power-law distribution of the World Wide Web, *Science*, 287, 2115-2116.

Albert, R., Jeong, H., & Barabasi, A-L. (1999) Diameter of the World-Wide Web, *Nature*, 401(9), 130-131.

Almind, T.C. & Ingwersen, P. (1997). Informetric analysis on the World Wide Web : methodological approach to "Webometrics", *Journal of Documentation*, 53(4), 404-426.

Bardford, S.C. (1934). Sources of information of specific subjects, *Engineering*, 137, 85-6.

Baskerville, R. and T. Wood-Harper (1996). A critical Perspective on Action Research as Method for Information Systems Research. *Journal of Information Technology*, 11, 235-246.

Benbasat, I., Goldstein, D.K. and Mead, M. (1987). The case research strategy in studies of information system. *MIS Quarterly*, 11(3), 369-386.

Berelson, Bernard (1952). *Content Analysis in Communication Research*. New York: Free Press.

Bjorneborn, L., & Ingwersen, P. (2001). Perspectives of webometrics, *Scientometrics*, 50(1), 65-82.

Bjorneborn, L. (2004). *Small-world link structure across an academic Web space: A library and information science approach*, Unpublished Doctoral Dissertation. Royal School of Library and Information Science, Copenhagen, Denmark.

Borgman, C.L., & Furner, J. (2002). Scholarly communication and bibliometrics, *Annual Review of Information Science and Technology*, 36, pp. 3-72

Bossy, M.J. (1995). *The last of the little: "Netometrics"*, Available at: http://biblio-fr.info.uni.caen.fr/ bnum/je;ec/Solaris/do2/ 2boddy.html

Brin, S., & Page, L. (1998). *The anatomy of a large scale hypertextual Web search engine*, Computer Networks and ISDN Systems, 30(1-7), 107-117.

Burrell, Gibson and Morgan, Gareth (1979). *Sociological paradigms and organisational analysis: elements of the sociology of corporate life*, London: Heinemann.

Busha, Charles H., and Stephen P. Harter (1980). *Research Methods in Librarianship: Techniques and Interpretation*. Orlando, FL: Academic Press, Inc.

Chakrabarti, S., Joshi, M.M., Punera, K. & Pennock, D.M. (2002). *The structure of broad topics on the Web*, Proceedings of the

WWW2002 conference. Available at: http://www.2002.org/CDROM/refereed/338

Cronin, B. (2001). Bibliometrics and beyond: Some thoughts on Web-based citation analysis, *Journal of Information Science,* 27(1), 1-7.

Cronin, B., Snyder, H., Rosenbaum, R., Martinson, A., & Callahau, E. (1998)., Invoked on the Web, *Journal of the American Society for Information Science and Technology,* 49(14), 1319-1328.

Devenport, E., & Cronin, B. (2000). *The citation network as a prototype for representing trust in virtual environments.* In: B. Cronin & H.N.B. Atkins (Eds.), *The use of knowledge: A festschrift in honour of Eugene Garfield,* pp. 517-534. Medford, N.J.: Information Today Inc.

Egghe, L. (2000). New informetric aspects of the internet: Some reflection many problems, *Journal of Information Science,* 26(5), 329-335.

Garfield, E.E. (1972). Citation analysis as a tool in journal evaluation. *Science,* 178, 471-479.

Glanzel, W. (2003). *On some principle differences between citations and sitation links: A methodological and mathematical approach.* Available at: http://www.niwi.knaw.nl/nerdi/lectures/glanzel.pdf

Gopinath, M.A. (1992). *Shiyali Ramamrita Ranganathan: A profile in relation to librametry.* In: I.K. Ravichandra Rao (Ed.), *Informetrics* 91 (pp.9-16). Bangalore: Sarda Ranganathan Endowment of Library and Information Management.

Guba, E.G. & Lincoln, Y.S. (1994). Competiting Paradigms in Qualitative Research. In Denzin, N.K. & Lincoln, Y.S. (eds) *Handbook of Qualitative Research.* London: Sage, pp. 105-117.

Harter, S., & Ford, C. (2000). Web based analysis of e-journals impact: Approaches, problems and issues, *Journal of the American Society for Information Science and Technology,* 51(3), 1159-1176.

Heimeriks, G. & van den Besselaar, P. (2002). *State of the art in bibliometrics and Webometrics,* Universiteit van Amsterdam, pp. 3.

Hood, W.W. (2001). The literature of bibliometrics, scientometrics, and informetrics, *Scientometrics*, 52(2), 291-314

Hulme, E.W. (1923). *Statistical bibliography in relation to the growth of modern civilization*, London: Gradton.

Ingwersen, P. (1998). The calculation of Web Impact Factors, *Journal of Documentation*, 54(2), 236-243.

Ingwersen, P., Larsen, B.,; Rousseau, R., & Russell, J. (2001). The publication citation-matrix and its derived quantities, *Chinese Science Bulletin*, 46(6), 524-528.

Kaplan, B. and Maxwell, J. A. (1994). Qualitative Research Methods for Evaluating Computer Information Systems. In *Evaluating Health Care Information Systems: Methods and Applications* Anderson, J. G., Aydin, C. E. and Jay, S. J.(Eds). 45-68.Sage publications, Thousand Oaks CA.

Kemmis S. & McTaggert R. (1988). The Action Research Reader. Geenlog, Deakin University Press.

Kim, H.J. (2000). Motivation for hyperlinking in scholarly article: A quantitative study, *Journal of the American Society for Information Science and Technology*, 51(10), 887-899.

Kretschmer, H. and Thelwall, M. (2004), From Librametrics to Webometrics. *Journal of Information management*, 1(1), 1-7.

Larson, R.R. (1996). *Bibliometrics and the World Wide Web: An exploratory analysis of the intellectual structure of the cyberspace*. (pp. 71-83). Proceeding of the 59th Annual Meetings of the American Society for Information Science. Available at: https://sherlock.sims.berkeley.edu/asis96/asis96.html

Lewis, I.M. (1985). *Social Anthropology in Perspective*. Cambridge University Press: Cambridge.

Lotka, A.J. (1926). The frequency distribution of scientific productivity. *Journal of Washington Academy of Science*, 16, 317.

Martin, P.Y. and Turner, B.A. (1986). Grounded Theory and Organizational Research. *The Journal of Applied Behavioral Science*, 22 (2), 141-157.

McCutcheon G. & Jung, B. (1990). *Alternative perspectives on Action Research. Theory into practice*. 24, 144-151.

Myers, M. D. (1997). Qualitative Research in Information Systems,"

MIS Quarterly, 21(2), 241-242.

Oppenheim, C., Morris, A., ; McKnight, C. & Lowley, S. (2000). The evaluation of WWW search engines, *Journal of Documentation*, 56(2), 190-211.

Orlikowski, W.J. and J.J. Baroudi (1991). Studying Information Technology in Organizations: Research approaches and assumptions. *Information Systems Research*, (2), 1-28.

Osareh, Farideh (1996). Bibliometrics, Citation Analysis and Co-Citation Analysis: A Review of Literature I. *Libri* 46 (September), 149-158.

Oxford English Dictionary Online (2002). *Search engine*, Available at: http://disctionary.oed.com/entrance.dtl

Potter, William Gray. (1988). Of Making Many Books There is No End: Bibliometrics and Libraries, *The Journal of Academic Librarianship* 14 (September), 238a-238c.

Powell R.A., Single, H.M.; and Lloyd, K.R. (1996). Focus groups in mental health research: enhancing the validity of user and provider questionnaires', *International Journal of Social Psychology*, 42 (3), 193-206.

Prytherch, R. (2000)(ed.). *Search engines. In:* Harrod's librarians' glossary. 9th ed. Aldershot, UK, Gower.

Rapoport R.N. (1970). Three dilemmas of Action Research. *Human Relations*. 23 (6), 499.

Rousseau, R. (1997). Sitations: An exploratory study. *Cybermetrics* 1(1). Available at: http://www.cindoc.csic.es/cybermetrics/articles/v1i1p1.html

Lewin, K. (1948) *Resolving social conflicts; selected papers on group dynamics.* Gertrude W. Lewin (ed.). New York: Harper & Row.

Smith, A.G. (1999). A tale of the two Web space: Comparing sites using Web Impact Factor. *Journal of Documentation*, 55(5), 577-592.

Tague-Sutcliffe, J. (1992). An introduction to informetrics. *Information Processing and Management*, 28(1), 1-3.

Thelwall, M. (2002). Methodologies for crawler based Web surveys. *Internet Research: Electronic Networking Applications and Policy*,

12(2), 24-138.

Thelwall, M. (2005). Link analysis: An information science approach. (pp.115). Amsterdam: Elsevier.

Vaughan, L., & Hysen, K. (2002). Relationship between links to journal Web sites and impact factor, *Aslib Proceedings: New Information Perspectives,* 54(6). 356-362.

Vaughan, L., & Shaw, D. (2003). Bibliographic and Web citation: What is difference? *Journal of the American Society for Information Science and Technology,* 54(14), 1313-1322.

Vaughan, L., & Shaw, D. (2005). Web citation data for impact measurement: A comparison of four science disciplines, *Journal of the American Society for Information Science and Technology,* 56(10), 1075-1087.

Vaughan, L., & Thelwall, M. (2003). Scholarly use of the Web: What are the key inducer of links to journal Web sites? *Journal of the American Society for Information Science and Technology,* 54(1), 29-38.

Walsham, G. (1993) *Interpreting Information Systems in Organizations* (Wiley, Chichester).

Wilson, T.D. (2002). Information Science and Research methods. Available at: http://eprints.whiterose.ac.uk/ 8055/

Yin, R. (2002). *Applications of case study research. Vol. 6,* 2nd ed. Thousand Oaks, CA: Sage Publications.

Zipf, G.K. (1949). *Human behaviour and the principles of least effort: An introduction to human ecology.* Cambridge Mass.: Mass Addison-Wesely. p. 573.

10
Information Society

"Information has become a talisman, a symbol of political potency and economic prosperity" - **William J. Martin**

It is undoubtedly state that information is always important for any society in any social existence. But the role of information and its degree of importance differed. With the evolution of the social order to a "post-industrial" society (Bell, 1976), or "post-capitalist" society (Drucker, 1993), or what we now commonly also call "information society," knowledge and information is assuming an increasing central role in every aspect of life. The primary aim of this chapter is to synthesize the essential facts and ideas regarding the information society. Firstly, we defined the concepts of "information" and "society" individually, and then examined what happens if we join the two terms. Finally, we examined how the society is transformed towards a new defined society. Since the subject of our interest is often identified with information and communication networks, and primarily with the Internet, our most significant task was to explain how these tool lead towards change in rational basis.

CONCEPTUAL BACKGROUND

Last few years world has witness a greater focus on the 'information society' than ever before. Everyone has his or her more or less well formed opinion about the information society, most of these opinions are fed by the discourses on information society and the Internet presented in the media. The information society not only differs from the Internet but also exceeds it. The Internet is only one of its significant features and techniques in such a society. Information society, in accordance with Castells' theory is the new mode of human existence where the organized production, storage, retrieval, and utilization of information play a central role. New structural elements and networks appear through which a certain "network society" is being created accompanied by appropriate institutions that are transformations of those already existing. As a result of this, on the macro level, politics, economics, and culture are reformulated, as are the institutions of the mezzo level and at the micro level, families and individuals experience similar changes (Castells, 1996: 13-18).

"Information society" - as the term appears straightforward, it is enough to understand the meaning conveyed by its two component parts: Information and Society. "Information" indicates a certain attribute of society where information as such plays a crucial role that transforms this particular society whose difference from others rests in its quality of, and access to information. Before we immerse ourselves in the exploration of the concept itself, let us focus on the meaning of the two components separately.

Information

Over the last few years, the concept of information, as it appears commonly, has expanded. This is mainly because we live in an information-centred world and because of the penetration of communication related technologies. In the industrially developed societies information has become something essential, a central, indispensable component of our society. From previous chapter we learnt that the term Information is relatively complex to define. Our intention over here, however, is primarily to understand the connotation of the term information in 'information society'. *The American Heritage Dictionary of the English Language* distinguishes seven different meanings of "information".

1. "Knowledge derived from study, experience, or instruction.
2. Knowledge of specific events or situations that has been gathered or received by communication; intelligence or news.
3. A collection of facts or data: *statistical information.*
4. The act of informing or the condition of being informed; communication of knowledge.
5. In *Computer Science* approach, it is processed, stored, or transmitted data.
6. A numerical measure of the uncertainty of an experimental outcome.
7. In context of *Law*, a formal accusation of a crime made by a public officer rather than by grand jury indictment."

With the exception of the field-specific meanings we can conclude that "information" is an expression related to: experience, the communication of knowledge and experience, data, knowledge, learning, communication, and news. In certain cases "information" appears to be identical with these concepts (e.g. experience, data, knowledge, intelligence), in other cases it is the subject of them (e.g. instruction, learning, communication).

Michael Buckland sums up the conceptual interrelations in a chart in the introduction of his work on information systems:

	Intangible	*Tangible*
Entity	Information-as-knowledge Knowledge	Information-as-thing Data, document, recorded knowledge
Process	Information-as-process Becoming informed	Information Processing Data processing, document processing, knowledge engineering

Source: Buckland, 1991: 6

Information-as-knowledge is exclusively subjective, it is linked to one particular person and gains its meaning in one particular context. As an entity, it is intangible but it can be communicated and also shared with others. *Information-as-thing* exists similarly to knowledge, yet it is recorded hence it is tangible; data also belongs here, that is recorded knowledge, since its employment requires the recognition of a certain context i.e. the structure of data recording, without which data could not be decoded.

The third group of information-exchange called *information-as-process* is essentially equal to the process of *becoming informed,* consequently, it links information-as-thing with information-as-knowledge. However, it can join two information-as-knowledge (*the process of cogitation)* or two information-as-thing entities *(data processing),* as well.

On analysing "information" one has to examine these groups and their components: knowledge, communication, data, information processing, thought, and other concepts of data processing.

Society

Defining "society" is apparently a much more simple task to accomplish, although it is problematic to define what we call society and what its relationship might be to a geographic unit, a nation, a language, a culture, the state and statehood. The Collins Dictionary of Sociology defines "society" as follows:

1. The totality of human relationships.
2. Any human group that perpetuates itself more or less linked to one specific geographical region, holding its own *institutions* and *culture;* both tribes and nation states in the modern sense belong to this category.

The most recent sociological trend shows, society as a basic concept may no longer be the key to getting to know our world since the examination of single societies may divert our attention from other interactions taking place between and beyond societies such as multi-lateralization or globalisation.

Information Society

Depending our understanding of the two terms, we may explain information society as a society in which information and related phenomena (knowledge, communication, data, information processing, thought, and data processing) gain unprecedented significance. Information is an indispensable pillar for the proper functioning of any society and social subsystem; it has played an active part in the process of every social formation, and in shaping industrial and agricultural societies historically, it is important element to change the society.

Alvin Toffler in his famous book *The Third Wave* identifies the three important revolution which causes significant change of our society: The first wave was associated with agricultural revolution, second wave with industrial revolution whereas, the third wave was associated with information revolution. This typology is identical with the typology used by Tadao Umesao, who divided the economy into *endodermal* (agriculture, fishing), *mesodermal* (transportation, heavy industry) and *ectodermal* (information, communication, training) sectors. Let us see some of the well known definition of information society

INFORMATION SOCIETY - "DEFINITIONS"

There is currently no universally accepted concept of what exactly can be termed information society and what shall rather not so be termed. However, following are some of the concept enunciate by various philosopher in context of information society as:

- A society that organises itself around knowledge in the interest of social control, and the management of innovation and change... *(Daniel Bell)*
- A new type of society, where the possession of information (and not material wealth) is the driving force behind its transformation and development [...] (and where) human intellectual creativity flourishes. *(Yoneji Masuda)*
- The information society is an economic reality and not simply a mental abstraction ...The slow spread/ dissemination of information ends [...] new activities, operations and products gradually come to light. *(John Naisbitt)*
- A society where [...] information is used as an economic resource, the community harnesses/exploits it, and behind it all an industry develops which produces the necessary information ... *(Nick Moore)*
- A social structure based on the free creation, distribution, access and use of information and knowledge [...] the globalisation of various fields of life. *((Hungarian) NationalStrategy of Informatics, 1995)*
- A new type of society in which humanity has the opportunity to lead a new way of life, to have a higher standard of living, accomplish better work, and to play a better role in society thanks to the global use of information and telecommunication technologies." *(Béla Murányi)*

It is evident from above definitions that there are so

many areas where the life changes significantly: some are centred around resources, others around products, or industries, or activities, or society and people. Some consider the representation of global dimensions extremely important, while others do not. Some are of the opinion that political dimensions (control) are basic, others do not even mention it. The classic study by Machlup (1962), followed by a number of similar studies (summary in Martin, 1998), documented the startling structural changes in the economy and society as driven by the growth of information and knowledge production and processing. Popularly, they were summarized by Drucker (1994, p. 42ff):

The change in the meaning of knowledge that began two hundred fifty years ago has transformed society and economy. Formal knowledge is seen as both the key personal and the key economic resource.... [K]nowledge proves itself in action. What we now mean by knowledge is information effective in action, information focused on results.. . . The actual products of the pharmaceutical industry is knowledge; pill and prescription ointment are no more than packaging for knowledge.

Dimensions of the information society according to Daniel Bell

	Pre-industrial	*Industrial*	*Post-industrial*	
Mode of Production	Extractive	Fabrication	Processing; Recycling	
Economic sector	Primary Agriculture Mining Fishing Timber Oil and gas	Secondary Goods producing Manufacturing Durable Non-durable Heavy Construction	Services Tertiary Transportation Utilities	Quaternary Trade Finance Insurance Real estate
			Quinary Health, Research Government Recreation	Education,

	Pre-industrial	*Industrial*	*Post-industrial*
Transfor-ming Resource	Natural power wind, water, draft animals, human muscle	**Created energy** Electricity - oil, gas, coal, nuclear power	**Information** Computer and data-transmission systems
Strategic resource	Raw materials	Financial capital	Knowledge
Technology	Craft	Machine technology	Intellectual technology
Skill base	Artisan, manual worker, farmer	Engineer, semi-skilled worker	Scientist, technical and professional Occupations
Methodology	Common sense, trial and error; experience	Empiricism, experimentation	Abstract theories, models, simulations, decision theory, system analysis
Time perspective	Orientation to the past	Ad hoc adaptiveness, Experimentation	Future orientation: forecasting and planning
Design	Game against nature	Game against fabricated Future	Game between futures
Axial principle	Traditionalism	Economic growth	Codification of theoretical knowledge

Source: Bell, 1976

Comparative Characteristics of industrial and information society

		Industrial society	*Information society*
Inno-vation Tech-nology	Core	Steam engine (power) computation, control)	Computer (memory,
	Basic function	Replacement, amplification of physical labour	Replacement, amplification of mental labour
	Productive Power	Material productive power (increase in per capita production)	Information productive power (increase optimal action-selection of capabilities)
Socio-economic	Products	Useful goods and services	Information, technology

		Industrial society	*Information society*
structure	Production centre	Modern factory (machinery, equipment)	Information utility (information networks, data banks)
	Market	New world, colonies, consumer purchasing power	Increase in knowledge frontiers, information space
	Leading industries	Manufacturing industries (machinery industry, chemical industry)	Intellectual industries, (information industry, knowledge industry)
	Industrial Structure	Primary, secondary, tertiary industries	Matrix industrial structure (primary, secondary, tertiary, quaternary/ systems industries)
	Economic Structure	Commodity economy (division of labour, separation of production and consumption)	Synergetic economy (joint production and shared utilization)
	Socio-economic Principle	Law of price (equilibrium of supply and demand)	Law of goals (principle of synergetic feed forward)
	Socio-economic Subject	Enterprise (private enterprise, public enterprise, third sector)	Voluntary communities (local and informational communities)
	Socio-economic System	Private ownership of capital, free competition, profit maximization	Infrastructure principle of synergy, precedence of social benefit
	From of society	Class society (centralized power, classes, control)	Functional society (multicentre, function, autonomy)
	National goal	GNW (gross national welfare)	GNS (gross national satisfaction)
	Form of Government	Parliamentary democracy	Participatory democracy

		Industrial society	*Information society*
	Force of social change	Labour movements, strikes	Citizens' movements, litigation
	Social problems	Unemployment, war, fascism	Future shock, terror, invasion of privacy
	Most advanced Stage	High mass consumption	High mass knowledge creation
Values	Value standards	Material values (satisfaction of physiological needs)	Time-value (satisfaction of goal achievement needs)
	Ethical standards	Fundamental human rights, humanity	Self-discipline, social contribution
	Spirit of the Times	Renaissance (human liberation)	Globalise (symbiosis of man and nature)

Source: Yoneji Masuda, 1980.

Webster (1997) provides a seminal approach to understanding the concept of information society. He provides five analytical criteria in defining the information society. These are: technological; economic; occupational; spatial and cultural.

Technological Definition

The technological definition of the information society highlights the huge innovations in technology. The key innovations being technological advancements in information creation, processing, storage and transmission that have impacted the application of information and communication technologies in every sphere of society. Some of these technologies include computer technology and telecommunications technologies, which have revolutionized the socio-economic milieus of modern society.

Economic Definition

The economic approach defines the 'information

society' by attempting to analyze the information industries in statistical terms. This approach looks at the role of the information industries and traces their contribution to the Gross National Produce (GNP) and the economic viability of a nation. Five broad information industry groups are identified:

(a) Education (e.g. schools, libraries and colleges)

(b) Media of Communication (eg. radio and television, advertising);

(c) Information machine (e.g computer equipment, musical instruments);

(d) Information services (e.g law, insurance, medicine)

(e) Other information activities (e.g research and development, non-profit activities).

Working with these different categories and groups, Webster (1997: 11) suggests: it is possible to ascribe an economic value to each and trace its contribution to gross national produce (GNP). If the trend is for these to account for an increased proportion of GNP, then one may claim to chart the emergence through time of an information economy.

Occupational Definitions

This measure highlights occupational change as a basis for a new form of society. The point here is that there is an emergence of the information society when the preponderance of occupation is found in information work. The contention is that:

It appears obvious that as work which demands physical strength and manual dexterity such as hewing coal and farming the land declines to be replaced by more and more manipulation of figures and text such as in education and large bureaucracies, we are entering a new type of society (Webster, 1997: 14).

Spatial Definition

The spatial approach to the concept of information society emphasises the role and importance of information networks, which connect locations and consequently impact on the organisation of time and space. The effects of these networks and the reordering of time and space can be seen in four interrelated elements in the transition to an 'information society':

- Information comes to occupy centre stage as the 'key strategic resource' on which the organisation of the world economy is dependent.
- Computer and communications technologies provide the infrastructure which enable information to be processed and distributed
- There has been a rapid growth of the 'tradeable information sector' of the economy in services such as the new media (satellite broadcasting, cable, video) and online databases
- The growing 'informatisation' of the economy is facilitating the integration of national and regional economies.

Cultural Definition

The cultural approach points to the extraordinary increase in information in social circulation and how it affects the pattern of our everyday lives. Webster (1997: 22) notes that: Contemporary culture is manifestly more heavily information laden than any of its predecessors. We exist in a media-saturated environment, which means that life is quintessentially about symbolisation, about exchanging and receiving - or trying to exchange and resisting reception - messages about ourselves and others. It is in acknowledgement of this explosion of signification that many writers conceive of our having entered an information society.

INFORMATION SOCIETY - A BRIEF HISTORY

The collocation "information society" as it is now used first emerged in Japanese social science (s) in the early 1960s. The Japanese version of the expression *(joho shakai, johoka shakai)* was born during a conversation in 1961 between Kisho Kurokawa, the famous architect, and Tudao Umesao, the renowned historian and anthropologist. Subsequently, in early 1971 a "dictionary" on information society was published in Japan (*Johoka ShakaiJiten,* Dictionary of Information Societies). Although, the first English language reference dates from 1970, however terms like **post-industrial society** and **white collar revolution** existed to explain the newly emerged social-economic entity, since 1914. The expression "post-industrial society" was coined in Great Britain by Ananda K. Coomaraswamy and Arthur J. Penty, and later revived from 1958 in America (primarily by Daniel Bell) and from the end of the 1960s in French social sciences (likewise by Alan Touraine). In fact, the term **post-industrial society** replaced the term "manual work" to "brain work" and opened the way towards the concept of information society. For a while the word intelligence seemed to be a popular choice to express the growing importance of those social groups in the labour market that emerged who were using their intellectual performance and knowledge to make a living.

The term "white-collar work", first coined by Upton Sinclair in 1919, spread more widely in the 1950s and it also became an "official" term used to denote a basic category in statistics and employment. At first the term was used exclusively for office workers and those officials who moved from manufacturing industry towards intellectual work; however, later it was extended to workers who carried out activities requiring certain (mainly high) qualifications.

However, due to the increasingly complicated patterns of information, knowledge processes and institutes, neither the term, "white-collar" nor "brain work" was able to reflect the process by which knowledge itself was upgraded in the case of each worker and by which traditional industries became increasingly information and knowledge intensive.

From the end of the 1960s until the beginning of the 1980s it seemed that the term "post-industrial society" would become more prominent to describe the major social transformation that had taken place. It was Fritz Machlup, who showed at the beginning of the 1960s that the production of knowledge is an economic activity and could be described with the terms used in the analysis of the industrial sector. He reviewed the conceptual field, and then described one of its sectors, the knowledge producing sector, in detail. Finally, he pointed out that the biggest and most important sector of this industry was education. Furthermore, the term "post-industriality" had not become materialize due to various political reasons. In the end the term "information society", which was become popular to describe the elemental social changes that took place in the second half of the 20th century, remained alone in the ring.

CHARACTERISTICS

The main characteristics of an information society are:

- Distribution of high intellectual technologies on the basis of computer information technologies in all economic and social activities;
- High employment in the services sphere - over 50% of all working population;
- Sharp increase of the amount of the data exchanged whose mastering by traditional means only is impossible;
- De-popularisation of specific social and economic processes - small series production, market segmentation, disintegration of part of the big industrial companies, etc.

- Increasing the role of the individual - the changes in the labour nature and in the management increase the individual's responsibility:
- Support of the qualification level in the dynamically changing world which requires from the people in information society to get educated and self-educated during their whole life;
- Globalisation, economic and social cohesion - conditions are established for building "borderless society", elimination of the "distance" factor, movement to social homogeneity.

While undoubtedly true, since all societies necessitate information flow, there is no society without information and never was. None of the previous societies, however, were so extensively influenced by the communication, reception, processing, recording, decoding, and flow of information as ours are. According to Frank Webster's work there are few perspectives through which we view changes in our society.

1. Technological

Technology simply means mechanismation of any thing using machine to achieve objectives. From the technological perspective we live in an information based society where telecommunication technologies play a vital role in all fields of social existence, which has shaken the foundations of social structures and processes and resulted in massive changes in politics, economy, culture, and everyday life.

2. Occupation structure and economy

According to this perspective we live in an information society because, when we have passed through the agricultural and industrial stages, the information sector and information oriented jobs dominate the economy.

3. Spatial structure

As the spatial theorists see it we live in an information society because through the use of information technologies and globalisation physical space tends to become closer. People are participating in networks that determine such social processes as production, division of labour, discussing politics for example.

4. Culture

Since our life is infiltrated by the globalised, extensively digitalized media culture that has become the primary means of providing sense and meaning for us and predominantly determines our life style, the cultural perspective may also claim that our society is informational.

INFORMATION COMMUNICATION TECHNOLOGY (ICT) AND ITS IMPLICATION IN SOCIAL CHANGE

Among the four perspectives, technological is one of the biggest area through which our society is knocking change. The very basic question arise in this regards: What kind of new information and communication technology was constructed in recent decades that determined the infrastructure of information society? Let us take some of popular technological innovations which highly influenced the society to change.

Ham Radio : Ham Radio or Amateur Radio is a communication device to communicate with other ham radio for public service, recreation and disaster management. It uses wireless communication technology and provide emergency communications when wireless, cell phones and other means of communication fail. Recent examples include the 2001 attacks on WTC, the 2003 North-American Blackout, the 2004 Indian Ocean Earthquake, Harrican Katrina and very recently Japan earthquake where ham radio was used to coordinate disaster relief activities when other system fails.

Governance to e-Governance : Government of almost all countries of the world is the largest and biggest generators and producer of information and the same time they are the largest consumers of information and knowledge too. Government collect, organize and disseminate statistical data on all its activities which constitute the most important and vital information resources for their planning and later implementation and execution. Before the widespread use of ICTs government memorandum, its order, plan of action was only concentrated to the office from where it originates. The delivery of such information to the destination took time which leads to undue delay in its implementation in the society. With the development of sophisticated ICT tool such policies disseminate to the destination without loss of any time. Government and governance converts into e-government and e-governance. e-Government could have been following varieties: digital interaction between a government and citizens (G2C), government and businesses/commerce/eCommerce (G2B), and between government agencies (G2G), Government-to-Religious Movements/Church (G2R), Government-to-Households (G2H). Application of e-government brings the opportunity to ensure good governance. Use of IT in government facilitates good governance, which is the efficient, effective, participatory, transparent and accountable democratic exercise of power in electronic form, and includes informal politics and non-governmental players. E-democracy is an opportunity for enabling and facilitating the provision of information and deliberation, enhancing civic participation in order to broaden political debate, and fostering better and more legitimate political decisions. There are so many service areas like Vehicle Registration, Driving License, Registration of Land Deeds, Arms License, Government Cash flow, Government Orders, Passport Application where e-governance is being applied for betterment of society. In

Indian context there are some initiatives by various government to implement e-governance. Under G2C, the Bhoomi Project in Karnataka, Gyandoot project in Madhya Pradesh, Lokvani Project in Uttar Pradesh, e-Mitra Project in Rajasthan, under G2B, e-Procurement Project in Andhra Pradesh, Gujrat, eSeva (Andhra Pradesh), and under G2G, the Khajane Project in Karnataka, SmartGov (Andhra Pradesh) are important.

E-Democracy and e-Parliament : The concept of E-democracy came into force with the establishment of a digital well-driven parliament database called POLIS (Parliamentary Online Information System). E-democracy is an integral part of the information society, which has ushered in a range of traditional and innovative tools that can usefully be applied in democratic processes and institutions. Access to the new information and communications environment can facilitate the exercise of democratic rights and freedoms, in particular participation in public life and democratic processes. E-democracy can bring together policy makers and citizens in new forms of engagement and policy making. This can lead, on the one hand, to a better understanding of public opinion and people's needs by policy makers and, on the other, to a better public understanding of the tasks and challenges facing policy makers, and thus to increased citizen identification with the democratic system and a higher regard for, and greater trust in, democracy. Because it opens up new channels for information, communication, deliberation and participation and enhances transparency and accountability, e-democracy has the potential to address shortcomings in democratic institutions and processes. By providing a means of reducing exclusion, e-democracy can foster social integration and social cohesion and thus contribute to social stability. E-democracy encompasses, in particular, e-parliament, e-legislation, e-justice, e-mediation, e-environment, e-election, e-referendum, e-initiative, e-voting, e-consultation, e-petitioning, e-campaigning, e-polling and e-surveying; it makes use of e-participation, e-deliberation and e-forums.

Agriculture to e-Agriculture : Only a few generations ago, nearly everyone was involved in agriculture. In many cases, the whole family - men, women and children - worked on the family farm or ranch. Today, only a few percent of total population is directly involved in agricultural production. But agriculture is the foundation of any society. It has social and economic significance and has important to every human health and environment quality. Since the beginning of the information revolution many applications of the internet and related technologies have been sought and deployed in agriculture. According to Food and Agricultural Organization, "e-Agriculture" is an emerging field in the intersection of agricultural informatics, agricultural development and entrepreneurship, referring to agricultural services, technology dissemination, and information delivered or enhanced through the Internet and related technologies. More specifically, it involves the conceptualization, design, development, evaluation and application of new (innovative) ways to use existing or emerging information and communication technologies (ICTs).

There are several types of activity related to e-agriculture applications that are widely recognized around the world today. The ICTs used in e-agriculture include mobile phones, digital personal assistants (PDAs), smart cards, Geographic Information Systems (GIS), radio, Radio-Frequency Identification Devices (RFID), imaging and acoustic technologies, websites and weblogs, and email-based information services. The selling of agriculture based products was previously concentrated only on local market. With this technology enabled society farmer have an opportunity to know the value of their products in global market and sell their products accordingly. The mobility of agriculture based products helps people to acquire better quality food. In some developed countries a new ICT based technological solution namely 'Precision agriculture' has emerged. In precision agriculture or site-specific farming, farmers are using ICTs and other technologies to obtain more precise information about agricultural resources which allow them to identify, analyze, and manage the spatial and temporal variability of soil and plants for optimum profitability, sustainability, and protection of the environment (Jefferson, 2000). Precision agriculture is an advanced e-agriculture application. It makes use of five major components of technology: 1) Geographical Information Systems (GIS) for analysis and management of spatial data and mapping; 2) Remote Sensing (RS) to identify and 3) Global Positioning Systems (GPS) to locate and define spatial features or activities that contribute to the quality of site-specific practices; 4) Variable Rate Technology (VRT) allowing targeted, site-specific input applications; and 5) Yield monitoring for recording crop productivity as an historical database for crop management (Rains, 2000).

However, E-Agriculture goes beyond technology, to promote the integration of technology with multimedia, knowledge and culture, with the aim of improving communication and learning processes between various actors in agriculture locally, regionally and worldwide. Facilitation, support of standards and norms, technical support, capacity building, education, and extension are all key components to e-Agriculture.

Till date, agriculture provides the principal means of livelihood for over 58.4% of India's population. It contributes approximately one-fifth of total gross domestic product (GDP). Ministry of Agriculture, Govt. of India has launched portals for mandi price online (AGMARKNET) to provide day-today market information to the farmers. There are number of portal are operationalble in India in the field of agriculture, for example, www.isapindia.org, www.agriwatch.com, www.fciweb.nic.in, www.agroindia.org, www.indg.gov.in, http://agmarknet.nic.in/

Education to e-education : APJ Abdul Kamal one of his presidential speech pointed that *"The whole purpose of education in a country like India is to develop and enhance the potential of our human resources and progressively transform it into a knowledge society"*. Education, one of the basic mean for overall improvement of a civilized society has severely changed by the use of ICT tools. The concept of e-education is associated with online delivery of information, communication, training and learning. The need of e-education has been developed due to various reasons, like, changing importance of capitalist economy to knowledge-based economy, a paradigm shift in the way education is viewed and delivered, and huge knowledge gaps demand educational system reform. According to the W.R. Hambrecht report in 2000, the new global economy poses more complex challenges to workers, requiring higher levels of education, computer literacy, critical thinking, information analysis, and synthesizing skills. However, educational deficiencies have brought the organization of curriculum and teaching methods as they relate to labour market preparation is needed. Academic and corporate environments must be redesigned to adequately prepare people to function in an information society. This new mode of education promises to transform the experience of the classroom in a number of fundamental ways: by augmenting traditional textbook materials with online resources; lectures through the use of rich multimedia and interactive content; and by extending student discussions beyond the walls of the classroom via a wide range of new communications platforms supporting inter classroom collaboration. As human capital becomes the chief source of economic value, education and training become lifelong endeavors for the majority of workers. E-education offers us potentially less expensive, more convenient, and richer ways of becoming educated, and of coming into contact with more diverse groups of fellow learners than ever before.

With the extremely rapid economic growth in recent years in India, there is increasing demand for higher education. However, there is a shortage of schools and teachers. In order to resolve these challenges, the development and adoption of electronic systems in education, as well as implementing remote e-education based on them, become more realistic in India. The scope of online education in India is actually much wider. Apart from proper course works, some E-learning portals in India are also conducting mock tests for various competitive examinations like engineering, medical, management etc. For example, the Indiatimes group has introduced the Mindscape test center where one can appear for mock IIT-JEE exams, online for making self-assessment. The Gurukul online Solutions, apart from providing various courses, set up a Jobs and Careers Centre (JCC), which, not only provides job-oriented vocational education in a variety of domains, but also provides career enriching courses via eLearning. They also offer Live Virtual Classroom connectivity to over 175 cities across India.

E-commerce : The integration of information and communications technology (ICT) in business has developed a new definition of business called e-commerce. In general, E-commerce can be defined as the use of ICT in business transactions to create, transform, and redefine relationships for value creation between or among organizations, and between organizations and individuals. However, E-commerce is more than simply another application of information and communication technology. People and institutions decide when, why, and where to acquire goods and services according to complex social and cultural criteria. The ability to valorize goods and services in a market economy was first learned in a "materially based" social context. In a digitized, dematerial environment, many of these social skills will have to be relearned (Neice 1998). Now, e-commerce and e business have increasingly become a necessary component of business strategy and a strong catalyst for social and economic development. With the expansion of e-commerce a totally new framework, the issues of trade competition, consumer protection, procedure of selling goods and services, structure and even operation of marketing businesses, are placed in a totally different framework from that which we have known until now.

Banking to e-Banking : The increasing importance of e-commerce and the use of internet in its communication along with the enhanced online security of transactions and sensitive information has been the core reasons for the penetration of online banking in everyday life. According to Pikkarainen et al (2004) many activities are handled electronically due the acceptance of information technology at home as well as at workplace. The transformation from the traditional banking towards e-banking is one of them and this change has been a 'leap' change (Heikki et al., 2002). The journey of e-banking started from the use of automatic teller machines (ATM) and has passed through telephone banking, direct bill payment, electronic fund transfer and the revolutionary online banking (Alter, 2002). The future of electronic banking according to some is the acceptance of WAP enabled banking and interactive-TV banking (Petrus & Nelson, 2006).

Health to e-health

In order to develop a healthy society, intervention of government towards people for their health is very essential. There is also need of planning of effective health programme for the child, old citizen and especially women. Every government of every nation in their agenda puts highest concerns towards health of their citizen. However, most of the time lack of information in right time, and delay in delivery of information creates huge losses to the society. By using various sophisticated communication technology, governments are now trying to eliminate these lacuna by providing right information to the right time about basic health services and public health education. It also helps to develop a prejudice free society where life is not controlled by speculations but by treatment. In fact health is one of the major areas where the role of ICT gives birth to a new generation of health. E-health is not only a health services by using technology, it exploits technology for betterment of those very common people who are surviving in remote region. Simply, ICTs plays an important role in reducing demographic and geographic disparities in access. It also helps to mobilize regional and local financial resources for promoting tele-medicine projects.

Several initiatives are presently underway across India to undertake GIS mapping in the health sector. However, information regarding these GIS initiatives remains largely fragmented and unavailable at a single point. The Ministry of Health & Family Welfare and the World Health Organization Country Office for India, has taken a major initiative to review the current status of health GIS in India and identify resources for developing health GIS infrastructure and mapping facilities. Some portal have also developed to promote telemedicine like: telemedicine module for Tropical Medicine in West Bengal, Telehealth education in Kerla, Telemedicine work for Naga, Kohima, Onconet network etc.

Web 2.0

The term Web 2.0, coined by Tim O'Reilly and Dale

Dougherty and popularized in 2004, is commonly used to refer to web formats such as blogs and social networking sites that are driven by social connections and user participation. The term is applied to virtually every new application or digital start-up business, resulting in conceptual vagueness at best and absolute meaninglessness at worst (Graham, 2005). For proponents of Web 2.0, YouTube, MySpace, and Wikipedia represent a second generation of websites that are widely transforming mainstream Internet experience. While most agree that Web 2.0 sites employ notions of collective intelligence, network-enabled interactive services, and user control, one is hard-pressed to find these core characteristics in Google, a website considered the poster-child of Web 2.0 applications (O'Reilly 2005).

Web 2.0 does employ a new generation of software and might be usefully understood not as an actual technology or group of technologies, but as 'a group of techniques' (Marsden 2006). Therefore, from the industry's perspective, the term Web 2.0 functions to represent a promising new way of 'doing' the Internet. From the user end, this translates into new ways of using the Internet that are quickly developing into new social practices and new forms of knowledge exchange.

While the earlier version, i.e. Web 1.0 refers to the 'Web-as-information source', Web 2.0 refers to the 'Web-as-participation-platform' (O'Reilly 2005). Web 1.0 of the mid-1990s is described as a 'repository of information and static content' or 'isolated information silos' (Tech Encyclopedia 2008). In contrast, Web 2.0 is framed as enabling interactivity and inviting user-generated content and comments.

E-learning 1.0 to 2.0

With the wide spread use of Internet, it became possible to acquire and store digitised versions of many different

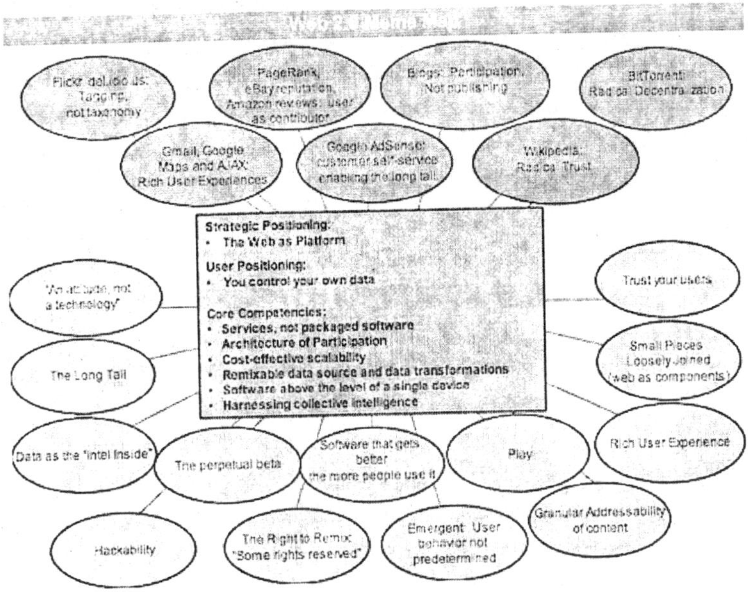

Fig. 1. Shows a "meme map" of Web 2.0 that was developed at a brainstorming session during FOO Camp, a conference at O'Reilly Media. Source: ©2011, O'Reilly Media, Inc.

kinds of learning content (texts, pictures, audio and video) and make it available through web portals . The concept e-learning 1.0 associated with accessing learning objects through static pages, homogenous database. This form of education, is actually the technologically supported variant of traditional knowledge distribution, the virtual extension of textbooks and classroom teaching. Even in this environment, learning remained a passive process, managed from above or outside. The formalized, centralized, bureaucratic world of education of industrialized societies was extended into a digital environment (Downes, 2005) The typical Internet user browsed the web pages and downloaded content, but did not actively participate in the content-creation process.

The concept e-learning 2.0 is associated with the concept web 2.0 which enable users not only searched for information on the web, but also became content providers themselves. With the wide available personal and institution information on web, the present form of world wide web allow individuals to harness collective knowledge and entertainment portals for their own purposes and exchange it with world community. Students can create and exchange content in a cooperative way, within networks of their contemporaries. Blogs, forums, chats, wikis, newsgroups, and networks of friends and acquaintances provide an immense communal information production and exchange framework. Increasingly sophisticated tools, from refined search engines through Wikipedia to well-maintained debate and knowledge portals, are available. By this means it has become possible to construct personally reflected knowledge adapted to one's individual needs from information represented in cyberspace. Internet is now not a medium for learning; it is the platform and the centre of personal study. In the milieu of eLearning 2.0, the opportunity exists to reconstruct an organic learning environment.

The Apple Education portal demonstrates the cultural differences between the new generation that uses web 2.0 (digital native users) and the teachers who were socialized in the paradigm of industrial society (digital immigrant teachers) as follows:

Digital Native Learners	*Digital Immigrant Teachers*
Prefer receiving information quickly from multiple multimedia sources.	Prefer slow and controlled release of information from limited sources.
Prefer parallel processing and multitasking.	Prefer singular processing and single or limited tasking.
Prefer processing pictures, sounds and video before text.	Prefer to provide text before pictures, sounds and video.
Prefer random access to hyper linked	Prefer to provide information

multimedia information.	linearly, logically and sequentially.
Prefer to interact/network simultaneously with many others.	Prefer students to work independently rather than network and interact.
Prefer to learn "just-in-time."	Prefer to teach "just-in-case" (it's in the exam).
Prefer instant gratification and instant rewards.	Prefer deferred gratification and deferred rewards.
Prefer learning that is relevant, instantly useful and fun.	Prefer to teach to the curriculum guide and standardized tests.

Source: Jukes - Dosaj, 2003

SIDE EFFECT OF ICT

Computer Virus

As computer progressed, the brain of intellectuals also stimulate to develop some unwanted/destructive codes/logic, which 'broke-the-bound' of useful program and would either perform operations on the data or programs belonging to different procedure, or actually transferred control to random areas and tried to execute data as program instructions.

A virus is code written with the express intention that the virus code replicates itself. A virus tries to spread itself from computer to computer by attaching itself to a host program. It may damage hardware, software, or data. A worm is a subclass of virus. A worm generally spreads without user action and distributes complete copies (possibly modified) of itself across networks. A worm can exhaust memory or network bandwidth, causing a computer to stop responding. A virus that appears to be a useful program, but that actually does damage, is a "trojan horse."

The term is some time also used for viral programs which spread by some method viz attachment, association with original code/ program and spread from one computer to another. One of the factors involved in the success of viral programs is a study of the mindset of the user: a study of the psychology or sociology of the computer community. Since the spread of viral programs generally require some action, albeit unknowing, on the part of the operator, it is instructive to look at the security breaking aspects of other historical programs.

Although the birth of virus is not as long as internet but since last decade its replication and number increased in such a manner that in present day its total number is anybodies guess. In present day more than 200 viruses are found in each month.

The first virus Brain was noted in 1986 which was written by Pakistan. The brain was a boot-sector virus, which means it only infected the boot records of 360K floppy disks, but not hard drives. It would occupy unused space on the disk so that it could not be used. It was also the first "stealth" virus, meaning it tried to hide itself from detection. If a computer user tried to view the infected space on the disk, Brain would display the original, uninfected boot sector. First file infecting memory resident Lehigh virus was noted in 1987 as executable file virus that attacks COMMAND.COM file. In 1988 first encrypted virus Cascade was found in Germany. Dark Avenger was introduced in virus history in 1989, which was designed to damage a system slowly, so it would go unnoticed at first and damage file would be backed up. During 1994-1999 number of notorious viruses has also developed such as Kaos4, Boza, Laroux, Melissa etc. But in year 2000 "I Love You Virus" wreaks havoc around the world. It is transmitted by email and when opened, it automatically sent to everyone in the user's address book. In 18 September, 2001 the birth of Nimda and subsequently CodeRed worms creates a panic to computer world. The differential feature of Nimda was that it requires no human interaction to spread, instead using known software vulnerabilities and multiple vector infection. It was estimated that during 2:30 PM on Sept 20 and 2:30 PM, Sept' 21 Nimda infected over 2.2 million servers and PCs which cause a total loss of $10.7 billion. Nimda propagate through network looking for unpatched Microsoft internet Information Server. It then attempts to use the specific exploit, called Unicode Web Traversal exploit, to gain control of the target server. It also propagate through email by harvesting email addresses from any MAPI compliant email program's mailbox and extract email address from html and htm files. Nimda attacks hard disks of systems that have enabled file sharing over network and create a guest account with administrative privileges.

In present day, PWSteal.lbank, Trojan. Anits, W32.Klez / Mydoom/ Spybot Bloodhound.Explot.13, Backdoor.Nemog.B, Beagle, W97/ MTX, VBS/SST@MM (Anna Kournikova) Blaster are some of the invention of most notorious virus/worms which all are based on network and spread computer to computer through Internet and LAN. These virus searches for .EXE, .INI, .COM, .DLL, .TXT, .GIF, .JPG, .JPEG, .MPEG, .MOV, .BAT, .PDF, .PNG, .PS, .ZIP, .VBS, .LOG files and also attack MY DOCUMENTS folder and attempts to send copies of these document to email recipients found in windows address book and address found in cache files.

Cyber Terrorism

According to Denning, *Cyberterrorism is the convergence of terrorism and cyberspace. It is generally understood to mean unlawful attacks and threats of attack against computers, networks, and the information stored therein when done to intimidate or coerce a government or its people in furtherance of political or social objectives. Further, to qualify as cyberterrorism, an attack should result in violence against persons or property, or at least cause enough harm to generate fear. Attacks that lead to death or bodily injury, explosions, plane crashes, water contamination, or severe economic loss would be examples. Serious attacks against critical infrastructures could be acts of cyberterrorism, depending on their impact. Attacks that disrupt nonessential services or that are mainly a costly nuisance would not.*

While Denning's definition is solid, it also raises some interesting issues. First, she points out that this definition is usually limited to issues where the attack is against "computers, networks, and the information storied therein", which we would argue is 'pure Cyberterrorism'. Indeed, we believe that the true impact of her opening statement ("the convergence of terrorism and cyberspace") is realized not only when the attack is launched against computers, but when many of the other factors and abilities of the virtual world are leveraged by the terrorist in order to complete his mission, whatever that may be. Thus, only one aspect of this convergence is generally considered in any discussion of cyberterrorism – an oversight that could be costly. Second, it is very different from the definition that appears to be operationally held by the media and the public at large.

Cybercrime

With the advent of WWW and its subsequent development like e-commence, online banking, e-trading irrevocably altered the criminal environment. Although the concept of computer virus and worms are not very old but the fashion of attack through web in 21st century is very much notorious and resulting huge loss in the economic and social life too. A generation of new criminals quickly learnt about money laundering and investigative methodologies from 'real life' criminals, adapting and adopting cybersystem to divert money to themselves using a mixture of simple and sophisticated schemes. In early 1980s when the concept hackers developed, the cyber criminals relied on early form of Internet Relay Chat. Through this chat service hacker enter into a computer system which is under the chat network and send malicious code to the system. With the passages of time the early form of cyber crime developed to a large extend and continuously disrupt regular activity to all people in all society, whether technically strong or week.

Phishing

Phishing is another form of online crime for hacking credit cards and bank accounts. The hacker, by providing some lucrative offer, sent spam emails to the account holder and tries to convince users to know their account detail, login, password etc.. Sometimes, phishers convinced the account holder to bot some scam site and to upload some files. It remains a lucrative endeavour, but each phishing attack lasts a matter of hours, from when spam requests for bank account information are sent out to when the phish site is abandoned. Even so, this is normally enough time for up to 10 to 15 legitimate account credential to be obtained.

Malware

It is another form of phish through which criminals pushes out huge volume of new malicious code to the computer every hour, each sufficiently different so as to overwhelm the response. In spite of filtering system in mail account, such malware enter into the system by by-passing filtering logarithm. Some malware, after entering into system sits in the background and mirrors every data input through keyboard, including password of online transaction, email account, online money transfer etc. to a third party. The very famous 'Trojan' is able to successfully keep online banking sessions alive after a victim successfully authenticates their identity.

Ripping

Ripping is the act of negotiating a deal and taking receipt of criminal goods or devices without providing remuneration and is very common for cheating other miscreants. With the increasing demand of society from commerce to e-commence the incidences of ripping are growing.

ATMs

There is an increasing preference of use of ATM in present day due to various shortcomings in traditional banking system. At the same time, the incidences of 'white plastic fraud' increasing sharply in present day society. The profile, including card number, password, branch code, name etc. are stored in a magnetic stripe and are encoded onto a plastic card. Criminals are continually researching and developing tools to exploit ATMs and point of sale (POS) terminals. Using skimmer criminal extracts card information in another blank card and withdraw money from other POS terminal located in different city, state or nation. Traditionally, skimmer uses 'pinhole camera' by physically presence on the ATMs, in sophisticated method, a new developed costly technology 'wiretapping' they use to obtain information. This wireless technology allow criminals to avoid detection once a skimmer or other intercept device is placed on an ATM or POS terminal.

Online payment

Paying various services through online is one of the most useable feature of citizen of this society. This enable a customer to initiate a payment to any entity based solely on a physical address. Criminals hacked the information relating to customer's bank account detail, routine number, and signature from previous deposited cheques and placed forged cheques with correct sequential numbers.

ROLE OF LIBRARIES IN SOCIETY

Libraries play a fundamental role in our society. They are the collectors and stewards of our heritage; they are organisers of the knowledge in the books they collect - adding value by cataloguing, classifying and describing them; and, as public institutions, they assure equality of access for all citizens. They take the knowledge of the past and present, and lay it down for the future. As an organization, they are also key links in the information chain in support of educational, cultural, technical, scientific and economic developments. In the information society they have a crucial role as gateways to the information resources on the global superhighways. Our societies are dependent on democratic access to information, and as citizen we should have access to our cultural heritage. The overall role of libraries in context of information society may be summarized as:

1. Libraries can play an important role in the information society as providers of electronic information and access points to information for citizens of the countries. It can be vital institutions in the efforts to bridge the gap between the information rich and poor. This is especially critical in promoting the development agenda because human resources are central to economic progress. The widening of this gap is a major threat to transform society towards progress. Copyright should be handled in a way that recognises the right of the citizen to have access to published material. They help to safeguard democratic values and universal civil rights impartially and by opposing any form of censorship.
2. They enable intellectual freedom by providing access to information, ideas and works of imagination in any medium and regardless of frontiers. Libraries have been identified as one of the key elements for open access to information, which is crucial to democratic information society development.

3. Libraries are especially important now when the whole idea of education is stressing more and more independent learning and acting. The importance of libraries as supporters of education on all levels is growing due to new ways of learning, in which access to and gathering of information is an integrated part of the process. They also build capacity by promoting information literacy and providing support and training for effective use of information resources, including Information and Communication Technologies. Media-competence is needed at a still broader level.
4. They should focus on the continuous training needs of the librarians themselves and on their role in guiding users in handling equipment and accessing information.
5. In the information society electronic access to information is of growing importance. However, physical library collections will remain necessary components in the information chain and vital parts of our cultural life for decades. A new library concept is evolving taking into account the intermingling and integration of the physical and the virtual role of most types of libraries. New kinds of meeting places and a new kind of cultural centre are developing, in which librarians are pro-active mediators of information. If efficiently supported, this concept could be extended to benefit all citizens. Likewise libraries can play a role in the ongoing efforts to revitalize the concept of citizenship.

IFLA urges national, regional and local governments as well as international organisations to:

- invest in library and information services as vital elements in their Information Society strategies, policies and budgets;

- upgrade and extend existing library networks to obtain the greatest possible benefits for their citizens and communities;
- support unrestricted access to information and freedom of expression;
- promote open access to information and address structural and other barriers to access; and
- recognise the importance of information literacy and vigorously support strategies to create a literate and skilled populace which can advance and benefit from the global Information Society.

CONCLUSION

Castells argues that the information society is the new mode of human existence, in which the production, recording, processing, and retrieving of information in organized networks plays the central role. There is no evidence, however, that such a society exists. Again, Castells' argues that it is legitimate to point to a newly created mode of communal existence, if quantitative changes (e.g. more computers, a wide range of TV channels, extensive information flow) result in *qualitative* changes with respect to social interaction. The novelty of a society cannot be established exclusively by our acquisition of new goods or phenomena such as the dotcom companies bubble in the economy. It is not this which denotes the renewal of the economy; this is simply the old system gathering some new participants. However, where we see the regeneration of prior processes through the creation of new expectations, which transform the accustomed logic of social interactions (cf. its culture, customs, political system, production system etc.) then we may claim a change. This fundamental change that creates information society is the transformation of the structure of society.

The growth of tension is also reflected in social movements. Some of these (religious fundamentalists, for instance, among other reactive movements) withdraw into traditions and religious values regarding stability, and lack of change as something precious. Others, (anti-globalisation proactive groups) turn against the network society, ironically enough, exploiting the latter's own means of globalised technology and culture. "Global criminal economy" presents another difficulty that societies have to face, and to make things even worse, in certain countries such crime is entangled with the legal political power. This circumstance in the end is something that poses a threat to the entire globalised world.

"Information society" is a term used to describe the most recent stage of social change in 20th century. The concept provides a paradigm for accelerated regional economic and social development. But regions *also* need to develop their strategic planning competence and development capability. To shape the Information Society at the regional level so as to ensure its benefits will be maximized and the risks minimised, it is necessary to engage in an *explicit* planning process. The outcome is an Information Society that facilitates and promotes consensus and social harmony, rather than division and conflict. There are another concept, *post-information society,* has also emerged, to demonstrate numerous future scenarios to describe possible futures surpassing the current institutions and technologies; biotechnological revolution, new generation of artificial intelligence, visions of the fusion of man and machine into functional systems.

In recent years the concept of the network society has gained importance in information society theory. For Manuel Castells network logic is besides information, pervasiveness, flexibility, and convergence a central feature of the information technology paradigm (2000a: 69ff). "One of the key features of informational society is the networking logic of its basic structure, which explains the use of the concept of 'network society'" (Castells 2000)

REFERENCES

Alter, S. (2002). *Information Systems.* 4th Edition, Prentice Hall

Bell, Daniel (1976). Welcome to post-industrial society, *Physics Today,* February.

Buckland, Michael (1991). *Information and Information Systems.* New York: Greenwood Press

Castells, Manuel (1996). *The Information Age: Economy, Society and Culture, Volume I: Rise of the Network Society.* Oxford : Blackwell

Denning, D. (2010). Cyberterrorism: Testimony before the Special Oversight Panel of Terrorism Committee on Armed Services, US House of Representatives, 23 May 2010. Available at: http://www.cs.georgetown.edu/ ~denning/infosec/ cyberter ror.html

Downes, Stephen (2005a): *E-learning 2.0.* Available at: http:// elearnmag.org/subpage.cfm?section= articles&article=29-1.

Drucker, P.F. (1993). Post-capitalist society. New York: Harper Business.

Graham, P. (2005). Web 2.0', [Online] Available at: http:// paulgraham.com/web20.html (6 June 2008).

Jefferson County Cooperative Extension Services. (2000). Precision agriculture - site specific farming. Available at: http:// jefferson.ifas.ufl.edu/ag_pages/PA-SST_page.htm>

Karjaluoto, Heikki; Mattila, Minna & Pento, Tapio (2002). Factors underlying attitude formation towards online banking in Finland, *International Journal of Bank Marketing,* 20(6).

Machlup, F. (1962). The production and distribution of knowledge in the United States. Princeton, NJ: Princeton University Press.

Manuel Castells (2000). *The Rise of the Network Society. The Information Age: Economy, Society and Culture.* Volume 1. Malden: Blackwell. Second Edition.

Marsden, R. (2006). What does Web 2.0 mean for the Internet?' The Independent (London), pp. 9, TechEncyclopedia (2008). Web 2.0, TechWeb Network, [Online]

Masuda, Yoneji (1980): *The Information Society as Post-Industrial Society*. Tokyo: The World Future Society.

Naisbitt, John (1984). *Megatrends – Ten new directions transforming our lives*. London: Futura Macdonald and Co.,

O'Reilly, T. (2005). *What is Web 2.0? Design Patterns and Business Models for the Next Generation of Software*. Available at: http://oreillynet.com/1pt/a/6228.

Petrus Guriting, Nelson Oly Ndubisi (2006). Borneo online banking: evaluating customer perceptions and behavioural intention, *Management Research News*; 29(1/2). Conceptual Paper

Pikkarainen, Tero; Pikkarainen, Kari; Karjaluoto, Heikki; & Pahnila, Seppo (2004). Consumer acceptance of online banking: an extension of the technology acceptance model, *Internet Research*; 14(3)

Rains, G. C. and Thomas, D. L. (2000). Precision farming: an introduction. Available at: http://pubs.caes.uga. edu/caespubs/pubcd/B1186.htm>

Toffler, Alvin (1980). *The Third Wave*. New York: William Morrow and Company

Webster, Frank (1997): *Theories of the Information Society*. London and New York : Routledge.

11
Information Industry

The information field has spread out of the libraries and information centers, and has been transformed into an industry that sells, organizes, and processes information. This chapter first outlines the concept and characteristics of industry and then examines then various types of industries that are associated with information.

THE CONCEPT

Industry in general sense is an organization where raw material processed to finish products. The basic purpose of any industry is production, it may agricultural production, or it may be industrial production. There are mainly five factors which control production. These are land, labour capital, organization and entrepreneur. With the increasing understanding about information as commodities, now every organization accepts that there is another factor which control production and that is the information. Since information and information products are used with each and every factor and stage of production thus information works as main ingredients of all factors of production and ensuring the best use of other factors. According to Churchill (1991) effective decision making depends on the quality of information input, and marketing research plays an essential role in providing accurate and useful information". In that sense all businesses are information businesses information play an important role to guide strategy and operations. However, here, the connotation of Information industry includes those players who produce/generate, process, store and disseminate information and collect revenue.

The post-industrial society is characterized by the centrality of theoretical knowledge as a commodity. A defining characteristic of an information society is an emerging or developing information industry. With the advent of the information era, IT and the information industry are becoming the main stimuli of world economy, driving the transformation from industrial society to information society, while causing the institutional reform and changing the realistic economic activities and social life. The "9/11" terrorist attack on the Unites States in September 2001 made the world economy even more sluggish, and brought the world information industry into depression and into a period of adjustment. However, it has again grown up.

Over the decade the world information industry has been developing very fast, which has played a vital role in the growth of world economy. In the middle 1990s, IT became the world first industry surpassing those industrial sectors, such as automobile and steel, etc. In the later 1990s, the average annual growth rate of world economy was around 3%, while the growing speed of IT and relevant industries was 2-3 times that of the economic growth. In 1998, the contribution rate of IT and information industry to the world economy growth was 14.7%, and actually exceeded 25% in view of a decreased value of products and services. In 1999, the merging and acquisition transaction in the global information industry amounted up to US$1 trillion, with an average annual 200% growth. Although the information industry of different countries in the world had been affected to certain degree due to the global economic depression starting from the second half of the year 2000, the world electronic information industry as a total still kept a stable increase since 2000.

CHARACTERISTICS

Information industry basically is a service industry, however, are distinct from computer and information technology services and distinct from many other professional services. As we know that marketing has its four "Ps": product, promotion, price, and place (distribution). In the case of information industry it has four "Gs.": generate, gather, group information, and then give (sell) information to others. Thomas W. Miller (2000) explains the function of these four Gs are:

Generate information : Every organization generate information when they develop new products, specify models, developed new techniques etc. Interpreting textual data from in-depth interviews or focus groups and writing research reports—these are creative, generative processes. It is their styles of information generation that often distinguish one research firm from another. Successful firms in the information industry are those who can generate information pin pointedly.

Gather information : Gathering relevant information for their need is the central activity of any organization. The primary source of gathering information is either from market or from consumer. However, they also gather information from a variety of secondary sources. Traditional modes of gathering include face-to-face and telephone interviews and focus groups, mail surveys, and observational studies. Today's methods of gathering include the additional methods of online research. Successful information industry firms are efficient gatherers.

Group information : George A. Miller (1956) called it

"chunking." By their day to day activities every organization generates huge quantity of data. To learn from data, aggregate according to need, and process those data for actual use is very important. They use model-based or data-adaptive statistical methods to transform, smooth, or reduce data. They convert data into summary statistics, parameter estimates, and probability statements. Although analysts may not reduce data down to what Miller (1956) called "the magic number seven, plus or minus two" chunks of information, their grouping activities should yield a more manageable, more understandable organization of the data. Successful information industry firms group information in meaningful ways.

Give information to others : Every organization is involved in information generating, gathering, and grouping. But for the firms in the information industry, the information providers, information generating, gathering, and grouping are primary activities. Information providers make and sell information. Information clients buy and use information. Successful information industry firms provide long-term value to their clients.

TYPES OF INFORMATION INDUSTRY

The concept of information as an economic resource can be approached from several angles. First, is an approach which divides the economy of a country into four sectors: This four sector approach may have first been popularized by Porat (1977) who carried out a landmark study, titled "*The Information Economy*" which replaced the three traditional sectors of the national economy - agriculture, industry and services with four sectors - by adding an information sector to them. The information sector itself was divided into several sections - the primary information sector whereby the primary product was information (publishing, libraries, telecommunications, insurance, computing) and a secondary information sector whereby the information component comprises a sizeable proportion of output (service sector, maintenance of ICT equipment, education etc.). Machlup (1962) is another important researcher closely associated with the concept of defining the information sector of the economy to determine its size relative to other sectors of the economy.

Although there is no standard or distinctively better way of organizing information sectors in present days, it is generally divided into few distinct segments: the first concerned with the creation of information – the content sector; the second concerned with the delivery of the information; and the third concerned with processing of information. In addition, there are other two categories of industries. They are: manufacturer of information processing devices and research intensive industries.

The Information-Content Industry

The information content industry can be classified into two groups: primary and secondary.

Primary

The primary information-content segment comprises the organizations in both the public and private sectors that produce and develop intellectual property. The information originates from creators like authors, composers, artists and photographers, assisted by editors, filmmakers, television producers, animators and allied occupations. The information creators sell their work to publishers, broadcasters, distributors and production companies to disseminate their creations, however, they take the raw intellectual property. For example, in book publishing context author submits his/her work to a publisher and the job of the primary publishers is to publish the primary literature, either in form of book, serial or monograph. They add value by identifying appropriate authors/creators, providing editorial oversight and control, often through peer review, and by providing marketing and promotion for their publications. Finally they distribute and sell the finished products to the information consumers and gain profit.

In the past, the work of creation and publication took place in quite separate organizations. Authors worked with publishers and rarely had much contact with video- or film-makers. But now that it is possible to present the different types of information in a common digital format, the boundaries are breaking down and it is possible to identify multimedia companies that bring written, audio and visual material together in the same information package. The primary publishers, a few years ago, produced predominantly print media, but that is changing rapidly with new providers for e-books and e-journals as well as web-enabled social media such as blogs.

Governments of all kinds are also major collectors and compilers of information. They hold, use and in some cases publish large amounts of information. In recent years a number of countries have encouraged the private sector information providers to exploit their information, partly to stimulate the dissemination of the information itself but also as a means of supporting the development of the information sector.

Some of the key players of primary information contents industries include Elsevier, Blackwell, Wolters Kluwer and Springer-Verlag, Sage, plus a wide range of professional association and academic presses.

Secondary

In addition to this genuinely creative information, a large part of the information-content segment is concerned with the compilation of information: the compilers of reference works, databases, statistical series and 'realtime' information services that supply constant flows of information about things like share and commodity prices. These publishers enable better access to primary publications by indexing and abstracting the primary publications. They may rely on cooperation with the primary publishers in order to have access to the source material, or may work directly with other types of source publications such as patents and trademarks. Before appearance of Web, the business of these publishers was based on print form, such indexes. However, with the appearance of Web these materials are now available mostly as databases in electronic format. Many secondary publishers offer access to their own database(s) via their website.

Some well known leaders of scientific and technical abstract and indexing providers are Thomson Scientific (Biosis, Derwent World Patent Index, ISI Science Citation Index), government agencies such as the National Library of Medicine (Medline) and the Department of Education (ERIC), and professional associations such as the American Chemical Society (Chemical Abstract Services) and IEEE (Inspec). NFAIS (National Federation of Abstracting and Indexing Services). These information providers account for a very significant proportion of the total revenues of the information-content sector. It is here that the public sector plays a key role.

There are another group of online services provider exists at present who job is not to generate but to aggregate information. They are well identified as information aggregator industry. They add value by aggregating many secondary and primary sources into a single environment, usually with a powerful search engine, and bundling in specialized capabilities for information delivery, formatting, analysis and customization. These services are evolving to more fully integrate the delivery of information with desktop or enterprise-wide software tools. Examples of online services are Dialog (part of Thomson Scientific, LexisNexis (part of Reed Elsevier), STN (part of ACS) and Ovid (part of Wolters Kluwer). The Software and Information Industry

Association (SIIA) is the representative professional association of this segment of the market.

The information-delivery industry

The second part of the information industry is concerned with delivery, that is the creation and management of the communication and dissemination networks through which we communicate information. This includes the telephone, broadcasting and book retail industries. They do not produce much more information, but their core business is to disseminate information to the clients. Today's many telecommunication companies, cable television networks companies, satellite broadcasters, cellular telecommunication companies, and radio (including FM) and television stations are under this category. These industries prove how much of an economy is about information, as opposed to materials.

Allied to these organizations is another set that is concerned with the use of these and other channels to distribute the information content. This is where we find the booksellers, libraries, and the providers of what are known as value added network services – these are services provided through the telecommunication networks, but which offer more than basic voice telephony: anything from information about the weather to traffic news.

The information-processing industry

This segment of the information industry is associated with information processing services. Here information is provided not as a tangible commodity but as a service. Some services, such as legal services, banking, insurance, computer programming, data processing, testing, and market research, require intensive and intellectual processing of information. Although those services do not necessarily provide information, they often offer expertise in making decisions on behalf of clients. These kinds of service industries can be regarded as an information-intensive part of various industries that is externalized and specialized.

In library context, these type of industries help in providing tools for managing, organizing and providing access to it through internal systems and to clients' desktops. A wide range of software providers operate in this space, including enterprise database management tools such as Oracle and SAP, content or document management systems such as Autonomy and Open Text, and intranet portal tools such as BEA's Plumtree. This is a rapidly changing arena, with a number of open source options available as well as major commercial players.

For library technical services, there are few such industries. They are providing tools for cataloging, circulation and public access. The library automation services that are commonly referred as integrated library systems (ILS) or Online Public Access Catalogs (OPACs) are also under this category. The largest player in shared cataloging - OCLC, a non-profit membership organization, is also comer under this category. Additionally, there are many stand-alone software and solutions providers including EOS, Sirsi-Dynix, ExLibris, and Innovative Interfaces which comes under this umbrella.

In order to support acquisition of books/serials there are some other players in market too. Examples of major players for materials acquisition management are EBSCO, SWETS, and Harrassowitz for journals and Blackwell Book Services, YBP, and Coutts for books. In the document delivery arena, key players are Infotrieve and the British Library Document Supply Center. However there are hundreds of regional and specialized suppliers belongs to this category.

With the increasing number of journals and books become available in electronic form, electronic book and journal delivery services are creating new types of distribution issues and services needs. The major players have entered the electronic arena and new services are emerging. Some of these new e-book services are Knovel, eBooks and Netlibrary. The e-journal services include Public Library of Science (PLOS), Open Content Alliance, Directory of Online Access Journals (DOAJ) and Highwire Press.

There are another category of service suppliers who are doing their business by helping librarian when a special project or internal requirement exceeds the bandwidth of library staff or requires special expertise. Information brokers typically have training and experience in librarianship, establishing their own consulting business to provide outsourcing services to information professionals. Some of the big players in this arena are Guideline, which encompasses the FIND SVP and Teltech services and Corsearch, which specializes in Trademark searching. However there are hundreds of other options and many brokers belong to the Association of Independent Information Professionals (AIIP).

Consultants or contract services can also be engaged for more permanent outsourcing of library functions, especially back room services. Where such outsourcing occurs, the relationship with the contractor may often be similar to working with a colleague in the same organization.

The information-processing device manufacturer industry

There are manufacturers of information-processing devices that require research and sophisticated decision-making. These products are vital to information-processing activities of above mentioned industries. The players include hardware producers and software producers. The hardware producers design, develop, manufacture and market computers, telecommunications equipment and consumer electronics. They tend to be concentrated in the United States and East Asia, deal in very high volumes and are operating in a market where unit prices have been falling steadily for over twenty years. Some of the prominent players in the market are IBM, DELL, Macintosh, HCL, HP, Compaq etc.

The software producers provide us with operating systems like UNIX, DOS or Windows, applications packages like spreadsheets and word processors, and increasingly computer games. In recent years most of the software industry has been concerned with producing software for mass consumption. There is still, however, a significant element that produces custom-built software systems for use in individual organizations.

In addition there are other types of industries under this category, the specialization of those industries in an economy is neither production of information nor sophisticated decision-making. Instead, this segment serves as an infrastructure for those activities, making production of information and decision-making services will be a lot less efficient. Printing and copying machines, measurement and recording devices of various kinds, electronic or otherwise, are also in this category.

Research intensive industries

Research intensive industries are not exclusively for information production or sophisticated decision-making, they played a vital role in decision making process. Industries that manufacture medical examination machines/devices and business farms that provide service to the client by using those devices and under this category. One can say these industries involve a great deal of sophisticated decision-making, although that part is combined with manufacturing or "non-informational" activities.

Finally, there are another group that are not research intensive, but serve as infrastructure for information production and sophisticated decision-making. Manufacturing of office furniture would be a good example, although it sometimes involves research in ergonomics and development of new materials, mostly they support infrastructure for various information generation industries.

CONCLUSION

Economics, although, has tended to treat information as something unproblematic, an auxiliary concept that can be left largely unanalyzed. Yet, in post-industrial economies, information has now become the main focus of economic transactions, and not merely a support for them. Economists, therefore, cannot afford the luxury of neglecting the conceptual foundations of an economics of information in this way.

Information industries are considered to boost to national economy. The increasing demand for information goods and services from consumers creates an opportunity for an urban, regional, or national economy to grow rapidly by specializing on these sectors. As information becomes the vital part of our economic activities we are moving towards an "information society", with an increased role of mass media, digital technologies, and other mediated information in our daily life, leisure activities, social life, work, politics, education, art, and many other aspects of society.

REFERENCES

Churchill, G. A., Jr. (1999). *Marketing Research: Methodological Foundations* (7th Ed.). Orlando, FL: Dryden.

Machlup, F. (1962). The production and distribution of knowledge in the United States. Princeton, NJ: Princeton University Press.

Miller, G. A. (1956). The Magic Number Seven, Plus or Minus Two: Some Limits on Our Capacity for Processing Information. *Psychological Review*, 63, 81-97.

Miller, Thomas W. (2000). Marketing Research and the Information Industry, *CASRO Journal*

Porat, M. (1977). The information economy: Definition and measurement. Office of Telecommunication, Washington, DC.

12 Marketing of Information

The future of marketing belongs to honest information, accurate data and clear claims based on truth. sold on the promise of a better future.
- Patrick Dixon

The increased importance of information in everyday life and in the economy prompted towards the development of an emerging sector commonly known as the 'information economy'. Perhaps, in the field of economics, the most important break with the past—one that leaves open huge areas for future work—lies in the economics of information. The Oxford American Dictionary defines economics as the science that deals with the production, distribution, and consumption of goods and services. If we considered information as goods and services (Pine and Gilmore, 1999) then economics of information simply means production, distribution, and consumption of information and these products have distinct cost and value characteristics. However 'economics of information' is not the same character as the 'economic of goods'. The value of information is one of the more difficult ideas to conceptualize.

During the past twenty years, academics have

produced a growing body of research about the value of information and its unique characteristics as an economic good (Repo, 1989). Some of the unique characteristics of information as an economic entity include:

- Information is expensive to produce but virtually costless to reproduce (Shapiro and Varian, 1999).
- Information can be a public good, a private good, or a hybrid good (Rafaeli and Raban, 2005).
- Depending on the type of good (public, private, or hybrid), the value of information may increase or decrease as a function of availability.
- Information is an experience good. Its value is revealed only after use (Shapiro and Varian, 1999).
- The value of information is largely subjective (Rafaeli and Raban, 2003).
- Information is transferred mostly by copying. Therefore, ownership rights do not, or at least should not, pose a problem (Cleveland, 1982).

In an organization, consumption of information is as common and necessary as the consumption of food. Unlike food, information when consumed does not go away, although it can become obsolete. The fundamental breakthrough in the economics of information was the recognition that information was fundamentally different from other "commodities." It possesses many of the properties of a public good—its consumption is nonrivalrous, and so, even if it is possible to exclude others from enjoying the benefits of some piece of knowledge, it is socially inefficient to do so; and it is often difficult to exclude individuals from enjoying the benefits. The issue of appropriating the returns to investments in information and knowledge is thus central.

INFORMATION AS RESOURCES

Now we will look information from different look. Resource basically is a tangible entity, however for the case of information we cannot be considered information as tangible until and unless we consider it as commodity or as a resource. In fact information is a resource on its own, as well as an asset to others. According to Cleveland there are six inherent characteristics of information as a resource:

1. Information is expandable : It is recognized that for specific purposes information may deplete, but in general, the more we have, the more we use, and the more useful it becomes. Information is certainly not scarce, and is available in profusion. This concept of "information-rich" may not necessarily be good, but may instead mean being "swamped". There are limits to the growth of information, but they lie in the time and capacity of people.

2. Information is compressible : It is possible to concentrate, integrate, and summarize information for easier handling.

3. Information is substitutable : Information can and does replace land, labor, and capital. It is the use of computers and telecommunications that aids in this phenomenon.

4. Information is transportable : Information can be tapped into just about anywhere; this has led to the idea of being remote as much more difficult to achieve since people and information can be taken to the remotest of places.

5. Information is diffusive : There tends to be an ability for information to leak. This leakage allows us to have more, and more of us to have it.

6. Information is shareable : No exchange transaction of information can take place, only sharing transactions, and this leads to an entire sharing environment.

ECONOMICS AND INFORMATION

The phrase 'economics of information' first appear in the terminology of economics nearly in 1960s. In information science it appeared primarily in connection with evaluation studies. The economics of information can be best described by naming the central areas of interests in the information market: a). information supply (economy of information production, pricing information products); b). information demand (acquisition and use of information; and c). special problems of information as a product or resources (e.g. pricing of use, public funding of information production).

INFORMATION ECONOMY - FEATURES

The most commonly cited definition of the "*information economy*" is that of Porat, who distinguishes between two economic domains: the domain of matter and energy, and the domain of information. An economy becomes an information economy when information-related work begins to exceed work related to the other sectors. Some of the feature as identified by Porat under *information economy* as:

1. An information economy is an economy where the information sector has become more dominant than the agriculture or industrial sectors of the economy.
2. The information sector is that part of the economy that deals with the creation, manipulation, processing, transmission, distribution, and use of information, where information is defined as the reduction of uncertainty, and uncertainty is a measure of the number of possibilities. The smallest unit of information is the bit, which resolves the uncertainty between two equally possible outcomes. Information is a non-material, non-energy entity and takes physical form only in so far as it is stored in a physical medium (as in a hard disk) or communicated in physical form (as in a radio signal).

3. Information by this definition includes software, databases, music, video, book content, designs, genetic information, human and organic memories, and other entities which may eventually be represented, stored and communicated as bits. These may be called information goods. They are sometimes placed under the category of information content. Information goods include goods which are not purely information, but whose amount of information contained is such that it contributes the biggest portion of the price of the good. They also include Internet Protocol (IP) numbers, domain names, formats, standards, and similar items used in information equipment and facilities.
4. The information economy also includes the physical equipment and facilities used for information generation and processing, although these equipment themselves may have been produced outside the information economy. These physical equipment include computers, communications equipment, switching equipment, networking equipment, audio and video equipment, printing presses, radio/TV studios and stations, ¬libraries, cinemas, DNA sequencing machines, and similar equipment. These may be called information equipment and facilities.
5. The information economy further includes the people engaged in generating and distributing information.
6. Information is a non-material entity/non-energy entity, and matter/energy is needed only in so far as information needs to be stored/communicated. As information technology continues to advance, ways of storing/communication information that use less matter/energy continue to be developed. Thus, the cost of reproducing (i.e., duplicating, making copies) information is approaching zero.

7. The preceding paragraph uniquely defines the economics of information: a good that may take a significant amount of matter or energy to create, but costs practically nothing to reproduce leads to an economy that is uniquely different from the economy of physical goods (i.e., goods which contain in each unit a fixed amount of matter and energy consumed, which will be inevitably reflected in the cost of such goods). Information goods may be reproduced at practically no cost (i.e., near-zero marginal cost of production), which means that once created, the scarcity of this good can be ended at practically no cost. Thus a study of the information economy should involve not only a conventional study of the economics of scarcity, but also a study of the economics of abundance.

8. Information goods today can be owned through a mechanism called intellectual property rights (IPR), which include such monopolistic statutory mechanisms as patents and copyrights. IPRs create an artificial scarcity, negating the potential abundance of an information good once it is created and enabling IPR holders to artificially maintain the price of an information good at an arbitrary level. An information economy that relies on such monopolistic mechanisms as IPRs to reward intellectual activity may be called monopolistic information economy. In the future, we may also see the emergence of non-monopolistic information economies, where intellectual activity is rewarded through non-monopolistic means only, enabling the public to enjoy fully the abundance of information goods once they are created. Information equipment and facilities are owned in the same traditional way as industrial equipment and land, even while individual aspects of such information

equipment and facilities may also contain patented or copyrighted material.

As digital technology made possible the production of exact copies of text, images, audio, video and other information materials over unlimited generations, the information economy grew rapidly. With the emergence of the Internet and later the World Wide Web, the information economy gradually matured into the full-blown economy that it is today.

WHAT IS MARKETING?

After understanding the concept information economy, let us try to understand how this resource can be used for generating money. One of the important steps for selling any product and generating money is marketing. So, let us first understand the concept of marketing and then how marketing of information can be done? Peter Drucker, the management guru, explained marketing as 'It is the whole business seen from the point of view of its final result, that is, from the customer's point of view... Business success is not determined by the producer but by the customer. 'Philip Kotler, calls *Marketing* 'a social and managerial process by which individuals and groups obtain what they need and want through creating, offering, and exchanging products of value with others'. On the other hand, Smith writes marketing is a stance and an attitude that focuses on meeting the needs of users. Marketing is a means of ensuring that libraries, librarians, and librarianship are integrated into both today's and tomorrow's emerging global culture. Marketing is not separate from good practice. It is good practice.

MARKETING OF INFORMATION PRODUCTS AND SERVICES

The concept of marketing in libraries began when

Philip Kotler formally propagated the marketing concept in non-profit organizations in the 1970s and was sharpened in the 1980s when the concept of services marketing emerged (Gupta, 2003).

As information is the main subject of interest and work for librarians and information professionals, many researchers believe that learning the economic aspect of information should be an integral part of information-related programs because "technology changes; economic laws do not" (Shapiro and Varian, 1999, p. 2). Researchers also propose that gaining a good understanding of the economic rules of information is important for the survival of librarians and information professionals. Marketing is a process that can help managers of libraries and information centres in achieving their objectives of improving access to their clientele, increasing the satisfaction of their clients and reaching financial self-sufficiency. The marketing process, in case of libraries and information centres, implies that these objectives be achieved by offering improved and competitive information products and services.

Why Marking Library Products and Services

1. Every type of library and information centre has some basic objectives to ensure the maximum use of its reading materials. The marketing of information products and services plays a dynamic role to attain the predetermined goals and objectives of library and information centres.
2. Today, with increased competition in this world of information, marketing is a factor for survival. Marketing of library services is concerned with satisfying the needs of the users. Hence, Narayana (1991) points out that the 'survival of a library depends among other things on its image in the minds of the users and the fund allocators. This image should be

the outcome of the quality and effectiveness of the services, the ability to anticipate the desires and requirements of actual and potential users and their fulfillment. Marketing is the instrument through which these library objectives can be fulfilled'.

3. Information products/services marketing can be considered as 'a bridge between information production and consumption' – encompassing all the activities performed in order to get information products and services into the hands of users (Ryan, 1981)
4. Any organization either profitable or non-profitable is likely to be more successful when a strong marketing viewpoint permeates the thinking and guides the decisions and actions of everyone in the organization. Like many other non-profitable organizations, library and information centres also need a strong and effective marketing programme to improve their image and gain acceptance among sponsors, government agencies, news media, and of course, consumers, all of which collectively determine an organization's success (Stanton, 1994).
5. In recent years, librarians and information managers are facing challenge due to:
   - Increase in clientele, their variety, their demands, and their expectations.
   - Complexity in their requirements, and servicing them.
   - Increase in the initial or capital cost of implementing information technology, and the need to leverage the technology and find new levels of economies of scale to serve the increasing potential clientele.
   - Decreasing the public sponsorship and subsidy

and the need to find alternate sources of revenue.

Librarians and information managers are, therefore, need to show their initiative and entrepreneurship. Time has come to rethink, shed many old beliefs, and find new ways of doing things. The traditional concept of a library or an information centre as a social service for knowledge, for the sake of knowledge, and library, for the sake of library, has outlived its need. The warehouse and custodian perspective of librarians and information managers needs a change. Preparing information products and services only when asked for, has to give in to a more systematic anticipation and research of the future requirements of different clients, leading to the preparation of appropriate products and services and making these available to the clients. Membership-patronage-subsidy comfort has ended.

Duncan Smith of CARL Corporation writes about libraries, librarians, and their role:

> Each generation of librarians must define for itself and its users what the library is and how it will add value to the information exchanges of its community. Libraries and librarians have traditionally added value to these exchanges in three major ways. They have provided physical access to information, they have organized this information for use, and they have provided assistance in locating and utilizing this information...

In this context, Mary C. Bushing of the Collection Development, Montana State University Libraries, raises the following questions:

> ... What will this library look like? What services, programmes, and materials will be offered? How can we find answers to important questions about such things as: the relationship of access

to ownership; the appropriate content and extent of collections; the right mix of services for a specific community of potential clients; and sources of adequate support for library activities? In order to address these concerns, we must first determine what the role of the library is to be. What is the business of the library? It is the answer to this question which is the crucial first step in defining the future.

6. As Leisner (1995) pointed the basis for library marketing is the need first to enhance the quality of services, and then, to improve the perceived value of these services and thus achieve the highest level of customer satisfaction to ensure survival of the organization. Alemna (2001) stated that effective marketing is the obvious means by which users can be made aware of the services of the library and their value.
7. A well-developed library marketing programme, as Narayana (1991) pointed is essential to:
   - Improved user satisfaction
   - Extension of the service to potential users and enlargement of the customers' circle
   - Efficient use of marketing resources
   - Improved resource attraction to the organization.
8. According to Gupta (2003) there are some other reasons that require marketing orientation in library and information services, such as:
   - It helps in managing libraries better;
   - It brings commitment to customer focus;
9. Changing is very common phenomenon in library environment. There is a change in concept about libraries Due to revolutionary changes in Information

and Communication Technologies (ICTs), the primary concept of the library (as a storehouse of knowledge) has been changed and become more dynamic. The mode of users' demand has also been changed and developed. Today, users are not so interested in getting their desired information in traditional ways. As a result library and information officials have been compelled to market their information products and services to users more actively.

Change of attitude has also noted among the users and librarians. Effective marketing is only one of the factors that determine library use. Effective marketing provides the means by which users are made aware of the services of the library and their value (Martey, 2000). Due to the dramatic change of users' attitudes towards information, the necessity of marketing information products and services has been realized by library officials. By implementing the marketing concept in libraries, Rowley (1995) renamed the librarian from storekeeper to salesman. Libraries must be run like commercial firms and professional librarians must be the managers.

10. Shariful & Nazmul Islam (2009) express the necessity of marketing in libraries and information centres because of the information explosion it has become difficult for users to find their desired information properly. Marketing of information products and services can help the users to get the information they want easily from the huge amount of information available.

How Marketing Libraries and Information Centres

The key steps for marketing stress that a library and information centre can achieve its goals by providing user satisfaction through coordinated activities. These activities are way of thinking or management philosophy about a library's total activities. Mishra (1994–5) describes those steps in the following five ways.

1. Market segmentation : Market segmentation for libraries depends on the type of library, its objectives, and the environment in which the library operates (Narayana, 1991). Public libraries do segment their clients on the basis of demographic characteristic and use 'community survey' to know about the actual and potential users of the library and quantify them. A public library may segment its users in different groups such as children, adults, senior citizens and the visually impaired (Mishra, 1994–5).

2. Market positioning : This is a process of arranging for a product to occupy a clear, distinctive, and desirable place relative to competing products in the minds of target consumers (Kotler and Armstrong, 2001). Having the market segmentation of the library, the librarian decides the major target group according to the objectives of the library and available resources (Mishra, 1994–5).

3. Consumer analysis : The process of determining the needs and preferences of the target group is known as consumer analysis. In libraries, we do user surveys to learn the needs and preferences of the users and call them 'Information Gathering Habits', 'Information Seeking Behaviour', and 'Information Needs' (Mishra, 1994–5). This is the most important step because the total marketing concept depends upon the consumer and his/her satisfaction.

4. Marketing programme : This is often called the marketing mix, which implies that it is possible to mix or blend the elements of the marketing concept in an infinite number of combinations in order to achieve marketing goals. These elements of marketing are product, price, promotion and place. For the sake of simplicity these are often called the 4Ps identified by McCarthy (Webber, 1999). Shapiro

(1981) recategorizes the 4Ps by adding advertising and policy for the purpose of non-profit organizations. We can describe, in brief, the marketing mix as:

- ***Product*** : The item or service being marketed, through its features, quality, benefits and quantities (Copley, 2004). The product can be ideas, services, goods or any combination of these three.
- ***Price*** : Price relates to the activities associated with establishing pricing policies and determining product prices (Rowley, 1995). Pricing is the marketing activity that determines the price of the product on the basis of costs as well as market factors, such as distribution channels, discount structure, competitors' prices, the ability or willingness of customers to pay, and so on.
- ***Place*** : Place is the marketing term for describing where the product or service is offered (Leisner, 1995). Place refers to location (such as a library), the distribution channel where a service is delivered, geographical coverage, telecommunications, travel and so on (Munshi, 2001).
- ***Promotion*** : The promotion variable is used to inform one or more groups of people about an organization and its products (Rowley, 1995). Promotion includes all the activities undertaken by the library to communicate its resources and services to the target user groups (Nicholas, 1998). Promotion activities include things like personal selling, advertising, sales promotions, publicity, public relations and packaging.

  Munshi (2001) also extends the concept of the 4Ps by adding people and process for the libraries and information centre.
- ***People*** : People cover staff/personnel that are responsible for providing effective information

services to users.

- *Process* : Process means techniques, methods or ways by which the products, goods or information services are managed and delivered to users. Booms and Bitner (1981) suggested a 7Ps mix by which they extended the traditional 4Ps (product, price, promotion and place) with including 3Ps (participants, physical evidence and process). • Participants: All human actors who play a part in reference and information services delivery, namely the library's personnel.
- *Physical evidence* : The environment in which the reference and information services are delivered that facilitates the performance and communication of the service.
- *Process* : The procedures, mechanisms and flow of activities by which the reference and information services are acquired.

5. Marketing audit

The marketing audit is a systematic, critical and unbiased review and performance appraisal of the marketing programme in the light of the data gathered from market segmentation, consumer analysis, and the objectives of the organization. On implementing a marketing programme, it is necessary to evaluate how far the programme has been able to achieve its set objectives. A few of the evaluation criteria are (Narayana, 1991):

- Size of market covered (population or geographic area)
- Market share of the library (percentage of neoliterate adults, minority sector, handicapped students and so on)
- Number and value of sales (number of on-line searches by customers and their sale value)

- Number of users
- Frequency of use of the library services (browsing, loan, reference)
- User satisfaction or library goodness

RANGANATHAN'S LAWS & MARKETING

If we consider Dr Ranganathan's concept of the Five Laws of Library Science, it had the marketing concept at their core. From five laws point of view the first law emhasise to maximize the use of books. In order to maximize the use there is a need of marketing. Similarly, the *Second law* 'Every reader his book' mainly explained that reader is the prime factor and his/her need must be satisfied. The *Third law* 'Every book its reader' mainly explained to find a reader for every book - for which marketing also essential. *Fourth law* 'Save the time of the reader' mainly explain to organize information in such a way that the reader finds the wanted information promptly. Finally, *Fifth law* 'A library is a growing organism emphasis is on comprehensive and evolutionary growth.

A closer examination indicates that modifications are needed in the interpretation of the laws. Firstly the definition of a customer, only as a reader, needs to be widened to include the purpose of reading and ways of using the information. Secondly, in today's context the process of use of information (like use of computers/information technology (IT) to process the information obtained from the library/information centre) may *give* rise to totally new needs and wants (like getting information through e-mail which can be used directly on the personal computer (PC). Thirdly, given the usefulness of information in one library/centre to customers in different and far off locations, reaching out to customers is becoming far more important. Thus, though customer focus has long been advocated in the library profession, it may be refined to suit the current context of the market.

The five laws of Ranganathan did imply a sharp focus on customer. However, a closer examination of the laws reveals that the focus is on a customer who came to the library rather than, the library reaching out to the customer. A focus on customer needs (second law) and wants through saving of time (fourth law) is clearly emphasized in these laws, as far back as 1931. Also, the third law relates to finding a reader, probably implying that the library should reach out to the customers.

Unfortunately, marketing concept, as presented by Kotler has hardly been used in libraries/information centres in developing countries. Seetharama in this regards points out that the concept of marketing of information services and products in India can be said to be still in infancy. This is in spite of the fact that, Dr S R Ranganathan had focused on the need for marketing, he did not use the term when he enunciated the Five Laws of Library Science in 1930. As a matter of fact, the Five Laws can be used as a basis for the development of marketing principles in the context of libraries and information centres.

IMPLICATION OF MARKETING TECHNIQUES IN LIBRARIES

Marketing strategy or technique varies with changes in environment, objectives of the organization, resources and the users. So it is not so easy to implement marketing techniques in libraries. A librarian can either employ an outside expert or do this activity him/ herself. Ojiambo (1994) identified five stages by which a librarian can simply apply marketing techniques in library or information centre. These stages can be illustrated on the basis of those ideas:

Stage-1: Determination of purpose and resources or product of library

This stage involves the following series of actions:

- Determine the purposes and goals of the library or information centre
- Identify the goals of the library for a marketing programme
- Know well the products that are being offered

Stage-2: Identification of competitors

Libraries and information centres are in competition with several non-profit and profit making organizations in providing information. Managers of libraries/information centres should identify those organizations with which they are in competition.

Stage-3: Identification of users

Applying marketing techniques to libraries requires that a library identifies various groups of users and modifies the library service and information based on those different groups and their different needs. This process is called segmentation. This will involve knowing libraries' patrons and their information needs by conducting user studies.

Stage-4: Establishment of a marketing strategy for the library

After defining library segments and establishing needs and matching these with information resources, the next stage is to identify particular goals for the marketing programme and to develop specific strategies to reach them, and to develop a timetable for all communication efforts. This includes advertising and public relations, channels of distribution and product policies. In general these factors can be referred to as communicating with the library/ information centre segments. Communication with the segments enables the library/information centre not only to provide its users with needed information but also to get feedback.

HURDLES IN IMPLICATING MARKETING TECHNIQUES IN LIBRARIES

Implementing marketing in libraries is a difficult task for a country like India. Most of the libraries here are still engaged only in providing assistance to users for finding books. There is also a common belief that marketing is relevant only to business, but not to libraries. So it is difficult task to implement such concepts. Here we are summing up some of the problems that the libraries of India are facing today to implement marketing concepts.

1. Ignorance about marketing concepts

Many of the library officials in Bangladesh do not understand what the term marketing means and why it is appropriate for libraries.

2. Lack of proper education and training of library staff

Due to lack of training and knowledge of marketing tools and techniques, librarians often do not promote library services properly.

3. Negative attitude of users

The attitude of users towards marketing also plays a passive role not to implement marketing concepts in libraries.

According to S. Sreenivas Rao the four barriers to the adoption of the marketing approach are:

- Attitudinal
- Structural
- Systemic
- Environmental

Attitudewise : Information professionals, like many other professionals, have been inward looking - happy with satisfying a limited clientele, that too when asked for, and happy with jealously guarding their importance. To be outward looking, from the client's point of view would require them to make a 180 degrees turnaround.

Structurewise : The staff which comes into contact with the public or clients are the counter clerks and less frequently, the reference librarian and the librarian. As a result, there is no staff to reach out and capture the point of view of the client. To introduce any such layer would be resisted from the existing staff and the turf holders. Moreover, the libraries and information centres are a part of a large organization which does not follow the marketing approach as well. Also, traditional security of the job, common to public institutions, and lack of involvement of professionals in the management of the library or the information centre, in developing countries, is conducive to a no-change syndrome.

Systemwise : Libraries and information centres, so far, have been more storage, security, and audit conscious. They do not allow the client or the client's point of view inside the system. Guarding or protecting the information is more important than utilizing it for the satisfaction of its clientele. Therefore, any changes in the system to make it more client or service oriented, would be to ask for both attitudinal as well as structural changes.

Environmentwise : The culture, especially in the developing countries, still believes that information should be free and should be sought by clients themselves. Dependence on government and private largesse in many areas is taken for granted. There is no attempt at seeking out clients. Marketing and payment for a variety of services, like education or information, is considered infra-dig both for the giver and the taker.

Seetharama explained following reasons for non-implementing marketing in library information centers:

- Confusion at the conceptual level among librarians and information scientists that marketing is nothing but promotion and sales.
- Lack of a definite marketing policy—end user policy, product policy, distribution policy, tariff policy, services policy—either at the national or at the local level.
- User Needs Assessment Studies are inadequate due to methodological deficiencies and due to the fact that they are not carried out on a continuing basis.
- Lack of proper market research and segmentation studies.
- Product development and targeting leaves much to be desired due to the absence of market research and segmentation.
- Reluctance on the part of the users to pay for information services resulting in the adoption of economy measures. As a consequence, the physical quality and get-up of products are adversely affected.
- Evaluation of information services and products is conspicuous by its absence (Gopalkrishnan, 1988). Marketing concepts are either not taught or least emphasized in library schools. In most cases, it does not form part of the curriculum.
- Information is a low priority item of users, and the motivation to share is even lower.
- Information consolidation activities/products, especially, value-added products which are very useful to users are not generated to the extent needed.

CONCLUSION

Being an non-profit making organization, marketing in libraries has become a buzz word. However, there is a growing need for understanding and employing marketing in libraries and information services. Library and information products/services are now being assumed as saleable and there is a growing market for these. The rationale behind this phenomenal change is may diverse but mostly associated with information explosion, influx of automated systems, rising costs of materials and services, adoption of sophisticated technologies in libraries and online services, demand for better services, staff shortage and harsh budget cutbacks compounded by soaring operating costs. It is the adoption of a marketing approach that will help libraries not only in their own sustenance, but also in the sustenance and self-sufficiency of their information products and services. Through marketing activities like user need analysis, determining user segment, analysis of the available products, definition of differentiated products, matching user profile with product profile, determining proper tools and techniques of trade, creating suitable publicity of products and defining outreach areas and levels can be possible properly. These ultimately helps libraries or information centres to provide better information products and services to users. With the emergence of concepts like virtual library and becoming a non-profitable organization in a society existence of a library depends on its image in the minds of the users and the fund allocators. This image should be the outcome of the quality and effectiveness of the services, and the ability to anticipate the desires and requirements of actual and potential users and their fulfillment.

REFERENCES

Alemna, A. A. (2001). The Need for Marketing and Total Quality Management Strategies in Libraries in Ghana, *INSPEL* 35(4):

265–9.

Booms, B. H. and Bitner, M. J. (1981). *Marketing Strategies and Organization Structures for Service*. In Donnelly, J.H., George, W.R. (Eds), Marketing of Services, Conference Proceedings: American Marketing Association, Chicago, IL, pp.47-51 .

Cleveland, H. (1982). Information as a resource. *Futurist*, 6(3/4), 1-5.

Copley, P. (2004). *Marketing Communications Management*. Oxford: Elsevier Butterworth-Heinemann.

Drucker, P.F. (1994). The age of social transformation. *The Atlantic*, 247. 53-80.

Firms', in J. H. Donnelly and W. R. George (eds) *Marketing of Services*, pp. 47–51. Chicago, IL: American Marketing Association.

Gupta, D. K. (2003). Marketing of Library and Information Services: Building a New Discipline for Library and Information Science Education in Asia, *Malaysian Journal of Library & Information Science*, 18(2), 95–108.

Islam, Md. Shariful and Islam, Md. Nazmul (2009). Marketing of library and information products and services : A theoretical analysis, *Business Information Review*, 26, 123

Kotler, P. and Keller, K.L (2006). *Marketing Management*. New York: Pearson Education.

Leisner, T. (1995). Should Libraries Engage in Marketing?, paper presented at the 61st IFLA General Conference, Istanbul, 20–5 August. Available at: www.ifla.org/IV/ifla61/61-leit.htm

Mishra, S. (1994–5). Marketing of Library and Information Services and Products: Old Wine in New Bottle', *Library Herald* 32(3–4), 153–6.

Munshi, M. N. (2001). Marketing of Information Services: A Conceptual Framework, *The Dhaka University Studies* 58(2), 127–38.

Narayana, G. J. (1991). *Library and Information Management*, pp. 175–87. New Delhi: Prentice Hall of India.

Nicholas, J. (1998). Marketing and Promotion of Library Services, *ASP Conference Series* 153, Available at: www.stci.edu/stci/meetings/lisa3/nicholasj/html

Ojiambo, J. B. (1994.) Application of Marketing Principles and Techniques to Libraries and Information Centres, *Library Review* 73(2), 46–51.

Pine, B. J., & Gilmore, J. (1999). The experience economy:Work is theatre & every business a stage. Boston, MA: Harvard Business School Publishing.

Porat, Marc U and Rubin, Michael R. (1977)., *The Information Economy* (9 volumes), Office of Telecommunications Special Publication 77-12 (US Department of Commerce, Washington D.C.).

Rafaeli, S., & Raban, D. R. (2003). Experimental investigation of the subjective value of information in trading. *Journal of the Association for Information Systems*, 4(5), 119-139.

Repo, A. J. (1989). The value of information: Approaches in economics, accounting, and management science. *Journal of the American Society for Information Science*, 40, 68-85.

Rowley, J. (1995). From Storekeeper to Salesman: Implementing the Marketing Concept in Libraries, *Library Review* 44(1): 24–35.

Ryan, W. T. (1981). *A Guide to Marketing*. Homewood, IL: Richard D. Irwin.

Seetharama, S. (1990). *Guidelines for Planning of Libraries and Information Centres, IASLIC*, Calcutta,.

Shapiro, C., & Varian, H. R. (1999). Information rules: A strategic guide to the network economy. Boston: Harvard Business School Press.

Smith, Duncan (1995). Practice as a Marketing Tool: Four Case Studies', *Library Trends*, 43(3).

13
Protection of Information

When you xerox a page of something the original doesn't disappear, and in the same way information isn't really lost when it's "stolen". — **Masamune Shirow**

World wide web and its subsequent development gives birth of huge information on the web. Creating, publishing and distributing information have become many times easier and faster as compared to the past decade. Simultaneously, it also brings those together who take advantage of the properties of digital information to copy, distribute, and use information illegally. The existence of virtual library has increased the violation of copyright and data security hazards, there are many obstacles and problems hindering digital resources in libraries. Existing copyright laws have not caught up with the technological developments in cyberspace. Many times there is no clarity as whether the content of electronic resources is free one or priced. This chapter basically handle some of such issues which are associated with lawful aspect of information, like intellectual property rights, digital rights management etc. We also touch the concept of fair use and explained creative common license in this chapter.

INTELLECTUAL PROPERTY RIGHT

Before going for the Intellectual Property Right we must understand what is 'Intellectual Property'. The term intellectual property (IP) generally refers to the creation of the human intelligence and the phrase intellectual property rights refers to the laws set forth to grant the legal rights to own and control the use of intellectual properties for a period of time, thereby creating the opportunity to profit from these properties. It includes the right to license or grant specific uses of these rights to a third party, typically for a fee. It is generally understood that IP includes rights relating to the following:

- Literary, artistic and scientific works;
- Performances of performing artists, phonograms, and broadcasts;
- Inventions in all fields of human endeavor;
- Scientific discoveries;
- Industrial designs;
- Marks and commercial names and designations;
- Protection against unfair competition; and
- All other rights resulting from intellectual activity in the industrial, scientific, literary, and artistic fields

It is a generic term covering patents, trademark, copyright, industrial property, registered design, trade secrets, layout of integrated circuits, geographical indicators and anti-competitive practices in contractual licenses The first step regarding the protection of intellectual property was first recognized in the Paris Convention for the Protection of Industrial Property in 1883 and the Berne Convention for the Protection of Literary and Artistic Works in 1886. Both treaties are administered by the World Intellectual Property

Organization (WIPO). Nations generally have laws to protect intellectual property has following main reasons.

- Give statutory expression to the moral and economic rights of creators in their creations
- To promote creativity and the dissemination and application of its results, and
- To encourage fair trade, which would contribute to economic and social development

Patent

A patent is a set of exclusive rights granted by a state to an inventor or their assignee for a limited period of time in exchange for a public disclosure of an invention. The procedure for granting patents, the requirements placed on the patentee, and the extent of the exclusive rights vary widely between countries according to national laws and international agreements. Typically, however, a patent application must include one or more claims defining the invention which must be new, non-obvious, and useful or industrially applicable. In many countries, certain subject areas are excluded from patents, such as business methods, treatment of the human body and mental acts. The exclusive right granted to a patentee in most countries is the right to prevent others from making, using, selling, or distributing the patented invention without permission. It is just a right to prevent others' use. A patent does not give the proprietor of the patent the right to use the patented invention, should it fall within the scope of an earlier patent.

Trademark

A trademark is a word, symbol, phrase or design, or a combination thereof, that identifies and distinguishes the source of the products or services from those of other entities. The term trademark is also used informally to refer to any distinguishing attribute by which an individual is readily identified. When a trademark is used in relation to services rather than products, it may sometimes be called a service mark. There is also a range of non-conventional trademarks comprising marks which do not fall into these standard categories, such as those based on color, smell, or sound.

The owner of a registered trademark may commence legal proceedings for trademark infringement to prevent unauthorized use of that trademark. However, registration is not required. The owner of a common law trademark may also file suit, but an unregistered mark may be protectable only within the geographical area within which it has been used or in geographical areas into which it may be reasonably expected to expand.

Copyright

Copyright refers to the legal protection of original works of authorship. Works covered by copyright include, but are not limited to: novels, poems, plays, reference works, newspapers, computer programs, databases, films, musical compositions, choreography, paintings, drawings, photographs, sculpture, architecture, advertisements, maps, and technical drawings. Copyright does not cover the ideas expressed in such works. But it covers the way ideas are expressed. Copyright protections are automatically provided to the author of both published and unpublished works at the moment they are affixed in a tangible medium. The copyright holder has the exclusive right to the following with his/her work:

- To reproduce the work
- To prepare derivative works
- To sell, lend, distribute copies or transfer ownership
- To perform the work publicly
- To display the copyrighted work publicly

Copyright is the body of laws which grants authors,

artists and other creators protection for their literary and artistic creations, which are generally referred to as "works". A closely associated field of rights related to copyright is "related rights", which provides rights similar or identical to those of copyright, although sometimes more limited and of shorter duration. The beneficiaries of related rights are: performers (such as actors and musicians) in their performances; producers of sound recordings (for example, cassette recordings and compact discs) in their recordings; and broadcasting organizations in their radio and television programs.

Industrial Property

Industrial property shall be understood in the broadest sense and shall apply not only to industry and commerce proper, but likewise to agricultural and extractive industries and to all manufactured or natural products, for example, grain, tobacco leaf, fruit, cattle, minerals, mineral waters, flowers, and flour. Industrial property include patents to protect inventions; and industrial designs, which are aesthetic creations determining the appearance of industrial products. Industrial property also covers trademarks, service marks, layout-designs of integrated circuits, commercial names and designations, as well as geographical indications, and protection against unfair competition. In some of these, the aspect of intellectual creation, although existent, is less clearly defined. What counts here is that the object of industrial property typically consists of signs transmitting information, in particular to consumers, as regards products and services offered on the market. Protection is directed against unauthorized use of such signs likely to mislead consumers, and against misleading practices in general.

Registered Design

Design is all about the way an object looks: its shape, its visual appeal. Designs look after the physical appearance and visual appeal of products - from the shape of flower pot to the body of a mobile-phone. It is a legal right which protects the overall visual appearance of a product or a part of a product in the country or countries you register it. For the purposes of registration, a design is legally defined as being "the appearance of the whole or part of a product resulting from the features of, in particular, the lines, colours, shape, texture or materials of the product or ornamentation." This means that protection is given to the way a product looks. The appearance of your product may result from a combination of elements such as shapes, colours and materials.

Trade secrets

To protect a trade secrets user can't go through an application process. A trade secret requires user to actively keep the information secret. User should consider keeping something as a trade secret if:

- it is not appropriate for intellectual property (IP) protection
- if the user want to keep it secret or
- user want protection to extend beyond the term of a patent

If it would be difficult to copy the process, construction or formulation from your product itself, a trade secret may give you the protection you need. However, a trade secret does not stop anyone from inventing the same process or product independently, and can be difficult to keep. Theoretically trade secret protection could last forever if the secret is carefully maintained. For example, user inventions and processes that do not meet patentability criteria can be protected under trade secret law. The advantage of a trade secret is that as long as the secret is properly maintained, the secret cannot be used by business competitors. One of the most famous examples is the Coca Cola formula that has now been kept secret for more than 100 years.

PLAGIARISM

The word plagiarism comes from a Latin word for kidnapping. Kidnapping is stealing a person, plagiarism is stealing a person's ideas or writing. Plagiarism is defined in dictionaries as the "wrongful appropriation," "close imitation". Terms like "copying" and "borrowing" can disguise the seriousness of the offense. In fact, plagiarism is not just about copying another's work, or borrowing someone else's original ideas, but it is an act of fraud. It involves both stealing someone else's work and lying about it afterward. All of the following are considered as plagiarism:

- turning in someone else's work as your own
- copying words or ideas from someone else without giving credit
- failing to put a quotation in quotation marks
- giving incorrect information about the source of a quotation
- changing words but copying the sentence structure of a source without giving credit
- copying so many words or ideas from a source that it makes up the majority of your work, whether you give credit or not

While preparing class assignment if a student read different books, attend lectures, discuss with colleagues and finally prepare the assignment assimilate different ideas into their own writing, this can not said to be plagiarism. But with the assistance of new emerging technology i.e. internet students can plagiarize by copying and pasting information from other sources. Here the concept of plagiarism comes into the picture. Plagiarism is using others' ideas and words without clearly acknowledging the source of that information. Plagiarism is not a crime but is disapproved more on the grounds of moral offence.

Reasons

The basic reason behind the plagiarism is unaware of the concept and its type. A person writing a article quote so many things from the paper already written on that topic without referring the original source. This normally happens for two reasons: lack of knowledge; and poor referencing

In the written article user never claim that it is his own contribution, but because of lack of knowledge and poor referencing he can be liable for infringement copyright act. Plagiarism does not only include the copy of the words but also the copy of expressions, ideas, and many other creative tasks.

Types of Plagiarism

The arrival of internet technology makes it easy for the user to copy the desired information and make it use for their own. Availability of e-book, database and other online information and material enhance the plagiarism. Easy access and quick results are the moto behind the plagiarism. The boundary between plagiarism and research is often unclear. There are different types of plagiarism based on the intensity of plagiarism and some of them are as follows:

Complete plagiarism

Complete plagiarism takes place where content are presented without making any change in the language, thoughts, flow, and even punctuation. Experts believe this is the act of a person having a little knowledge on the define subject.

Partial/Substantial Plagiarism

When content are present with some sort of modification, complying different sources, using synonyms, adding more details in the text, changing the patterns of the text and the technique of rephrasing, it is known as partial or substantial Plagiarism.

Minimalistic Plagiarism

This kind of plagiarism mostly takes place in academic sector, where students plagiaries someone else concept, ideas, thought, or opinions in their own words and in a different flow.

Source Citation

There are certain cases where user quotes the original sources, but the information or material provided in the articles are not match with the source provided at the end of the article. While in other cases user copy the information and merge all at one and provide the false reference.

Sources Not Cited

Under this category user copy the information from different sources, regroup the word combination, rephrase the paragraph, add words and make the whole new article.

Self-plagiarism

This form of plagiarism is also known as "recycling fraud". When the user uses significant, identical, or nearly identical portions of his own work in another article without giving the credit to the original sources is known as self-plagiarism. Publishing the same material through different mediums without referencing it correctly is a very common habit among many writers.

Justification for Plagiarism

In the year 1994 Pamela Samuelson acknowledged the various factors which present justification in the favour of plagiarism. The factors are as follow:

- The previous work needs to be restated in order to lay

the groundwork for a new contribution in the second work.

- Portions of the previous work must be repeated in order to deal with new evidence or arguments.
- The audience for each work is so different that publishing the same work in different places was necessary to get the message out.
- The author thinks they said it so well the first time that it makes no sense to say it differently a second time.

Ways to avoid Plagiarism

Internet and other various networking technologies open immense possibilities to copy and paste material and publish it with one's name. Detection of plagiarism of such cases is relatively a simple process but preventing it a difficult task. Here are some of the way to prevent plagiarism:

Use Templates : It is better to use templates, because copying of template is a difficult task and if anyone wants to copy he/she can easily identified by the original contributor. Suppose if you want to post something in online journal use image of the same colour matching with background behind the text and if someone copies your text from the page and publish it with their own name he easily detected online. What the original contributor has to do just change the image and plagiarized material also show the same changed image. Use of the Digital Millennium Copyright Act with a file and takedown notice is the most common method of dealing with plagiarism.

Preserve Evidence : Preserving the evidence is another option to overcome plagiarism. Use a bookmarking site like Furl to keep a cached copy of the plagiarist's site. This is good for user's own records and if a dispute comes up later. Though it is not a full proof evidence but it is useful in future.

Use Licensing Wisely : By using Creative Commons Licensing users can avoid persuing people that are merely reusing your content and focus on those that are plagiarizing it or using it for commercial gain. Though this isn't right for everyone, it can reduce the burden of fighting content theft while increasing legitimate distribution.

Take help from Copyright Attorney : Though the vast majority of plagiarism cases on the Web can be easily resolved without an attorney. But cases involving large sums of money and very large distribution may resolve with the help of copyright attorney.

Copyright and Plagiarism

These two aspects of intellectual property are the most relevant to our everyday activities. Copyright protects a person's work from being used without the express permission of the copyright holder. Plagiarism is misrepresenting someone else's work as your own and can include the taking of their words, ideas or other creations. Even if you give permission for someone to use your work for a specific purpose and he uses it for another without acknowledging you, thus misleading the audience, it's plagiarism. "Plagiarism" is not mentioned in any current statute, either criminal or civil. Some cases may be treated as unfair competition or a violation of the doctrine of moral rights. The increased availability of intellectual property due to a rise in technology has furthered the debate as to whether copyright offences are criminal. In short, people are asked to use the guideline, "...if you did not write it yourself, you must give credit." Plagiarism is not the same as copyright infringement. While both terms may apply to a particular act, they are virtually different concepts. Copyright is a legal issue that can be enforced in a court of law. Plagiarism is not in itself a legal issue, but is best described as a "respect and integrity" issue. IP violations are not always a legal issue.

Copyright and Electronic Publishing

- The same copyright protections exist for the author of a work regardless of whether the work is in a database, CD-ROM, bulletin board, or on the Internet.
- If you make a copy from an electronic source, such as the Internet or WWW, for your personal use, it is likely to be seen as fair use. However, if you make a copy and put it on your personal WWW site, it less likely to be considered fair use.
- The Internet IS NOT the public domain. There are both uncopyrighted and copyrighted materials available. Assume a work is copyrighted.

IPR & EXISTING ACTS

Each and every country has accomplished laws to protect intellectual property right of its creator or owner. In spite of that his many infringements take place and end up in legal Institution. The vital implementation of information and communication technologies made the situation much intimidating. To cope up with current situation different countries made the different laws to protect intellectual property of the owner. USA is the first country among others who take the initiative and implement the Digital Millennium Copyright Act in 1998, followed by the Australia and India named as Digital Agenda Act and Information Technology Act in 2000 respectively. Another laws implemented by the Indian Government for the easy access of information and promote transparency in Public authorities are Freedom of Information Act 2002 and Right to Information Act 2005.

Freedom of Information Act 2002

Freedom of Information Act, 2002 is an Act to provide for freedom to every citizen to secure access to information under the control of public authorities, consistent with public interest, in order to promote openness, transparency and accountability in administration and in relation to matters connected therewith or incidental thereto. Freedom of information is the right to obtain information from any public authority by means of

- inspection, taking of extracts and notes ;
- certified copies of any records of such public authority;
- disketts, floppies or in any other electronic mode or through printouts where such information is stored in a computer or in any other device.

Information in this context means any material in any form relating to the administration, operations or decisions of a public authority. The Act provides for making information held by executive agencies of the State available to the public unless it comes within any one of the specific categories of matters exempt from public disclosure. Virtually all agencies of the executive branch of the government are required by the Act to issue regulations to implement the provisions of the Act. These regulations inform the public where certain types of information may be readily obtained, how other information may be obtained on request and what internal agency appeals are available if a member of the public is refused the requested information. The freedom of information Act is designed to prevent abuse of discretionary power of the Governmental agencies by requiring them to make public certain information about their working and work product. This Act was severely criticized for permitting too many exemptions, not only under the standard grounds of national security and sovereignty, but also for requests that would involve "disproportionate diversion of the resources of a public authority". There was no upper limit on the charges that could be levied. There were no penalties for not complying with a request for information. The Freedom of Information Act, consequently, never came into effective force. The inactive Freedom of Information Act led to sustained pressure for a better Act which results the Right to Information Act.

Right to Information Act 2005

The Right to Information Act was passed in 2005 by Parliament of India. The first draft of the Right to Information Bill was presented to Parliament on 22 December 2004. After intense debate, more than a hundred amendments to the draft Bill were made between December 2004 and 15 June 2005, when the bill finally passed. This law was passed by Parliament on 15 June 2005 and came fully into force on 13 October 2005. It is the implementation of freedom of information legislation in India on a national level "to provide for setting out the practical regime of right to information for citizens." The Act applies to all States and Union Territories of India, except the State of Jammu and Kashmir - which is covered under a State-level law. Under the provisions of the Act, any citizen (excluding the citizens within J&K) may request information from a public authority which is required to reply expeditiously or within thirty days. The Act also requires every public authority to computerize their records for wide dissemination and to proactively publish certain categories of information so that the citizens need minimum recourse to request for information formally. Information disclosure in India was hitherto restricted by the Official Secrets Act 1923 and various other special laws, which the new RTI Act now relaxes.

Scope

The Act covers the whole of India except Jammu and Kashmir, where J&K Right to Information Act is in force. It is applicable to all constitutional authorities, including the executive, legislature and judiciary; any institution or body established or constituted by an act of Parliament or a state legislature. It is also defined in the Act that bodies or authorities established or constituted by order or notification of appropriate government including bodies "owned, controlled or substantially financed" by government, or non-Government organizations "substantially financed, directly or indirectly by funds" provided by the government are also covered in it. Private bodies are not within the Act's ambit directly. However, information that can be accessed under any other law in force by a public authority can also be requested.

Right to Information

Subject to the provisions of this Act, all citizens shall have the right to information.

Every public authority shall—

(a) maintain all its records duly catalogued and indexed in a manner and the form which facilitates the right to information under this Act and ensure that all records that are appropriate to be computerised are, within a reasonable time and subject to availability of resources, computerised and connected through a network all over the country on different systems so that access to such records is facilitated;

(b) publish within one hundred and twenty days from the enactment of this Act,—

1. the particulars of its organisation, functions and duties;
2. the powers and duties of its officers and employees;
3. the procedure followed in the decision making process, including channels of supervision and accountability;
4. the norms set by it for the discharge of its functions;
5. the rules, regulations, instructions, manuals and records, held by it or under its control or used by

its employees for discharging its functions;

6. a statement of the categories of documents that are held by it or under its control;
7. the particulars of any arrangement that exists for consultation with, or representation by, the members of the public in relation to the formulation of its policy or implementation thereof;
8. a statement of the boards, councils, committees and other bodies consisting of two or more persons constituted as its part or for the purpose of its advice, and as to whether meetings of those boards, councils, committees and other bodies are open to the public, or the minutes of such meetings are accessible for public;
9. a directory of its officers and employees;
10. the monthly remuneration received by each of its officers and employees, including the system of compensation as provided in its regulations;
11. the budget allocated to each of its agency, indicating the particulars of all plans, proposed expenditures and reports on disbursements made;
12. the manner of execution of subsidy programmes, including the amounts allocated and the details of beneficiaries of such programmes;
13. particulars of recipients of concessions, permits or authorisations granted by it;
14. details in respect of the information, available to or held by it, reduced in an electronic form;
15. the particulars of facilities available to citizens for obtaining information, including the working hours of a library or reading room, if maintained for public use;

16. the names, designations and other particulars of the Public Information Officers;
17. such other information as may be prescribed and thereafter update these publications every year;

Process

Under the Act, all authorities covered must appoint their Public Information Officer (PIO). Any person may submit a request to the PIO for information in writing. It is the PIO's obligation to provide information to citizens of India who request information under the Act. If the request pertains to another public authority (in whole or part) it is the PIO's responsibility to transfer/forward the concerned portions of the request to a PIO of the other within 5 days. In addition, every public authority is required to designate Assistant Public Information Officers (APIOs) to receive RTI requests and appeals for forwarding to the PIOs of their public authority. The applicant is not required to disclose any information or reasons other than his name and contact particulars to seek the information.

The Act specifies time limits for replying to the request.

- If the request has been made to the PIO, the reply is to be given within 30 days of receipt.
- If the request has been made to an APIO, the reply is to be given within 35 days of receipt.
- the PIO transfers the request to another public authority (better concerned with the information requested), the time allowed to reply is 30 days but computed from the day after it is received by the PIO of the transferee authority.
- Information concerning corruption and Human Rights violations by scheduled Security agencies (those listed in the Second Schedule to the Act) is to be provided within 45 days but with the prior approval of the

Central Information Commission.

- However, if life or liberty of any person is involved, the PIO is expected to reply within 48 hours.

Since the information is to be paid for, the reply of the PIO is necessarily limited to either denying the request (in whole or part) and/or providing a computation of "further fees". The time between the reply of the PIO and the time taken to deposit the further fees for information is excluded from the time allowed. If information is not provided within this period, it is treated as deemed refusal. Refusal with or without reasons may be ground for appeal or complaint. Further, information not provided in the times prescribed is to be provided free of charge.

For Central Departments as of 2006, there is a fee of Rs. 10 for filing the request, Rs. 2 per page of information and Rs. 5 for each hour of inspection after the first hour. If the applicant is a Below Poverty Card holder, then no fee shall apply. Such BPL Card holders have to provide a copy of their BPL card along with their application to the Public Authority. States Government and High Courts fix their own rules.

Exemption from disclosure of information

1. Notwithstanding anything contained in this Act, there shall be no obligation to give any citizen,—
   I. information, disclosure of which would prejudicially affect the sovereignty and integrity of India, the security, strategic, scientific or economic interests of the State, relation with foreign State or lead to incitement of an offence;
   II. information which has been expressly forbidden to be published by any court of law or tribunal or the disclosure of which may constitute contempt of court;

III. information, the disclosure of which would cause a breach of privilege of Parliament or the State Legislature;

IV. information including commercial confidence, trade secrets or intellectual property, the disclosure of which would harm the competitive position of a third party, unless the competent authority is satisfied that larger public interest warrants the disclosure of such information;

V. information available to a person in his fiduciary relationship, unless the competent authority is satisfied that the larger public interest warrants the disclosure of such information;

VI. information received in confidence from foreign Government;

VII. information, the disclosure of which would endanger the life or physical safety of any person or identify the source of information or assistance given in confidence for law enforcement or security purposes;

VIII. information which would impede the process of investigation or apprehension or prosecution of offenders;

IX. cabinet papers including records of deliberations of the Council of Ministers, Secretaries and other officers: Provided that the decisions of Council of Ministers, the reasons thereof, and the material on the basis of which the decisions were taken shall be made public after the decision has been taken, and the matter is complete, or over: Provided further that those matters which come under the exemptions specified in this section shall not be disclosed;

X. information which relates to personal information the disclosure of which has no relationship to any public activity or interest, or which would cause unwarranted invasion of the privacy of the individual unless the Central Public Information Officer or the State Public Information Officer or the appellate authority, as the case may be, is satisfied that the larger public interest justifies the disclosure of such information.

2. Notwithstanding anything in the Official Secrets Act, 1923 nor any of the exemptions permissible in accordance with sub-section (1), a public authority may allow access to information, if public interest in disclosure outweighs the harm to the protected interests.

3. Subject to the provisions of clauses (a), (c) and (i) of sub-section (1), any information relating to any occurrence, event or matter which has taken place, occurred or happened twenty years before the date on which any request is made under section 6 shall be provided to any person making a request under that section:

Provided that where any question arises as to the date from which the said period of twenty years has to be computed, the decision of the Central Government shall be final, subject to the usual appeals provided for in this Act.

Grounds for rejection to access in certain cases

Without prejudice to the provisions of section 8, a Central Public Information Officer or a State Public Information Officer, as the case may be, may reject a request for information where such a request for providing access would involve an infringement of copyright subsisting in a person other than the State.

1. Where a request for access to information is rejected

on the ground that it is in relation to information which is exempt from disclosure, then, notwithstanding anything contained in this Act, access may be provided to that part of the record which does not contain any information which is exempt from disclosure under this Act and which can reasonably be severed from any part that contains exempt information.

2. Where access is granted to a part of the record under sub-section (1), the Central Public Information Officer or State Public Information Officer, as the case may be, shall give a notice to the applicant, informing-

    I. that only part of the record requested, after severance of the record containing information which is exempt from disclosure, is being provided;

    II. the reasons for the decision, including any findings on any material question of fact, referring to the material on which those findings were based;

    III. the name and designation of the person giving the decision;

    IV. the details of the fees calculated by him or her and the amount of fee which the applicant is required to deposit; and

    V. his or her rights with respect to review of the decision regarding non-disclosure of part of the information, the amount of fee charged or the form of access provided, including the particulars of the senior officer specified under sub-section (1) of section 19 or the Central Information Commission or the State Information Commission, as the case may be, time limit, process and any other form of access.

DIGITAL RIGHTS MANAGEMENT

Digital rights management (DRM) is a term used to restrict the unauthorised access of digital content bring out by publishers, copyright holders and individual. It poses one of the greatest challenges for content communities in this digital age. Traditional rights management of physical materials benefited from the materials' physicality as this provided some barrier to unauthorized exploitation of content.

Digital rights management is a systematic approach of copyright protection for digital media. The main purpose of digital rights management is to prevent unlawful redistribution of digital media and restrict the ways users can copy content they've purchased. DRM products were developed in response to the rapid increase in online piracy of commercially marketed material, which proliferated through the widespread use file exchange programs. Typically DRM is implemented by embedding code that prevents copying, specifies a time period in which the content can be accessed or limits the number of devices the media can be installed on. Although digital content is protected by copyright laws, policing the Web and catching law-breakers is very difficult. DRM technology focuses on making it impossible to steal content, However, today we already see serious breaches of copyright law because of the ease with which digital files can be copied and transmitted.

Initially, Digital Rights Management focused on security and encryption that is, lock the content and limit its distribution to only those who pay for it. The first-generation of DRM substantially narrow the real and broader capabilities of DRM. The next generation of DRM covers the description, identification, trading, protection, monitoring and tracking of all forms of rights usages over both tangible and intangible assets including management of rights holders relationships. Additionally, it is important to note that DRM is the "digital management of rights" and not the "management of digital rights".

DRM & E-BOOK

Electronic book or e-Book is a new medium of scholarly communication where the contents (soul) of the book is available in digital format and can be downloadable from the Internet. As it is available in digital, there is no as such physical size (gross body) of the e-book like traditional books. One can read e-book by using computer or laptop as well as new device called e-book readers (An eBook reader can be a software application for use on a computer, or a book-sized computer that is used solely as a reading device). Still today there is no common standard is available for e-book reading/ viewing and due to that e-book are mostly available with the *de factor* standard format of the company who published/ distribute it. Although it is not necessary to use a reader application or device to read an Ebook, they are popular because they enable options similar to those of a paper book - readers can bookmark pages, make notes, highlight passages, and save selected text. Additionally, e-Book readers also include built-in dictionaries, and alterable font sizes and styles. Typically, an e-Book reader can store from four thousand to over half a million pages of text and graphics. Most of e-book readers are enable with back-lit screen which makes easy reading of text in the dark too.

DRM technologies have enabled publishers to enforce access policies that not only disallow copyright infringements, but also prevent lawful fair use of copyrighted works, or even implement use constraints on non-copyrighted works that they distribute. DRM is a copy protection tool generally used by the e-Book publishers to restrict the user to converting their e-Books format from one to another and limit them to copying, printing, and sharing of e-books. When we consider e-Books format we must keep in mind that each of these formats there are at least two versions of each format: a "secure" version that has some kind of DRM (Digital Rights Management) attached to it and a non-DRM version, i.e., Adobe Secure/DRM PDF, secure EPUB, etc. There are several different DRM schemes. E-Books with one DRM scheme can't be read on a device that uses a different DRM scheme. Some DRM schemes limit e-Books to one device only, so if the user want to read that eBook on a different device, it's necessary to download the e-Book again.

One of the greatest limitations of e-book is that reading and vioewing e-book is format and device dependent. E-books from Amazon, Barnes & Noble, and other vendors can come in different file formats, and Kindles, Sony Readers, Nooks, Kobos, and other e-readers may read certain e-book formats and not others. A DRM attached with the e-books restrict the users from converting the format to others. For eg. a MOBI e-book format of Amazon is different than e-Pub format of Barnes & Noble and vice-versa. As a result, it prevents e-books from being read on a different e-book reader – even one that reads the same format! So, while Nooks and Sony eReaders both read the ePub file format, an e-book bought from B&N that has DRM attached can't be read on the Sony eReaders.There are a few exceptions, but generally e-books with DRM attached that are bought from one retailer can only be read by that retailer's corresponding e-book device:

- Amazon.com e-book store: Kindle e-reader
- Barnes andNoble.com e-book store: Nook e-reader
- Sony eReader Store: Sony eReaders
- Kobo.com e-book store: Kobo e-reader
- Apple iBook Store: Apple iPad, iPhone, & iPod

e-Book Formats

There are several eBooks format are available in the digital market. Some of them are discussed below:

EPUB/.epub : This is the proposed "universal" format from the IDPF that is having trouble taking hold with dedicated readers and mass-market book retailers. In 2009, Sony started supporting EPUB and discontinued its own DRM format. Some retailers have started offering books in secure EPUB, but it is not widespread. ePub is the closest we have to an industry standard e-book format, as it's used by Barnes & Noble, Sony, Kobo, Apple, and others, however, not by Amazon. ePub is based on HTML, and allows for re-flowable text and other e-book features.

Adobe eBook (EPUB) : Adobe e-Book EPUB files are often synonymous with Adobe Digital Editions which is actually a software offered by Adobe that is used to read EPUB files. DRM is almost always involved. The format is readable on several different e-reader devices, including the Nook and several iPhone applications. Google adopted Adobe EPUB in Dec. 2010 for its e-Book store.

PDF/.pdf : PDF is a not only specific to e-books, but was designed by Adobe as a "Portable Document Format" that retains formatting in different computers or devices. It is available in both secure and non-secure formats. It's useful because PDFs can be read on almost any computer or e-book reader, and because the formatting and any pictures or charts should be well preserved. However, it's not an ideal format for e-books because it doesn't normally allow for re-flowable text. In this format a printed book page looks like a photograph, so you can't adjust the font size or style.

eReader/.pdb : It is developed by Palm and bought by Barnes&Noble in 2009. eReader software is compactable in various devices including the iPhone/iTouch. eReader format is the basis of the books that are delivered to the B&N Nook.

Mobipocket/.prc/.mobi : Mobi probably the most popular of all, since it's the format used by Amazon and read by the Kindle. MOBI, also called PRC, is quite similar to ePub, as it's also based on HTML and has many of the same features, like re-flowable text. Mobipocket is available to be read on several devices.

Microsoft Reader/.lit : Microsoft's ebook format is readable on several types of devices. This format seems more or less dead in the water.

Device-specific formats

Kindle/.azw format is based on Mobipocket technology. From March 2009, Kindle books is readable on the iPhone and from November 2009, on PC too. Both options are available without having to actually buy a Kindle.

Sony Reader/.lrx/.lrf format works as imaginable, with Sony Readers.

Non-Commercial Formats

- **Text/.txt**: no special formatting available, these files are plain text with line breaks. Some use CAPS or special characters (**) to help with readability.
- **Rich Text/.rtf**: more formatting available than plain text.
- **HTML/.html**: can be read in web-browsers, and some special formatting can be used. The concept of pages is not easily embedded or utilized with HTML ebook files.
- **Others**: Windows Word Document .doc, JPG Image .jpg, Portable Network Graphics / .png, Bitmap / .bmp

e-Book Reading Devices

Reading eBooks on devices are basically classified in to the three categories computers, dedicated eReaders and smart phones.

Computers : In present day almost all computers having with operating system, either Windows or Mac is capable to read e-book. While it is very uncomfortable sit in front of computer for hours to read a book, ultraportable computer or netbooks are the better option to read.

Dedicated E-book readers : There are so many e-Book devices available in market. The feature of these devices is that most of them are utilize E Ink technology, which is a non-backlit electronic display that simulates text printed on paper. Below mention are a few of the most well-known e-book reading device:

- **Apple iPad :** Apple iPad is an eBook reader but it does so much more. It is often cited as an eBook reader and most iPhone applications to read eBooks also work on the iPad.
- **Amazon Kindle :** This device is well popular due to its better looking, cheaper and with more storage inside. It is appreciated above all for the ability to buy and download books wirelessly. In October 2009, a Kindle International version was made available for use outside the U.S.A. A large selection of books is available in the Kindle format, with support for other non-DRM/secure formats like HTML and TXT.
- **Sony Reader :** This device is available in both a pocket and regular version. It displays Sony's ebook format BBeB (.lrx / .lrf), PDF, and EPUB in both secure/DRM and non-DRM formats; and other non-secure formats like HTML and TXT.
- **Barnes & Noble "Nook" :** B & N's 'Nook' format appeared in 2009. It is compatible with color touch screen, with 2GB space and expandable for more. I supports e-eader formats and EPUB, both in DRM and non-DRM formats.
- **eBookwise** is one of the first dedicated readers, though

it does not use electronic ink technology and therefore has a backlit screen. Formats like Rocket Book (.rb) files and other non-secure formats like HTML, .doc and text.

- **Foxit eSlick Reader :** One of the reader available using e Ink, it seems to only support PDF and TXT formats.
- **Smartphone :** Smart phones are the newly developed device and need very little to set up to read eBooks. Blackberry, iPhone and iPod are all examples of Smart phones.

FAIR USE

The term fair use was originated in the United States. According to Abend Stewart "An equitable rule of reason, which permits courts to avoid rigid application of the copyright statute when, on occasion, it would" undermine the purpose of copyright". Fair use is the condition under which user can use material that is copyrighted by someone else without paying royalties. It is exclusive right granted by the copyright law to use of copyrighted material without requiring permission from the right holders, such as for commentary, criticism, news reporting, research, teaching, library archiving and scholarship. The only guidance for fair use is provided by a set of factors outlined in copyright law. These factors are weighed in each case to determine whether a use qualifies as a fair use. Unfortunately, if the copyright owner disagrees with the fair use interpretation, the dispute may have to be resolved by legal recourse. If it's not a fair use, then users are infringing upon the rights of the copyright owner and may be liable for damages

Condition Under which user seek permission to use another's work

As "fair use " is the law under which one can use copyright materials without permission under limitations, the question arises why we need another's work? And, if we needed then, is there is any need for asking permission to use another's work? To determine whether the user needs to seek permission to use the work of another, user asks these three questions to himself

1) Am I using the expression of the other author?

While asking this question, if the answer comes as 'yes' or 'may be' then, user must remember the facts and ideas are not copyrightable, but the specific expression of them may be. And, photocopying, scanning, faxing, etc., always involve using the expression of another.

2) Is the author's expression protected by copyright?

While asking this question, if the answer comes as 'yes' or 'may be' then, remember that works in the public domain are not protected by copyright, but that organized summaries or compilations of such work may be. And, certain works can't be copyrighted, such as work by U.S. Government employers, some simple (even if lengthy) listings, blank forms, etc.

3) Does my intended use fall within the bounds of "fair use"?

If the answer is 'no', or 'may be', then look for permission.

Fair use principle

The basic motto of copyright is: "*to promote the progress of science and the useful arts*". By copyright authors are given a mini-monopoly to reproduce, distribute, adapt, perform and display their work, as an incentive to encourage development of new work. Some, but not all, educational uses fall under the principle of "fair use". Fair use gives scholars, researchers, authors, etc, permission to make limited use of the work of another without asking permission. To determining whether the use made of a work in any particular case is a fair use, fall under the Fair use principle;

consider all four of these issues:

- Purpose and character of the intended use
- Nature of the copyrighted work
- Amount and substantiality
- Effect upon work's value

1. Purpose and character of intended use : Fair use is a mean to stimulate creativity for the enrichment of the commons. To justify the use as fair, user must demonstrate how it either advances knowledge or the progress of the arts through the addition of something new. A key consideration is the extent to which the use is interpreted as transformative, as opposed to merely derivative. If the work is "transformative" then fair use is more likely to be applicable.

Typical acceptable transformations include:

- *Comment and Criticism* : e.g., a quote used to illustrate a comment;
- *News reporting* : e.g., summarizing a report, and including a quotation, in a news piece;
- *Research and Scholarship* : e.g., a quote used to illustrate a comment or observation.

Fair use is more likely to apply in the above situations if the use of the otherwise protected work in the situation is intended to advance new knowledge. It is less likely to apply if the intention is simple commercial gain.

2. Nature of the copyrighted work : Fair use is more likely to apply if the original is a factual work (e.g., scientific or technical work) than a work of fancy (e.g., novel or poem). Fair use as applied to unpublished materials is a very complicated topic. An extreme oversimplification is that a major limitation to its fair use involves any potential negative impact on the later value of publishing the original. Fair use does not mean that one's can automatically re-use out-of-print work, but it does suggest that less-strict guidelines are applicable when a previously-published work is no longer readily available through normal means. The common question arises whether the work:

- Is the copyrighted work a published or unpublished works? Unpublished works are less likely to be considered fair use.
- Is the copyrighted work out of print? If it is, it is more likely to be considered fair use.
- Is the work factual or artistic? The more a work tends toward artistic expression, the less likely it will be considered fair use.

3. Amount and substantiality : The third factor assesses the quantity or percentage of the original copyrighted work that has been imported into the new work. In general, the less that is used in relation to the whole, e.g., a few sentences of a text for a book review, the more likely that the sample will be considered fair use. The larger the amount, and proportion, of original expression you want to use, the less likely it is covered by fair use. The more important the specifics are to the original work, the less likely it is covered by fair use. The amount and substantiality of the portion used:

- The more you use, the less likely it will be considered fair use.
- Does the amount you use exceed a reasonable expectation? If it approaches 50 percent of the entire work, it is likely to be considered an unfair use of the copyrighted work.
- Is the particular portion used likely to adversely affect the author's economic gain? If you use the "heart" or "essence" of a work, it is less likely your use will be considered fair.

4. Effect upon work's value : The fourth factor measures the effect that the allegedly infringing use has had on the copyright owner's ability to exploit his or her original work.

- The more the new work differs from the original, the less likely it will be considered an infringement.
- Does the work appeal to the same audience as the original? If the answer is yes, it will likely be considered an infringement.
- Does the new work contain anything original? If it does, it is more likely the use of the copyrighted material will be seen as fair use.

In a legal dispute, as the copier it will be up to you to show that your use did no harm to the value of the original. Unless your intended use meets all four criteria for fair use, then you must get the copyright holder's permission before you can use protected material.

Practical Effect of Fair Use

The practical effect of this law is that it is usually possible to quote from a copyrighted work in order to criticize or comment upon it, teach students about it, and possibly for other uses. Certain well-established uses cause few problems. A teacher who prints a few copies of a poem to illustrate a technique will have no problem on all four of the above factors (except possibly on amount and substantiality), but some cases are not so clear. All the factors are considered and balanced in each case: a book reviewer who quotes a paragraph as an example of the author's style will probably fall under fair use even though he may sell his review commercially. But a non-profit educational website that reproduces whole articles from technical magazines will probably be found to infringe if the publisher can demonstrate that the website affects the market for the magazine, even though the website itself is non-commercial.

General Fair Uses

Subject to some general limitations discussed later in this article, the following types of uses are usually deemed fair uses:

- **Criticism and comment :** If user commenting upon or critiquing a copyrighted work – for instance, writing a book review – fair use principles allow to reproduce some of the work to achieve the purposes. Some examples of commentary and criticism include:
  - quoting a few lines from a Kishore Kumar's song in a music review,
  - summarizing and quoting from a medical article on prostate cancer in a news report,
  - copying a few paragraphs from a news article for use by a teacher or student in a lesson,
  - copying a portion of a Sports Illustrated magazine article for use in a related court case.

The underlying rationale of this rule is that the public reaps benefits from one's review, which is enhanced by including some of the copyrighted material. Additional examples of commentary or criticism are provided in the examples of fair use cases.

- **Parody :** A parody is a work that ridicules another, usually well-known work, by imitating it in a comic way. Judges understand that, by its nature, parody demands some taking from the original work being parodied. Unlike other forms of fair use, a fairly extensive use of the original work is permitted in a parody in order to "conjure up" the original.
- **News reporting :** Summarizing an address or article, with brief quotations, in a news report.
- **Research and scholarship :** Quoting a short passage in a scholarly, scientific, or technical work for

illustration or clarification of the author's observations.

- **Nonprofit educational uses**: Photocopying of limited portions of written works by teachers for classroom use.

In most other situations, copying is not legally a fair use. Without an author's permission, such a use violates the author's copyright.

Non-commercial use is often fair use : Violations often occur when the use is motivated primarily by a desire for commercial gain. The fact that a work is published primarily for private commercial gain weighs against a finding of fair use.

Benefit to the public may be fair use : A commercial motive doesn't always disqualify someone from claiming a fair use. A use that benefits the public can qualify as a fair use, even if it makes money for the user.

For example, in its advertising a vacuum cleaner manufacturer was permitted to quote from a *Consumer Reports* article comparing vacuum cleaners. Why? The ad significantly increased the number of people exposed to the *Consumers Reports'* evaluations and thereby disseminated helpful consumer information. The same rationale probably applies to the widespread practice of quoting from favorable reviews in advertisements for books, films, and plays.

What Counts as Fair Use

While writing article, the primary attention should be to cite all materials that are used someway or other way. However one might be used following extends for academic reasons under fair use for a limited period of time:

- A chapter from a book (never the entire book).
- An article from a periodical or newspaper.
- A short story, essay, or poem. One work is the norm

whether it comes from an individual work or an anthology.

- A chart, graph, diagram, drawing, cartoon or picture from a book, periodical, or newspaper.
- Poetry
  - Multiple copies of a poem of 250 words or less that exist on two pages or less or 250 words from a longer poem.
- Prose
  - Multiple copies of an article, story or essay that are 2,500 words or less or excerpts up to 1,000 words or 10 percent of the total work, whichever is less.
- Illustrations
  - Multiple copies of a chart, graph, diagram, drawing, cartoon, or picture contained in a book or periodical issue.

Types of media and permissible amounts

- Motion media:
  - Up to 10 percent of the total or three minutes, whichever is less.
- Text material:
  - Up to 10 percent of the total or 1,000 words, whichever is less.
  - An entire poem of less than 250 words may be used, but no more than three poems by one poet or five poems by different authors in an anthology. For poems exceeding 250 words, 250 words should be used but no more than three excerpts from one poet or five excerpts from different poets in the same work

- Music, lyrics, and music video:
  - up to 10 percent of the work but no more than 30 seconds of the music or lyrics from an individual musical work.
- Illustrations or photographs:
  - no more than five images from one artist or photographer.
  - no more than 10% or 15 images, whichever is less, from a collection.
- Numerical data sets:
  - up to 10 percent or 2,500 fields or cell entries, whichever is less, from a copyrighted database or data table.
- Copying of a multimedia project:
  - no more than two copies may be made of a project.

What Should Be Avoided

- Making multiple copies of different works that could substitute for the purchase of books, publisher's reprints, or periodicals.
- Copying the same works from semester to semester.
- Copying the same material for several different courses at the same or different institutions.
- Copying more than nine separate times in a single semester.

Fair Use and Internet

The spread of Internet technologies challenges copyright laws to maintain a balance between the free flow of information and the protection of intellectual property rights. Merely browsing a web site containing copyrighted material may, theoretically, constitute copyright infringement. When a person browses a web site, a copy of the website is temporary store either in RAM or in Temp

Directory of Operating system, or history directory of web browser. And in making a copy, even a temporary one, copyright's reproduction, distribution, and public display rights are potentially violated. Copyright laws have held web sites and other Internet service providers liable for infringements conducted through various Internet-related functions such as linking, media streaming, file sharing and storage, the maintenance of electronic bulletin boards, and posting. Now-a-days Copyright law is facing new digital environment that are significantly deviate from traditional fair use analysis. Followings are some of the fair use factor, as discussed in the Library of Congress Report, in the context of particular Internet technologies.

Hyper linking

Any web page contains a number of inlinks (a link from other page to a page) and outlinks (a link from a page to other page). The use of these technologies to appropriate copyrighted material raises a number of issues. If a linked site contains infringing material, the link may give rise to secondary liability for contributory or vicarious infringement on the part of the linking site, particularly if the linking site is promoting the copying, transmission, public display or public performance of material at the linked site. To the extent that the linked material is not infringing in itself, the reproduction, distribution, performance, or display that results from the link may not be authorized, and therefore may constitute an infringement in its own right

The fair use doctrine may apply to hyperlink, because it is likely the case that many site owners will want their material disseminated as widely as possible. However, where a link causes harm, fair use may not be appropriate. For example, unauthorized links may burden the linked site's server by increasing traffic to the web site. To the extent that the links pull in users that the linked site is not targeting, the owner of the linked site could argue that such traffic is unwanted and prevents the distribution of copyrighted material to its desired audience. Specific kinds of outline links, such as deep linking, may raise other issues.

Thumbnails

Thumbnails is the reduced size, low resolution, scaled down images that are widely exploited by different web sites. When a website uses thumbnail as embed a link in the image, it may potentially infringe on a number of exclusive rights, including the reproduction, distribution, public display rights, and, arguably, the right to make derivative works.

Use of thumbnail images implicated the photographer's reproduction right, but was, nonetheless, a fair use. While the use of the images served a commercial purpose, the search engine neither used the images to directly promote its web site nor tried to profit by selling them. As the search engine did not directly benefit from the images and did not use them in a "highly exploitative way, the commercial nature of the use only slightly weighed against a finding of fair use. The thumbnails also served a transformative use, since they "were much smaller, lower-resolution images that served an entirely different purpose than original images, as a tool to help index and improve access to images on the Internet

Streaming Videos and Audios

Streaming videos and audios (through YouTube etc.) allow access to a wide variety of visual and musical works, to listen the retransmissions of radio programs, concerts and other musical events and services. It also allow to view popular/useful videos, television shows, movies, cartoons, and other transmissions of visual content. A single transmission of music or video can simultaneously infringe on a copyright holder's reproduction, distribution, public display and performance rights, in addition to the right to make derivative works. Even though the length of the previews are usually less than two minutes, whereas the length of the motion pictures was over one and a half hours, the small amount used can not be termed as fair use. From a qualitative perspective, it relied heavily upon the "expressive value" of copyrighted works.

File Sharing

File sharing refers to a process to interact directly with each other to transfer files between them, rather than using an intermediary, such as a central server, to transfer files. Music, literature, motion pictures, photographs, and other examples of copyrightable content can be traded over a file sharing network. These networks are architecturally diverse. The design of some file-sharing networks employs a central server to house a publicly accessible and searchable index of files available over the network. When users engage in the unauthorized trade of copyrighted material, the copyright holder's reproduction and distribution rights are implicated. The Internet service that provides for the functionality of these networks may be held secondarily liable for the infringing acts of its users, even though it does not reproduce, store, or directly distribute copies of the infringing files on its servers.

Bulletin Board and Blogs

Making copyrighted works publicly available over the Internet raises obvious copyright issues. The most common means of doing this is by storing copyrighted works on publicly accessible servers or by posting copyrighted material on Internet related services, such as bulletin board services or web sites. These uses can violate a host of exclusive rights, but may, in some circumstances, constitute a noninfringing fair use. The user always remember followinh things in mind while using internet:

- Always credit the source of your information
- Find out if the author of a work (e.g., video, audio, graphic and icon) provides information on how to use his or her work. If explicit guidelines exist, follow them.
- Whenever feasible, ask the owner of the copyright for permission. Keep a copy of your request for permission and the permission received.

Fair Use Myths

When the user deals with the internet he must be careful about the extent and quantity of use, it is important for the user to distinguish between myth and fact. Some of the myths that many people has are, if it is on the Internet, it is not copyrighted; if the copyright notation is not present, the material is not copyrighted; if the material is for educational purposes, copyright does not apply. It is time to correct these myths. It is also important to be aware that while the Internet is the "wild side" of the Information Age, copyright still applies. Although fair use covers educational purposes, but it does not give user unlimited opportunities, rather, it still provides guidelines for use within the educational setting. Fair use is commonly misunderstood because of its deliberate ambiguity. Brad Templeton pointed some of the common misunderstandings on fair use with explanations of why they are wrong:

1. The Lack of a Copyright Notice : The absence of a copyright notice on a work does not essentially mean that users can freely use that work. Previously works may have needed copyright notices to protect them. A copyright notice generally includes:

- a copyright symbol "©," or the word "Copyright"
- the date the work was copyrighted, i.e. created, and
- the owner of the copyright

It is critical to realize that the copyright notation is no

longer required. So it is more judicious to acknowledge that everything is copyrighted unless otherwise noted.

2. It's copyrighted, There Can Be No Fair Use of that Work : Fair use applies only to copyrighted works, describing conditions under which copyrighted material may be used without permission. If a work is not copyrighted, fair use does not come into play, since public-domain works can be used for any purpose without violating copyright law. Fair use is a defense to the use of copyrighted materials - the work must actually be copyrighted for the fair use doctrine to even apply.

3. Uses looks fair is not always Fair use : In the law, the term fair use has a specific meaning that only partly overlaps the plain-English meaning of the words. While judges have much leeway in deciding how to apply fair use guidelines (purpose and character of the intended use, nature of the copyrighted work, amount and substantiality and effect upon work's value) , not every use that is commonly considered "fair" counts as fair use under the law. So, it is generally better to error on the side of caution when evaluating whether a use would be fair or involve copyright infringement

4. Interpretations are unique and limited : Fair use is not a static concept. In other words, the definition of what constitutes fair use changes with time and circumstances. That's because if you're using a work under the fair use doctrine today, that same use of the work at a later time might not still be considered fair use.

Fair use is decided on a case by case basis, on the entirety of circumstances. The same act done by different means or for a different purpose can gain or lose fair use status. Even repeating an identical act at a different time can make a difference due to changing social, technological, or other surrounding circumstances.

If user use a work that clearly falls within the "fair use" doctrine it does not mean that he is free from a lawsuit. The owner of the copyrighted work could still threaten to or even sue user for use of the copyrighted work - even if the use falls under the "fair use" doctrine. Why? Because the owner might not feel that your use was "fair," and may want a judge or jury to decide whether your use falls under the fair use doctrine.

5. Acknowledgment makes a use fair : Giving the name of the author is not sufficient on its own. While plagiarism and copyright violation are related matters—-both can, at times, involve failure to properly credit sources—-they are not identical. Plagiarism—using someone's words, ideas, images, etc. without acknowledgment—is a matter of professional ethics. Copyright is a matter of law, and protects exact expression, not ideas. For example, reprinting a copyrighted book without permission, while citing the original author, would be copyright infringement but not plagiarism.

6. Disclaimer is not enough to prevent Fair use : Fair use is a right granted to the public on all copyrighted work. Fair use rights take precedence over the author's interest. Thus the copyright holder cannot use a non-binding disclaimer, or notification, to revoke the right of fair use on works. However, binding agreements such as contracts or license agreements may take precedence over fair use rights.

7. Copying an entire work is not fair use : While copying an entire work may make it harder to justify the amount and substantiality test, it does not make it impossible that a use is fair use.

8. If you're selling for profit : While commercial copying for profit work may make it harder to qualify as fair use, it does not make it impossible. Not necessarily. If user use another's copyrighted work and make no money off of it, user may still have committed copyright infringement.

9. The Less Words You Quote, the More "Fair" the Use : Sometimes this is true, but not always. Often people think that if they only quote a small number of words, then the quote automatically constitutes fair use. While this may be true under many circumstances, there are other circumstances where this is not true. For example, if user quoted 40 words from an 80 word story, user may have committed copyright infringement. In contrast, if he quoted 40 words from a 200,000 word novel, it would more likely be considered fair use - depending on how you used those words and the importance of the quote

CREATIVE COMMONS

Creative Commons is a nonprofit organization that develops, supports, and stewards legal and technical infrastructure that maximizes digital creativity, sharing, and innovation. In order to make universal access to research, education, and culture on the Internet, a new method of copyright evolved during recent past - The Creative Common (CC) license. It consists of a set of copyright licenses and tools that create a balance inside the traditional "all rights reserved" setting that copyright law creates. This tool give everyone from individual creators to large companies and institutions a simple, standardized way to keep their copyright while allowing certain uses of their work — a "some rights reserved" approach to copyright — which makes one's creative, educational, and scientific content instantly more compatible with the full potential of the internet. Creative Commons License is developed to promote the idea of free access of originative works. It comes in to existence by getting inspiration from Open Source Software.

In fact, creator may not want to exercise all of the rights granted by the copyright laws, especially if they are engaged in creative activities on the Internet, as full copyright protection may prevent extensive diffusion and exposure of their works. To overcome this, a group of researchers from the fields of intellectual property rights, and information technology dedicated themselves to the formation of Creative Commons, and founded this non-profit organization in 2001. Now more than 400 million CC-licensed works are available on the Internet, from music and photos, to research findings and entire college courses. Creative Commons created the legal and technical infrastructure that allows effective sharing of knowledge, art and data by individuals, organizations and governments. The license allow creators to keep some right protected and waive others for the benefit of users. Creative Commons was invented to create a more flexible copyright model, replacing "all rights reserved" with "some rights reserved". Wikipedia is one of the notable web-based projects using one of its licenses.

Major Creative Commons Licenses

To help creators, organisation lay out the specific terms and conditions under which they can publish their work to keep some right reserve and other open for public. CC developed six different licenses based on the four principles, creator can select a license they find most appropriate for their works. Following are the major license under creative commons

Attribution-Noncommercial-No Derives : The most restrictive license. Often called the "free advertising" license because it allows others to download works and share them with others as long as they mention the source and link back to it, but they can't change the work in any way, or use them commercially.

Attribution-Noncommercial-Share Alike : Others can remix, tweak, and build upon a work non-commercially, as long as they credit the creator and license their new creations under the identical terms. All new work based will carry the same license (derivatives will also be non-commercial in nature).

Attribution-Noncommercial : Lets others remix, change, and build upon the work only non-commercially, and new works must acknowledge the original, but they don't have to license those derivative works on the same terms.

Attribution-No Derives : Allows for redistribution, commercial and non-commercial, as long as it is passed along unchanged and in whole, with credit to the creator.

Attribution-Share Alike : You can change and build upon the work, even for commercial reasons, as long as you credit the creator and license your new creation under the identical terms.

Attribution : This is the least restrictive license. You can distribute, remix, change, and build upon the work, even commercially, as long as you credit the original creation.

"Attribution" has been the default element of all CC licenses since v. 2.0 was released. It means that the licensee can copy, distribute, display, and perform the licensor's works, and derivative works based on it, provided that the licensee credits the licensor.

"Noncommercial" means that the licensee can copy, distribute, display, and perform the licensor's works only for noncommercial purposes.

"No Derives" means that the licensee can copy, distribute, display, and perform only verbatim copies of the licensor's works.

"Share Alike" means that the licensee can distribute derivative works only under a license identical to the license that the licensor chose for his/her works. All Creative Commons licenses allow the "core right" to redistribute a work for non-commercial purposes without modification.

CONCLUSION

From books to bytes, the library & information centres have faced amazing challenges and we should be proud of our accomplishments. We're waist-deep in the information age and all of the challenges that come along with it, including intellectual property rights should be welcomed. From the scholarly work and beyond, IP rights are about respect and value. On many levels this is a very complex issue. Still, it should be obvious that, we have a lot to lose by ignoring it. To not ignore it is to develop awareness, encourage education and discussion. We'll be protecting ourselves now as well as investing in our future—a future ideally that continues to build on our tradition of "helping each other to be successful for each other." That, by the way, is one of the means that allowed us to survive over the last two decades and, interestingly enough, is the very spirit of what IP rights are about.

ACKNOWLEDGEMENT

Some part of this chapter is prepared by Prashant Kumar. Author acknowledge to the concerned.

WEB REFERENCES

Copyright and the fair use. Available at: http://www.intellectualpropertylawfirms.com/topics.cfm/copyright-fair-use-laws.html

Creative Common License. Available at: http://creativecommons.org/

Donde, Rahul. What aspects of intellectual property were covered by the Paris Convention for the protection of industrial property? What significance does this treaty have in relation with international patents? Available at: http://ipmall.info/hosted_resources/ip_india/paris_convention.pdf

Government of India (2002). The Freedom of Information Act, 2002. Available at: http://orissa.gov.in/e-magazine/

orissaannualreference/ORA-2004/pdf/the_freedom_of_inf_act2002.pdf

Government of India (2005). Right to Information Act, 2005. Available at: http://righttoinformation.gov.in/rti-act.pdf

Intellectual property. Available at: http://en.wikipedia.org/wiki/Intellectual_property

Jennings, C. A. (2002). Fair use of the Internet. Available at: http://www.scribd.com/doc/22454657/Uses-of-Internet\

Patents and Trademark Organization (n.d.) Definition. Available at: http://trademarkorganisation.org/ en/definitions

Plagiarism in the Digital Age: Voices from the Front Lines. Available at: http://www.plagiarism.org/

Plagiarism: How to Avoid It. Available at: http://www.aresearchguide.com/6plagiar.html

Ross. S. (2009). How to Read an ebook: Formats, Devices, Dedicated Readers and iPhone Applications. Available at: http://whenihavetime.com/2009/03/10/how-to-read-an-ebook-formats-devices-dedicated-readers-and-iphone-applications

Stanford University (n.d.) Copyright and Fair use. Available at: http://fairuse.stanford.edu/Copyright_and_Fair_Use_Overview/chapter9/9-a.html#2

The law Fair use. Available at: http://www.benedict.com/Info/FairUse/FairUse.aspx

The meaning of fair use. Available at: http://www.geom.uiuc.edu/events/courses/1996/cmwh/Copyright/ fairuse.html

Thom, Karen (2000). Copyright: Fair Use or Foul Play. Available at: http://frank.mtsu.edu/~itconf/proceed01/ 14.html

Types of Plagiarism. Available at: http://www.duplichecker.com/Plagiarismtypes.asp

U.S. Government. Overview of Intellectual Property Rights and the TRIPs Agreement. Available at: http:// www.osec.doc.gov/ogc/occic/ipr.htm

University Maryland University College. Types of media and permissible amounts. Available at: http://lib. jcu.edu/files/Types_of_Media_and_Permissible_Amounts.pdf

University of Alberta (2011). Guide to Plagiarism and Cyber-Plagiarism. Available at: http://guides.library.ualberta.ca/content.php?pid=62200&sid=457755

University of Cambridge (2005) Intellectual Property and Copyright in the Digital Environment. Available at: http://www.caret.cam.ac.uk/copyright/

University of Maryland. Copyright and Fair Use in the UMUC Online or Face-to-Face Classroom. Available at: http://www.umuc.edu/library/copy.shtml

World Intellectual Property Organization (2011). What is intellectual property? Available at: http://www.wipo. int/about-ip/en/

14 Knowledge Management

Knowledge is of two kinds. We know a subject ourselves, or we know where we can find information upon it.

- Samuel Johnson

CONCEPTUAL BACKGROUND

During the second wave of industrial world, the organizations that made use of cost-effective, efficient and advanced technologies were assumed as productive organization. However, in the third wave of information world, the importance of managing and utilizing organizational knowledge started gaining popularity. In this knowledge-based economic system, the organizations are realizing the importance of their intellectual assets i.e., the knowledge possessed by the employees, their skills of the organization just like any other corporate resource and are now devising ways to harness this previously unforeseen power for organizational success. Today, the main source of competitive advantage of an organization is represented by the organization's learning capacity and its knowledge assets. Knowledge Management (KM) enters the scenario at this point. Before attempting to address the issues associated with KM, it's probably appropriate to develop some perspective regarding this stuff called 'knowledge'. Neil Fleming (1996) explained that a collection of information is not knowledge. Instead, 'information' relates to description, definition, or perspective (what, who, when, where), whereas, 'knowledge' comprises strategy, practice, method, or approach (how). Tom Davenport and Laurence Prusak (1998) defined knowledge as "a combination of experience, values, contextual information, and expert insight; and knowledge provides a framework for evaluating and incorporating new experiences and information." Where as, Applehans, Globe & Laugero (1999) explained knowledge as the ability to turn information and data into effective action, which brings desirable outcomes for an organisation.

The relationship between knowledge with data and information has been explained in different ways. Traditionally, it is explained that knowledge is above data and information; data is a prerequisite for information; and information is a prerequisite for knowledge. This may be simply illustrated as

Data → Information → Knowledge

However, in a different look Tuomi (1999) suggested that we first need to have the knowledge about what information we want, and then we will know what data to look for. In other words, data emerge only after we have information, and that information emerges only after we already have knowledge. This view can be simply illustrated by the following diagram:

Knowledge → Information → Data

Even, a third view is also possible. We have a large amount of data collected but fail to make use of the data to create information because of our lack of relevant knowledge. Meteorologists usually collect weather data for long time.

The usefulness of these data is possible only when they have the relevant knowledge about how to process data, how to visualize data. In this situation, the knowledge is the catalyst that transforms data into information. This process can be simply illustrated by the following diagram:

Data → Knowledge → Information

These differing logics and understandings about the relationships and the sequences between data, information, and knowledge are meaningful, depending on the context. The development of the traditional information systems (TPS, MIS, DSS) basically follows the traditional view of data, information, and know1edge while scientific research and inference statistics generally follow the second view (the reverse hierarchy) on data, information, and knowledge. In terms of knowledge management, the third view bears more impacts and implications. In library perspective, this third view suggests a fundamental fact in many organizations—there are a lot of documents (data) accumulated over years, and we need to know what may be best option to utilize these documents in optimum. The document is one place where information about knowledge can be found. Another place is the human mind, and the identification of the right human mind (expert) for a given task must be a responsibility of knowledge management. This help explains why the awareness of corporations to identify and utilize inside expertise for a given task has increased in recent years.

TYPES OF KNOWLEDGE: EXPLICIT, IMPLICIT AND TACIT

Explicit Knowledge

Explicit knowledge is knowledge that has been or can be expressed, codified, and stored in certain media. It can be readily transmitted to others by using various communication channels. The most common forms of explicit knowledge are manuals, documents and standards. Knowledge of this type also can be audio-visual, graphic form. The organization however, is skilled at continuously expanding, renewing, and refreshing its knowledge in all categories.

Tacit Knowledge

Michael Polanyi (1962), a Hungarian physical chemist turned philosopher was the first to introduce the concept of tacit knowledge by explaining as "We know more than we can tell." However the reference to this undocumented form of knowledge can be traced to Helmholtz's work in the 19th century. Nonaka and Takeuchi describe tacit knowledge as non-linguistic, non-numerical form of knowledge that is highly personal and context specific and deeply rooted in individual experiences, ideas, values and emotions. It is difficult to communicate such type of knowledge to the rest of an organization. One example of tacit knowledge as mentioned in wikipedia is the skill of riding a bicycle - there is no manual of how to do so you have to be taught by someone who already can. Tacit knowledge can be understood to be knowledge that is embedded in a culture (for instance a regional culture, organizational culture or social culture) and is difficult to share with people not embedded in that culture. Tacit knowledge has been described as "know-how" (as opposed to "know-what" [facts], "know-why" [science] and "know-who" [networking]) It involves learning and skill but not in a way that can be written down.

The organization promotes the learning of tacit knowledge to increase the skill and creative capacity of its employees and takes advantage of explicit knowledge to maximize efficiency. Tacit knowledge is cultivated in an organizational culture that motivates through shared vision and common purpose. Personal knowledge is leveraged with explicit knowledge for the design and development of innovative products, services and processes. Strategic vision and operational expertise are fused in creative action. The process of transforming tacit knowledge into explicit knowledge is known as codification or articulation

The diagram illustrated below explains the types of knowledge.

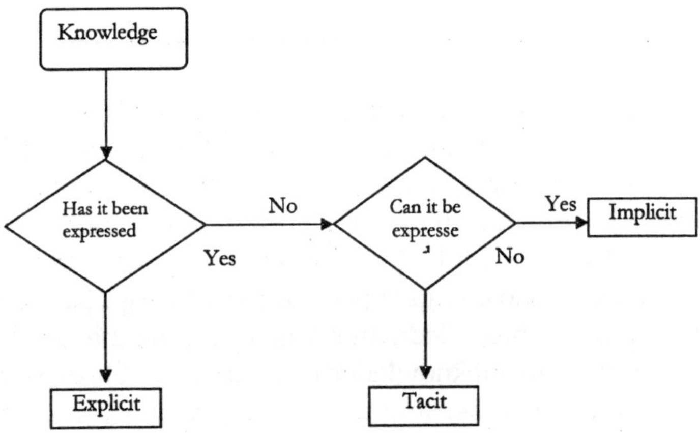

Source: **Nickolos, F (2010). The knowledge in knowledge management..**

Implicit Knowledge

Knowledge that can be expressed but hasn't is implicit knowledge. The existence of such knowledge is implied by or inferred from observable behavior or performance. "The 'implicit' is that which is available to your consciousness but which you have not conceptualized. This type of knowledge

Explicit and Tacit Knowledge

Explicit knowledge	*Tacit knowledge*
Also known as formal knowledge	Also known as implicit, informal or unstructured knowledge
Can be processed by information systems; can be codified	In one's mind, beliefs, experiences and perspectives; personal
Can be directly expressed by knowledge representations	Difficult to document or process; cannot be expressed easily by knowledge representations
Easy to use technology to communicate	Difficult to use technology to communicate and share
Tangible assets	Intangible assets: A source of competitive advantage

Source: Lee (2008)

can often be teased out by task analyst, knowledge engineer or other person skilled in identifying the kind of knowledge. One very common example of such knowledge is that we know explicitly that all men are mortal and that I am a man. Thus, I also have implicit knowledge that I am mortal. we can make that knowledge explicit by performing a particular act of consciousness (deduction) and by saying the result: "I am mortal." Implicit knowledge is mostly available in pieces; have not put together into a concept, principle, or theory; and have not named, stated, or formulated. Once these outcomes were formulated, it was a comparatively simple matter to identify the criteria used to determine the response to a given application. In so doing, implicit knowledge became explicit knowledge.

KNOWLEDGE MANAGEMENT

Knowledge has become a much greater factor of production than land, labour, and capital. The increasing dimensions in KM have given emphasis on promoting, rewarding, pooling together of knowledge resources (i.e., documents, experiences, expertise, etc).

The term Knowledge Management (KM) was first introduced in a 1986 key node address to a European management conference. Today, there are numerous definitions of KM to be found in various publications printed as well as Web. KM can be defined as the management of corporate knowledge that can improve a range of organizational performance characteristics by enabling an expertise to be more 'intelligent acting'. It is a process that helps an organization to find, select, organize, disseminate and transfer important information and expertise necessary for activities such as problem solving, dynamic learning, strategic planning and decision making.

Bessie : "Knowledge management is defined as the process of creating, capturing and using knowledge to enhance organisational performance."

Ruggles : "Knowledge management is a newly emerging, interdisciplinary business model dealing with all aspects of knowledge within the context of the firm, including knowledge creation, codification, sharing, learning, and innovation."

The Economist, Yankee Group : "Knowledge management involves efficiently connecting those who know with those who need to know and connecting personal knowledge in to organisational knowledge."

Skyrme (2003) defines knowledge management as a "process or practices of creating, acquiring, capturing, sharing and using knowledge, whenever it resides, to enhance learning and performance in organizations" Similarly White (2004) defines knowledge management as " a process of creating storing, sharing and re-using organizational knowledge (know-how) to enable an organization to achieve its goals and objectives." In more practical aspect knowledge management may be defined as the capabilities by which communities within an organization capture the knowledge that is critical to them, continuously improve it and make it available in the most effective manner to people who need it, so they can exploit it creatively to add values as a normal part of their work (Hayes, 2004; Butler, 2000).

Thus, knowledge management is an ongoing process, which comprises of various methods, steps and strategic efforts of an organization to gain competitive advantage by utilizing its knowledge assets which resides in its employees, products, processes and clients, but the most important step is to identify knowledge which can be considered as an asset for the organization and utilize it to enhance learning and performance.

During the past few years, Knowledge Management (KM) has been emerged as one of the important topics of discussion among academicians and professionals of many fields of knowledge. There are several disciplines that took interest in the research and development of KM, including Information Technology (IT), Strategic Management, Cognitive Science, Management Science, Knowledge Engineering, Artificial Intelligence, Sociology, Library & Information Science, Economics and many more. There are several academic and professional journals that are publishing scholarly articles on KM. Professional Associations (such as International Federation of Library Associations and Institutions (IFLA), Knowledge Management Society (KM Pro), Knowledge management Society of Malaysia and International Society for Information Science (ISI) are promoting the interest of KM among professionals and practitioners by organizing national and international seminars, conferences and workshops on KM.

NEED OF KM

The under mentioned reasons justify the **need** of Knowledge Management.

- Knowledge is the basic input to transform the society. It is the important source for economic wealth and there is an emerging recognition that the most valuable resource of any country is its inherent intellectual assets/effectively exploited innovation.
- Knowledge helps to cope up with changes in redesigns, re-expanding, and re- casting the production and services.
- Knowledge helps in streamlining operations and reduces costs by eliminating redundant processes.
- Increasing completion in market needs rising of innovation. Innovation needs knowledge.
- Reductions in staffing, early retirements and increasing mobility of the work force lead to loss of knowledge. There is possibility of changes in strategic direction. So there is a need to replace informal knowledge with formal methods.

STEPS IN KNOWLEDGE MANAGEMENT

The basic goal for any KM System is simple and straightforward - to enable right information to flow to the right people at the right time with a consequence of helping them take quicker, more informed and effective decisions.

Nonaka[6] addresses the important issues of knowledge transfer and knowledge creation in his 1991 article. He cites four such transfers or creations:

1. Tacit to tacit : Acquiring someone else's tacit knowledge through observation, imitation and practice. For example learning how to make pastry by someone else through observation.

2. Explicit to explicit : Combining discrete pieces of explicit knowledge to form new explicit knowledge, for example, analyzing data through SPSS software and preparing a logarithmic graph. The output represents new explicit knowledge.

3. Tacit to explicit : Converting tacit knowledge to codified form. For example writing book on 'how to cook tasty food'.

4. Explicit to tacit : Internalizing explicit knowledge. For example, the broachers for various company's Mixer-grinder machine and understating the best by comparing various features. This type of knowledge might have been implicit knowledge at one point but was never truly tacit knowledge because that cannot be articulated.

Nonaka and Takeuchi (1995) explained four knowledge conversion processes: socialization, externalization, combination, and internalization. Each process involves converting one form of knowledge (tacit or explicit) to another form of knowledge (tacit or explicit). This model explains on the important issue of how knowledge may be created through organizational sharing and is useful for identifying and evaluating certain key activities in the management of knowledge. Hlupic, Pouloudi and Rzevski (2002) refer to Ruggles (1998) who identified three main types of activities: knowledge generation involving the creation of new ideas and new patterns; knowledge codification, and knowledge transfer, ensuring exchange of knowledge between individuals and departments. Another model, proposed by Oluic-Vukovic (2001) outlines 5 steps in the knowledge processing chain: gathering; organizing; refining; representing; and disseminating.

Beckman (1997) has proposed a seven-stage process for knowledge management:

Identify → Collect → Select → Store → Share → Apply → Create

I. The *identify* stage determines which core competencies are important to academic success. Every department needs robust knowledge about its pedagogical needs and expectations from its members, services and administration. An understanding needs to be developed to settle its place in the pedagogical world and in other organizational and environmental aspects such as research endeavors and consulting services offered by the department.

II. The *collect* stage deals with acquiring the internal and external knowledge, educational skills, fundamental theories and human experience needed to create the selected core responsibilities and knowledge domains.

III. The *select* stage takes the continuous stream of collected, formalized knowledge and assesses its value. Initially, one framework should be selected as the basis for organizing and classifying knowledge to be stored in the Knowledge Bank.

IV. Departmental memory resides in three different forms: in human minds, on paper and electronically. The *store* stage takes the nuggets of knowledge and classifies them and adds them to the departmental memory. Much of this knowledge can be represented in electronic form as expert systems. This is where even tacit, intangible knowledge assets are transformed to tangible one.

V. The *share* stage retrieves knowledge from the departmental memory and makes it accessible to the users. Individuals, teams and departments often share ideas, opinions, gossip, knowledge & expertise in meetings held in person or through groupware.

VI. The *apply* stage reclaims and uses the needed knowledge in performing tasks, solving problems, making decisions, researching ideas and learning. To reclaim just the knowledge, requires that the system understand the user's purpose and context. To receive the knowledge at the right time requires a proactive system that monitors the user's actions and behavior and determines his/her purpose.

VII. The *create* stage uncovers new knowledge through many avenues, such as observing students, student feedback and analysis, research, experimentation, creative thinking and automated knowledge discovery and data mining.

Bouthillier, and Shearer (2002) diagrammatically explain KM process as:

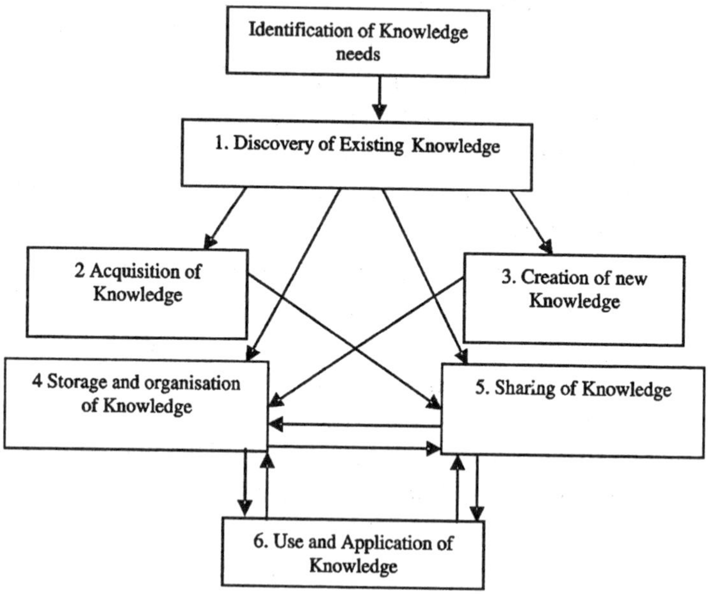

Fig. 1 : Knowledge Management Process

Liebowitz (2000) presented a nine step approach to Knowledge Management

- Transform information knowledge
- Identifying and verify knowledge
- Capture and secure knowledge

- Organise Retrieve and apply knowledge
- Combine knowledge
- Create knowledge
- Learn knowledge
- Distribute sell knowledge

Factors critical to knowledge management success

Despite the best efforts of organizations, many face challenges implementing and sustaining successful knowledge management initiatives. This may stem from a variety of reasons, such as unrealistic expectations, a one size-fits-all approach to knowledge management, lack of understanding of knowledge management, overemphasis on technology, lack of strategic alignment, or information.

Knowledge management success is believed to be dependent on various factors as they provide a context within which knowledge flows among individuals, whose actions in turn are influenced by their environment. Appropriate organizational context enables an organization to execute better, learn faster, and change more easily.

Gold et al. (2001) analyzed knowledge management success from the perspective of organizational capabilities. Organizational capabilities have two aspects: knowledge infrastructure capabilities and knowledge process capabilities. Knowledge infrastructure capabilities include technology, organizational structure, and culture, while knowledge process capabilities cover acquisition, conversion, application, and protection. The model developed by Gold et al (2001) matches the principles of knowledge management success proposed by Hostler (2005), which are technology, people and process. Technology focuses on the application of technological resources to maximize the knowledge management functions. Knowledge management involves change management and requires organization culture and structure to support the new change. The Hostler's principles of knowledge management success are similar to knowledge maturity model developed by Tata Consultancy Service (TCS) which consists of three basic pillars- People, Technology and Process. TCS believes that the states of knowledge maturity can be achieved by systematically addressing these three pillars: people and culture address the "mindsets" and relate to attributes of assessing people and culture; technology and infrastructure are the enablers that help people harness maximum of out the knowledge management initiative; process, policy and strategy facilitate and guide the efforts of the people to capture and use the knowledge in the organization to achieve the business benefits (Mohanty and Chand, 2005).

Conley and Zheng (2009) grouped KM success factors into two categories, organizational factors and factors related to the KM initiative. Organizational factors capture the general characteristics of the organization, such as top management and leadership support, organizational culture, structure, technology infrastructure, and strategy. KM-initiative-related factors encompass those that are targeted to KM practices, including processes, training and education, measurement, and incentives.

Differences between Information and Knowledge Management

Information Management	*Knowledge Management*
Information management deals with management of explicit knowledge	Knowledge management deals with tacit knowledge
In IM, information is a tangible entity.	In KM, knowledge is an intangible entitle
This type of management basically deals with handling or managing of resources like document, materials, entities.	In this process of management there is a need to understand the skill, capacity lying with the human brain of that organization.

It has no universally accepted meaning	It depends on a higher degree of certainty and validity.
It is a flow of information.	It is formed by this flow.
It achieves its success through the preservation and retrieval of information.	Successful KM involve identifying, learning codifying and storing of implicit knowledge available in the forms of skills, experiences etc. of the human of working on that organization
It is organized data.	It is extrapolative and future - oriented.
IM is mainly for clients and their service.	KM mainly for organization itself, for its future.
Timeliness, accuracy, authority, veracity, speed, cost, storage space and retrieval are the main concerns.	It recognizes value in originality, innovation, adaptability, intelligence and learning.
Information is passive in nature	Knowledge is dynamic

TOOLS OF KNOWLEDGE MANAGEMENT

KM techniques are based on two-fold principles, firstly to measure the intellectual capital of an organization by developing measurement ratios or indexes and benchmarks, and secondly, for knowledge mapping , i.e., capturing knowledge gained by an individual and disseminating it throughout the organization, mainly through information technology. However, the main drawback in the KM strategy used nowadays is that it only takes into account the management of explicit knowledge within an organization whereas the implicit or tacit knowledge that forms a major chunk of the intellectual resources of the organization is ignored. The basic goal of knowledge management is to harness the knowledge resources and knowledge capabilities of the organization in order to enable the organization to learn and adapt to its changing environment (Auster & Choo, 1995).

The first known human discovered knowledge management tools that transformed the ancient world was the alphabet which brought with it the ability to alphabetically index information for future retrieval. All writing, whether video graphic or alphabetic is a knowledge management tool, so is the human ability to classify ideas and objects intelligently into logical hierarchies. Present day KM covers three main knowledge activities: generation, codification and transfer. In order to perform these activities various tools are used. There is now wide applicability of information technology tools in KM arena. Ruggles (1998) in this regard pointed that "Knowledge management tools are technologies, broadly defined, which enhance and enable knowledge generation, codification, and transfer." Although, IT tools are becoming increasingly important to many of the stages of knowledge management, they are by no means the only tools available. KM tools are used to tie organizational objectives to the achievement of specific business outcomes such as improved performance, competitive advantage, and higher levels of innovation. Broadly, the KM tools can be categorized in to the three categories.

- Traditional tools of knowledge management
- Contemporary tools of knowledge management

A. Traditional Tools of Knowledge Management

Given below are certain techniques to manage the various forms of tacit knowledge available within an organization.

Knowledge Generation tools

Authority files are the files from where the leaving employees share their methods of work, style of working, Procedure to be follow to get best utilisation of resourses and so many other important things witch helps the new employee to work with ease.

Community of Practice is a way of sharing knowledge where a group of people comes together and share each others experience over a particular subject of a common interest. This experience sharing helps each other in solving day to day problems and updating themselves with new knowledge in the area of their work. A group of doctors staffs share each others experience about patient while taking coffee together in canteen is example of a natural learning community interaction.

Seminars, meetings, symposiums, conventions and other informal social activities amongst the employees which helps employees to share their experiences and views of their day-to-day work. In this way, the tacit knowledge of the employees is shared amongst themselves, which improves their performance in turn benefiting the organization.

Mentorship

The term mentors means adults who introduce students to ideas, theories, tools, activities, or careers in their own fields of expertise. Douglas and Mc Cauley (1999), define "mentorship as a relationship that motivates individuals to learn and grow through exposure to new opportunities and the provision support". Effective relationships and learning are the mainstays of organizational success today. Organizations that find meaningful ways for their employees to connect are more likely to realise greater productivity, enhanced career growth, freely flowing innovation and overall improvement in employee performance. Group mentoring is a value-added tool for connecting employees and advancing learning within the organization. It has also become one of the strongest drivers of knowledge management contributing to the 'soft' interpersonal aspects that balance the aggressive dissemination of technological solutions to the capture and dissemination of knowledge. For the junior employee especially the politics of the organisation can be a minefield. A mentor with greater experience can help the protégé to develop a mental map about what to cultivate, what to avoid, what behaviours and track record are most and least valued – all factors that help make the juniors more effective and that are useful in managing their career options.

Knowledge Codefication tools

Knowledge audit : tries to understand and analyze the existing knowledge level of employees with relation to the processes of the organization and to an extent even its operations, information sources available to them, level of productivity at performing tasks etc. It is a also systematic process to identify an organisation's knowledge needs, resources and flows as a basis for understanding where and how better knowledge Management can add value.

After Action Review : is a structured review process that allows project participants to discover for themselves what happened, why it happened, and how it can be done better. After-action reviews were originally developed and are extensively used by the U.S. Army. Their use has now extended to business as a knowledge management Tool

B. Contemporary Tools of Knowledge Management

Although knowledge management is not about technology, technology plays an important role in KM. The main roles of information technology in knowledge management are to accelerate the speed of knowledge transfer and creation. Knowledge management tools intend to help the processes of collecting and organizing the knowledge of groups of individuals in order to make this know ledge available in a shared base. The following are most popular contemporary Knowledge Management tools:-

Knowledge Generation Bureau (KGB)

KGB is a pay-based service, mostly available in developed nations like US, Spain etc. through which one can get an instant answer from authoritative persons by sending text message. The advantage of using text messages for the question is that virtually any mobile phone can use it, you don't need a data plan, and you don't have to rely on a slow and unreliable browser. Of course, people with an advanced (3G) smartphone may find it easier to use their Internet browser, but I've found that the KGB service is sometimes able to get an answer back to me quicker than I could using the Internet on the road.

Knowledgemail

This is an innovative system for eliciting tacit knowledge and providing partial managerial control over it. It is a product from 'Tacit Knowledge Systems', a premiere organization in developing expert systems for managing tacit knowledge. It is no meant for storage of the knowledge, but mainly for pinpointing the knowledge islands'. The developers of this system recognized that reading through the e-mails, papers, memos and other documents that people created, provides a basic insight into their understanding of the concept led them to develop KnowledgeMail, which monitors the outgoing e-mails and other documents that the employees of the organization create.

Take the example of a distress call from an employee of an organization dealing with computer maintenance. The employee has a technical question, the answer to which is neither mentioned in the technical manuals nor- in the training manuals of the organization. He may then write up his question in natural language and ask - the KnowledgeMail system for the e-mail addresses of people who are likely to know the answers. The system searches the database and presents a list of several people, along with small graphic indicators of the likelihood they have of that particular knowledge. A mouse-click then sends his questions to the people he had picked from the list. Thus, in this way, the tacit knowledge of the employees of the organization is successfully used for the improvement of services.

The Xerox Story

There are numerous cases where knowledge management techniques are successfully applied to tacit knowledge. However a typically interesting project is the 'Eureka Project', (now called Smart Service), a project created by Xerox France and Xerox Palo Alto Research Center (PARC) in California. The engineers at Xerox receive around a million customer calls every month worldwide. A study done by PARC revealed that these engineers narrated their experiences to each other about diagnosing and fixing the machines -whenever there was an informal or formal gathering. Xerox found that many of the problems that they discussed were not mentioned in their training manuals. It was at this instant that Xerox recognized that the really current know-how is in the heads-and-hands of the service technicians. This led to the development of the project Eureka that aimed at facilitating sharing of tacit knowledge among the peers.

Groupware

It is one of the most prevalent computer network based electronic means for eliciting, sharing and organizing quantities of information. Using this technique, the participants can share their ideas, views and suggestions with each other without any social hindrances and obstacles. Presently, this technique is being used in Hewlett-Packard's Human Resources Division in Rohnert Park, California. Dennis Hong, World Wide Web curriculum manager for corporate information systems at Hewlett- Packard's headquarters in Palo Alto says, "Everybody's seeing information electronically, so you do not have bullies, no shy guys, you're focusing on ideas. Everybody's ideas get equal footing. It 'a great leveler. It's like a big core dump. You can get people's knowledge out and discuss it a new way."

Wiki

'Wiki' is the Hawaiian word for 'quick'. The first wiki, implemented in 1995 by the Portland Pattern Repository group, permitted users to create, edit, and organize content in a Web format (2004). It is a website that allows visitors to add, remove, edit and change content, typically without the need for registration. Wiki technology can impact knowledge management, and can support knowledge creation and sharing (Leuf & Cunningham, 2001; Wagner,2004; Lamb, 2004). Wikis permits asynchronous discussion in that it enables students and instructors to engage in continuous discussion, when they have the time. This permits ability to share and update the knowledge base (Bergin, 2002). It also supports many-to-many communication and enables creation of new knowledge based on a given knowledge history (Wagner, 2004). However, sometime it may be argued that it is not a pure tool of KM, however, wikis are a powerful replacement for conventional knowledge management software, because they make knowledge easier to capture, find and consume.

Blog

A blog is a user-generated social website on a particular subject where people share their experiences. Blogs often provide commentary or news on a particular subject, such as professional development, culture, travel, food, politics, or local news; some function as more personal online diaries. It is a very effective tool for sharing knowledge and can link similar items together. Tim Sanders has a blog that tries to educate people about email usage and etiquette. Please read it. Tim Ferriss advocates checking email only a couple of times a day. However, some of the notable drawback of such tool is that the intervention of limited experts and ignorance about the authority of expertise.

Intranet

Intranets can have a great impact on knowledge management, particularly in the fields of information collection, collaboration and communication, and task completion. Following the necessary approach, this tool can substantially increase the likelihood of an effective, useful system within an organisation.

Social Technologies

Social Technologies cover a broad swathe of tools, all using technology to build collaboration and sharing of tacit knowledge. There are many different fora for this, chiefly internet-based tools but also including telecommunications, radio and face-to-face socialising.

Data Warehousing

Data warehousing is the key component of Knowledge Management tool. It facilitates data search from the heterogeneous databases and also serves functions of various query formulation for the intensive search. Data Warehouse can serve as a storage medium for keeping the corporate memory, or at least concerning certain types of data. It helps gaining new knowledge by delivering well integrated data to analysis tools, e.g. On-Line Analytical Processing or Knowledge Discovery in Databases, and thus becomes an important part of Decision Support Systems or Executive Information Systems. In this way a Data Warehouse, storing only data, results in growth of knowledge and may lead to enhance the enterprise's success (Erdmann, 1997).

ROLE OF LIBRARIAN IN KNOWLEDGE MANAGEMENT

Like other business management trends, knowledge

management is also a commercial concept, emerging first in the for-profit sector and then entering into the non-profit sector. Knowledge management within libraries involves organizing and providing access to intangible resources that help librarians and administrators carry out their tasks more effectively and efficiently. Kim (2000) said that 'Knowledge Management is not about managing or organizing books or journals, searching the inherent for clients or 'arranging for the circulation of materials'. Knowledge Management is one way to develop and apply the organizational knowledge needed to improve library operations and ultimately, library effectiveness through sound practices of management and organisalional learning. With the help of the knowledge management processes, libraries convert data and information stored in various sources into knowledge and deliver only relevant knowledge to users. The human action and the information flow shall be the two most dominant inputs to any sound development strategy. For them right information needs to be in the hands of the right people at the right time.

A report in the US noted that, currently, 13 per cent of librarians don't work in a traditional library setting. Instead they are functioning throughout business in roles that command salaries much higher than the profession has traditionally seen. It has also been noted that, whichever part of society is the focus; the information profession has unprecedented opportunities.

How to manage tacit knowledge is an important subject for libraries in preset days. It can be possible if a library can focused on effective research and development of knowledge, creation of knowledge base, exchange and sharing of knowledge between library staffs (including its users), training of library staff, speeding up explicit processing of the implicit knowledge and realizing of its sharing (Shanhong,2000). It is believed that "Tools of

Knowledge Management consists 70% of services and 30% of Technologies. Librarians provide these 70% services. This indicates the role of Librarians as Knowledge Manager." Libraries and Information centres since their inception are epic centre of delivering the strategic knowledge to the users of their organization. In changing perspective the work culture of libraries and their tools and techniques have undergone several changes. Their roles have been changing with social advances. With the re-designation as Chief information Officer, the scope and meaning of the term librarian is expanded. The terms such as knowledge manager, resource manager, information specialists, technological gatekeeper and web navigator are some of the examples that are commonly applicable to professionals.

Roknuzzaman et al. (2009) argues that library itself is a knowledge-based organization where collection and maintenance of recorded knowledge by librarians is a practice as old as civilization itself. The library and information professionals have been acknowledging for years that it is a burgeoning field of great interest to them, since they possess the necessary skills in the organization of knowledge, and are well aware of the benefits of properly organized and codified information, as the aim of codification is to put organizational knowledge into a form that makes it accessible to those who need it.

Kebede (2010) pointed out that the goal of KM in Library and Information Science (LIS) is basically to help facilitate human access to information and knowledge for effective decision making and problem solving in work situation as well as everyday life. Further, he argued that the goal of KM in LIS is broader than the goals of KM in other disciplines interested in KM because facilitating access to knowledge by LIS is not limited to serving specific contexts and environments such as gaining sustainable and competitive advantage or market positions in management sciences, or improving organizational learning in organizational sciences.

The basic goal of knowledge management within libraries is to leverage the available knowledge that may help librarians to carry out their tasks more efficiently and effectively Knowledge management is also aimed at extending the role of librarians to manage all types of information and tacit knowledge for the benefit of the library (Dillon, 1999). Supporting this view, Shanhong (2000) argues that the objective of knowledge management in libraries is to promote knowledge innovation, closer relationships in and between libraries, and between a library and its users, to strengthen knowledge inter networking and to quicken knowledge flow. Townley (2001) points out that knowledge management is a way to develop and apply the organizational knowledge needed to improve library operations and, ultimately, library effectiveness. Further, he stressed that knowledge management enables libraries to generate organizational knowledge for higher education institutions. Jantz (2001) believe that knowledge management can transform the library into a more efficient knowledge-sharing organization.

Librarians, of these days are trained perfectly in the skills that a knowledge manager or a business intelligence analyst often needs. It is our endeavour to understand the importance of classification schemes or cataloguing codes, author table, We understand that without taxonomies, finding specific subject in the diversified format based vast collections, whether virtual or real, is very hard. We understand the importance of metadata, or context, in facilitating the correct identification of a document after it has been contributed to a digital library or an online repository, especially if it is an image or an audio clip.

Navigation in web pages is probably one of the biggest shortcomings of present day. Much more research in ongoing throughout the world in this regard. This is essentially about search and taxonomy and clarity in instructions. This is very much a task for librarians to tackle.

Knowledge management has been seen as a survival factor for libraries to overcome the challenges library professionals faces in the changing and competitive environment (Sinotte, 2004; Wen, 2005). Respondents in a study by Sarrafzadeh et al. (2010) agreed by strong majority that knowledge management can contribute to an improvement in the future prospects of libraries. Libraries can also improve their knowledge-based services for internal and external users through creating an organizational culture of sharing knowledge and expertise within the library. In order to perform such jobs, the present day librarians or knowledge manager must possess certain quality. Webb (1998) pointed following per-requisites of a present day librarian:-

- Knowledge about library's information sources or assets, products and services;
- Knowledge about where these sources stored are and what is its use.
- Knowledge about users including teaching staff and researcher and, who is using these information sources.
- Knowledge about information and records management: indexing methods, database development, thesaurus construction, retrieval/ delivery methods, electronic storage, retention policy, structuring records, legislation, standards and controls.
- What are the current usage of these sources and bow to increase its uses?
- Knowledge about the library's own competencies and capabilities.
- Knowledge about the emerging library trends and technologies.

Some Specific Role

In area of Information Literacy/User Education:-

The goal of information literacy is to ensure that people understand how to, and why they need to, learn about sources in the information society. There is a growing recognition of the need to train users in information literacy skills. Libraries should take on the role of imparting information literacy skills. The traditional card catalogue are become outdated with the development of concept like online searching, OPAC etc. Now users mostly prefer to access electronic data and catalogs in electronic form. In this changing requirement Librarians should serve themselves as guardians of searching in electronic environment. Librarians should not only bring collections to the user, but service as well. With their vast knowledge they can guide users to access authoritative literature than less-authoritative with the loss of nominal time. They can also help the users to provide authoritative open source literature and can guide them to search various online databases.

In 1990, Matarazzo and Prusak (1990) conducted a study to determine the value of LIS professionals in a corporate sector in the growth and development of company. They found the role of library manager as: the online search performed by librarians was the most valuable service offered. They also found that most companies surveyed had no methods or process in p1ace to evaluate the effectiveness, efficiency or productivity of what librarians do. While every one appeared to 'like' libraries and librarians, few firms thought of them as 'mission critical'. They concluded that with no methods to evaluate library contribution to productivity and profits, the stature of librarians within the firm was likely to sink further in terms of compensation, status, value and impact.

Another study conducted by Fleck and Bawpen (1995)

in the professional field of Law and Medicine revealed the findings of study as: The working librarians in their associated institutions were highly regarded by their clients but they fulfilled very much a service oriented and reactive function serving clients by responding of their needs rather anything more dynamic and proactive. Their active clients perceived the librarians as efficient, intelligent, helpful, and processing specialized knowledge. They were also seen as un-ambitious people whose satisfaction was in helping others to their ends.

In area of Indexing

Indexing is the oldest technique for identifying the contents of documents to assist in their retrieval. The indexing process is typically performed by professional indexers associated with library organizations. Indexes need to convey more intelligence than the contents of text, in the sense that it should be able to structure or indicate every possible route a user might take into the text. Discussions and writings about searching the Internet frequently mention the difficulty of finding what is wanted and the need for good indexing. A prepared index to a site with a specific depth should offer a thesaurus of controlled entry terms closely related to the outline and bring together material from disparate sources. Indexing the Internet is an exciting and challenging project. It is exciting to develop approaches to search the growing amount of online materials.

CONCLUSION

To conclude it would be say that KM is not only to manage or organise books or journals, searching content on the Internet or arranging the circulation of materials. However, each of the activities can in some way be part of the KM spectrum and process. Knowledge management is about enhancing the use of organizational knowledge through sound practices of knowledge management and organizational learning. Thus, KM is a combination of information management, communication and human resources. In the business world, knowledge management has been implied to gain a competitive advantage over their competitors, to add value to their products, and to win greater satisfaction from their customers. In the library world, there is a lesson to be learned from the business world. Knowledge management is as important for libraries as for the businesses minus the competitive, proprietary, and moneymaking concerns. In fact, libraries have had a long and rich experience in the management of information. Many of such knowledge and skills of librarianship can be applied to knowledge management. Information technology and systems can provide effective support in implementing knowledge management. Librarians should work together with IT professionals and others to develop the appropriate knowledge management systems.

REFERENCE

Applehans, W., Globe A., Laugero G. (1999). *Managing Knowledge,* Boston MA, Addison-Wesley (1999).

Auster, E & Choo, Chun Wei (1995). ed., Managing Information for the Competitive Edge. NewYork, NY: Neal Schuman.

Bassie, L J. (1997). Harnessing the power of intellectual capital, *Training and Development,* 51(12), 25-30.

Beckman, T. (1997). A methodology for knowledge management. *IASTED International Conference on AI and Soft Computing, Banff, Canada*

Bergin, J. Teaching on the Wiki Web, *ACM SIGCSE Bulletin,* (2002) 1.

Bouthillier F and Shearer K. (2002). Understanding knowledge management and information management: the need for an empirical perspective" *Information Research,* 8(1) Available at: http://InformationR.net/ir/8-1/paper141.html

Butler, Y. (2000). Knowledge management, if you knew what you knew. *Australian Library Journal*, 49(1), 31-43.

Conley, C. A. and Zheng, W. (2009). Factors Critical to Knowledge Management Success, *Advances in Developing Human Resources*, 11, 334.

Davenport, T. and Prusak L. (1998). *Working knowledge: how organizations manage what they know*. Cambridge, MA: Harvard Business School Press.

Dillon, M. (1999). Knowledge management opportunities for libraries and universities. *Library and Information Science Annual*, 7, 3-11.

Douglas C A & Mc Cauley C D. (1999). Formal developmental relationships: a survey of organizational practices. *Human Resource Development Quarterly*, 10(1), 203-220.

Erdmann, M. (1997). The data warehouse as a means to support knowledge management. Availe at: http://www.dfki.uni-kl.de/~aabecker/Freiburg/Final/Erdmann/dwh_km.doc.html

Fleck, I and Bawden, D. (1995). The information professional: attitudes and images: Examples from information services in law and medicine, *Journal of Librarianship and Information Science*, 27(4), 215-26.

Fleming, N. (1996). Coping with a revolution: Will the Internet change learning? Lincoln University, Canterbury, New Zealand.

Gold, A. H.; Malhotra, A., and Segars, A. H. (2001). Knowledge Management: An organizational Capabilities Perspective", *Journal of Management Information systems*, 18(1), 185-214.

Hayes, H. (2004). The role of libraries in the knowledge economy. *Serials*, 17(3), 231-8.

Hlupic, V.; Pouloudi A. and Rzevski G. (2002). Towards an integrated approach to knowledge management: 'hard', 'soft', and 'abstract' issues. *Knowledge and Process Management*, 9(2), 90-102.

Hostler, J. (2005). The Path to Advancement-Centered Knowledge Management: Transforming Advancement Services,

Available at: http://www.supportingadvancement.com/potpourri/trans_as_km/trans_as_km_ presentation.pdf.

Jantz, R. (2001). Knowledge management in academic libraries: special tools and processes to support information professionals. *Reference Services Review*, 29(1), 33-39.

Kebede, G. (2010). Knowledge management: An information science perspective. *International Journal of Information Management*, 30 (2010) 416–424

Kim, S. (2000). The roles of knowledge professionals for knowledge management. 65th IFLA Council and General Conference Bangkok, Thailand, August 20 - August 28, 1999, 1-8

Lamb, B. (2004). The standard wiki overview. *EDUCASEUSE Review*, 39(5), 36-48.

Leuf, B. and Cunningham, W. (2001). The wiki way: Quick collaboration of the Web. Addison-Wesley.

Liebowitz, J. (2000). Building organizational intelligence: A knowledge management primer, *CRC Press, Boca Raton, FL.*

Matarazzo, J. and Prusak, J. (1990). Valuing corporate libraries: a senior management survey, *Special Libraries*, 81(2) 102-10.

Mohanty, S.K. & Chand, M. (2004). 5iKM3-Knowledge Management Maturity Model. Knowledge Management Practices. Mumbai: Tata Consultancy.

Nonaka, I and Takeuchi, H. (1995). The knowledge creating company: How Japanese companies create the dynamics of innovation. New York: Oxford University Press.

Nonaka, I. (1991). The knowledge creating company. *Harvard Business Review*, November-December, 96-104.

Oluic-Vukovic, V. (2001). From information to knowledge: some reflections on the origin of the current shifting towards knowledge processing and further perspective. *Journal of the American Society for Information Science and Technology*, 52, 54-61.

Polanyi, M (1962). Personal knowledge. Chicago, IL.: University of the Chicago Press.

Roknuzzaman, M., Kanai, H., & Umemoto, K. (2009). Integration of knowledge management process into digital library system: a theoretical perspective. *Library Review*, 58(5), 372-86.

Ruggles R. (1998). The state of the nation: Knowledge management in practice, *California Management Review*, 40 (Spring), 80-89.

Ruggles, R L. (1977). ed., Knowledge management tools. Oxford, Butterworth-Heinemann.

Sarrafzadeh, M., Martin, B., & Hazeri, A. (2010). Knowledge management and its potential applicability for libraries. *Library Management*, 31(3), 198-212.

Shanhong, T. (2000). Knowledge management in libraries in the 21st century. 66th IFLA Council and General Conference. Jerusalem, Israel, 13-18 August (2000). Available at: http://www.ifla.org/IV/ifla66/papers/057-110e.htm

Shanhong, T. (2000). *Knowledge management in libraries in the twenty-first century. In: 66th IFLA Council and General Conference,* August 13-18, Jerusalem.

Sinotte, M. (2004). Exploration of the field of knowledge management for the library and information professional. *Libri*, 54(3), 190-8.

Skyrme, D. (2003). Knowledge management: Making sense of an oxymoron. Available at: http://www.skyrme.com/isights/22km.htm.

The Economist, Yankee Group, A little knowledge (2000). Available at: http://www.economist.com/surveys/displaystory.cfm?story_id=E1_QTSDNJ

Townley, C.T. (2001). Knowledge management and academic libraries. *College and Research Libraries*. 62(1), 44-55.

Tuomi, I. (1999). Data is more than knowledge: implications of the reversed knowledge hierarchy to knowledge management and organizational memory. Proceedings of the 32nd Hawaii International Conference on Systems Sciences, IEEE Computer Society Press.

Wagner, C. (2004). WIKI: A technology for conversational knowledge management and group collaboration, *Communications of the Association for Information Systems*.13, 265-289.

Wagner, C. (2004). WIKI: A technology for conversational knowledge management and group collaboration, *Communications of the Association for Information Systems*.13, 265-289.

Wagner, C. (2004). WIKI: A technology for conversational knowledge management and group collaboration, *Communications of the Association for Information Systems*.13, 265-289.

Webb, S. P. (1998). Knowledge management: Linchpin of change. Some practical guidelines, London: Aslib, The Association for Information Management.

Wen, S. (2005). Implementing knowledge management in academic libraries: a pragmatic approach. In: *3rd China-US Library Conference*, Shanghai, March 22-25.

White, T. (2004). Knowledge management in an academic library: based on the case study KM within OULS. In: 70th IFLA General Conference and Council, August 22-27, Buenos Aires.

Wikipedia.

Index

L

M

O

P

R